UNRAVELING
THE MEGA-CHURCH

UNRAVELING
THE MEGA-CHURCH

True Faith or False Promises?

WILMER E. MACNAIR

PRAEGER

Westport, Connecticut
London

Library of Congress Cataloging-in-Publication Data

MacNair, Wilmer.
  Unraveling the mega-church : true faith or false promises? / Wilmer E. MacNair.
    p. cm.
  Includes bibliographical references and index.
  ISBN 978-0-313-37778-5 (alk. paper)
  1. Big churches.   I. Title.
  BV637.9.M33   2009
  262'.2—dc22   2009010333

British Library Cataloguing in Publication Data is available.

Library of Congress Catalog Card Number: 2009010333
ISBN: 978-0-313-37778-5

First published in 2009

Praeger Publishers, 88 Post Road West, Westport, CT 06881
An imprint of Greenwood Publishing Group, Inc.
www.praeger.com

Printed in the United States of America

The paper used in this book complies with the
Permanent Paper Standard issued by the National
Information Standards Organization (Z39.48–1984).

10 9 8 7 6 5 4 3 2 1

CONTENTS

Introduction   vii

1   The Mega-Church: New Kid on the Block   1

2   The Mega-Church: What Happened to Righteousness and Truth?   35

3   Worship in the Mega-Church: The Church and Its Music   57

4   The Sermon in the Mega-Church   75

5   The Mega-Church Program: Education and Groups   97

6   The Mega-Church and the Necessary Moment of Uncertainty   119

7   The Mega-Church: Fundamentalism and Certainty   141

8   Ecumenicism and Its Limits: The Boundary Looks Outward   163

9   Ecumenicism and Its Inclusiveness: The Boundary Looks Inward   183

10   A Theological Baseline   203

11   Reaching Out in an Era Plagued by the Problem of Meaning   223

Bibliography   249

Index   251

INTRODUCTION

The mega-church is a modern phenomenon, a creature taking form within and among all ethnic and racial groups, a life form parading under the auspice of Christian faith, perhaps quite rightly, because there is no other handy label. The stunning largeness of the mega-church is fueled and maintained by its leaders, who have made their goal to bring about ever more growth. But before calling this mega-church a case of uncontrolled growth, we must see that the mega-church has other characteristics that should be examined as closely as this growth factor.

For example, the mega-church features a *regal pastor* who is the church's head minister and is totally in charge and in control. Although a sizable roster of "members" does exist, the people on this roster do not act or think independently of the head minister and his staff. Only in extreme situations could they act as a self-directing and more traditional congregation. Indeed, tradition itself is missing from the mega-church venue, or at least it is distorted beyond almost all recognition. We see that the mega-church architecture and interior decoration bear little resemblance to the traditional church. And the music heard in the mega-church is altogether new. Neither traditional hymns nor traditional types of hymns or songs are heard. What is heard is simple, nonmelodic, and repetitious. Moreover, even traditional doctrines are transformed to mega-church standards and perceptions. Doctrines pertaining to the Bible and the Christian Gospel are certainly affirmed by the mega-church, as are the common Christian views on morality. But they are affirmed not because they are matters of great concern, but because they are matters of indifference. Church growth is the single priority. All else is a means to that end.

The mega-church is strong in its ability to attract people in large numbers, but it has two weaknesses. These weaknesses are built in to its project of growing ever larger and cannot be overcome. First, the mega-church does not conceive of God as *awesome* and *holy*. The God who looks on the mountains and they shake; who comes on a day of clouds and thick darkness and who is awesome in his deeds among men is totally alien. His place is taken by the smiling deity who is our Best Friend. And, second, the mega-church cannot have a concept of *righteousness*. It has ideas about what is good, but the *righteous*—in the sense of a perspective on right and wrong that is distinct from what people think, individually and collectively, is alien and incomprehensible. What is left is an insubstantial, even mushy, sense of good and bad. Clergy and lay leaders of authentic (nonmega) churches would do well to emphasize these built-in deficiencies of mega-churches in their work with congregants, divinity students, and theologians. Otherwise we will begin to lose perspective on what is happening to Christianity as this giant expands beyond all norms and becomes all we know of Christianity and even of religion in general.

This book, *Unraveling the Mega-Church*, is intended to be more than the last whimper of a lost understanding of religion in the face of the emerging God-industry. It is meant to be a call to awareness, even action, a cry for us to open our eyes to see where the notion of God is going, or perhaps retreating, when we make religion a business—a mega-business indeed.

Rev. Wilmer E. MacNair, B.D., PhD
Lafayette, Louisiana
October, 2008

1

THE MEGA-CHURCH: NEW KID ON THE BLOCK

In the panorama of religious events in the United States, the mega-church is something new. Nothing quite like it has appeared before. True enough, it did have precursors. The evangelist or the revival preacher came in many types and used many means for proclaiming his message. But although they have roots in certain earlier traditions, these very large mega-churches are a "new kid on the block" among religious organizations in the United States. They are different from the churches that most American church-goers are familiar with. They are different not only in being very large, but in other characteristics as well. They are a new *kind* of church and not just a larger size church. Certainly, they are big, but they differ from smaller size churches in qualitative ways and not just in the numbers of people involved.

THE MEGA-CHURCH IN THE HISTORY OF THE CHRISTIAN CHURCH

There is nothing new about large churches. However the case may be in particular times and places, there have been many large churches. Some had massive buildings. Others were large in having substantial numbers of people. And these people were numerous in varying ways. Sometimes, the abundance was in the collection of those who were baptized and qualified to participate in the church's Sacraments. In other cases, it was the numbers present for Mass or other ceremonies. In still others, the numbers were of those who reside in a parish or zone surrounding a church building in which preaching and the celebration of sacraments take place. Later, members were listed as belonging to a community of believers in which the people have rights and obligations.

But the mega-church is something new. Just being very large in any way does not qualify a church as mega. The churches that can claim that title certainly are large, however large is determined. But, in addition, a mega-church is a religious enterprise that has special characteristics; most notably the indefinite increase in numbers is an *intention and a project*. The people who organize and lead it set out to build an operation that would be large and that would become ever larger. Everything that they did was designed to bring about this outcome.

TOP DOWN AND BOTTOM UP AUTHORITY

As a way of approaching the mega-church in its historical context, we distinguish two kinds of authority in churches: top down and bottom up. In the top down authority, officials of some sort define what a community, an organization, or a congregation exists for, including what assertions about God and human beings (doctrines) are to be affirmed, what its organizational structure will be, and what it will require of its adherents. These may be referred to as members, communicants, participants, attendees, or simply "one of us." In bottom up authority, basic features are determined from the "rank and file" who make up the majority of the people involved.

In the New Testament, both forms of authority are present. As the evangelists went from place to place, they converted people to the Christian Faith. Of necessity, they presented themselves as authorities and guides to the nascent Christian communities. Because the essence of a congregation was that it was founded on faith in Jesus Christ crucified and raised from the dead, authority had to be given to those who understood this faith and all that it involved. Initially, it was the evangelists themselves who assumed this role. Then, as they wandered further, they appointed "elders" to guide the flocks. These were presumably men (usually men) who had shown that they understood the Faith.

On the other hand, the bottom up feature of the Faith was present in the form of the gift of the Holy Spirit. At some point in receiving the Gospel, or

Good News, the people in a congregation were gripped by the Holy Spirit. This force or presence then moved them to say and do certain things, and in so doing it endowed them, singly or collectively, with a certain authority. There was an inevitable back-and-forth between the authority of evangelists and elders, on the one hand, and the spirit-gripped congregation on the other. This bipolar locus of authority was destined to remain in the Christian tradition from that point on.

In time, the top down feature of the Christian community came to imitate the authority structures of the sociopolitical units in which the churches flourished. Because kings or emperors were basic to those units, similar authority figures came to be basic to the churches as well. Before long, the churches in an area were presided over by *bishops*. The bishops gave structure and dependability to the churches, just as kings did for whole societies. And the bishops provided the sense of unity or oneness that was cherished by the churches. And because the emperor in Rome made a single empire of the many kingdoms included within the reach of his administration, so the bishop of Rome, by around the year 400, came to be a head or "first among equals." In time, he was assigned a special title, the *pope*.

Although the top down authority seems to have been dominant, the bottom up was not missing. It took two forms. First, there were the *monastic orders* in which men were recruited to live a special kind of Christian life. They were *monks*. Women were also embraced in such a life. They were *nuns*. Compared with the hierarchy of pope, bishops, and priests, the monasteries were scenes in which the Spirit was given free expression. The second form of bottom up authority was found in the *saints*. These people appeared apart from the top down collection of bishops and priests. They could be men or women. They could be of any social category. They had no official position in the Church. The Church might canonize (grant official recognition to) the saints, but it did not create or ordain them; the free-flowing Holy Spirit did that. In the evolution of the Roman Catholic tradition, the monastic orders and the saints are every bit as important as the hierarchy with its higher and lower officials.

In the era around 1000 to 1400 A.D., the Roman Catholic Church achieved the form and content that mark its personality as a church until the present day. The very large cathedrals and other buildings were constructed in this period. They were not, however, churches as we understand the term today. They did not have congregations in the sense of a community of people bound together as a particular unit of the worldwide Christian Church. Nor were the church buildings thought of as housing such a congregation. Rather, they were temples of *Christendom.* That is, they were embedded in political, social, and territorial units. The congregations were the people resident in a certain area. And just as someone living in America is an American, so the people living in an area were the people of the parish viewed as a piece of land that was a subdivision of a kingdom or a princedom. We can see that such a parish church bears no resemblance to the mega-church of our day.

The back-and-forth between top down and bottom up authority continued with the Protestant Reformation. The kings and princes assumed the role of bishops in the Lutheran territories—parts of Germany and the Scandinavian countries. In Calvinist or "Reformed" areas—parts of England, Scotland, Holland, Germany, Switzerland, and some Eastern European territories—a similar role was played by the presbytery, which is a body consisting of representatives of the churches. In both branches of the Reformation, the minister or pastor continued to be an instance of top down authority, although with more emphasis on his stature as a learned individual and preacher. In these traditions, the identity of the congregation and of the residents of an area continues, but with somewhat greater emphasis on the church building being a "church" in the sense that it houses a congregation.

Alongside the churches of the Reformation and the Counter-Reformation Roman Catholic Church, there were innumerable sect churches. There were Ana-Baptists of many kinds, Baptists, Brethren, and others. In these, the bottom up emphasis strengthened to the point that the top down withered to almost nothing. Rather than being churches of a certain territory, these groups defined themselves as against the larger society of which they were part. They had a sense of distinctiveness that defined, for them, who they were. In many cases, the bottom up emphasis was so strong that the top down side went into almost total eclipse.

REVIVAL OF RELIGION IN THE UNITED STATES

The big break came in the United States with the efforts to carry Christianity to the people of the Western frontier. Before the movement away from the Eastern seacoast began, almost all life was that of the village or town. People lived in settled communities. And, as residents of a village, they allied themselves with Catholic, Lutheran, or Reformed (Calvinist) forms of religion. In this sense, church life was also community life. But on the frontier, there were disconnected people. They had little in the way of family and less in the way of community. If, for this reason, people were to be evangelized for Christianity, they had to be reached one person—or one family—at a time.

This project of converting the tough and hardy folk of the frontier left little space for top down authority. The question confronting the gifted lay preacher of the Baptists or the circuit rider of the Methodists was what manner of preaching, singing, and, in general carrying out evangelistic activity would in fact bring a hard-working and hard-drinking frontiersman to his knees in quest of divine forgiveness and renewal. Other considerations that might occupy top down leaders, considerations such as the dicta of theological scholarship, had to be set aside while a simple message of "saved by the blood of Christ" induced hardened frontier farmers and merchants to abandon the thrill-seeking life and to take up regular work, marriage, fatherhood, and, of course, weekly church attendance.

TOP DOWN AUTHORITY AND VALUE

It is in the nature of a top down authority that something is taken to be of inherent dignity and value. This may be a treasured body of thought or of sensibility that was considered to be good in and of itself. Its value did not depend on whether it would sell. It depended only on itself, or on a higher Source of Value. With the Old Testament prophets, this Source was the Word of God. This Word had its own nature, quite apart from whether people did or did not pay heed to it. If they did not, it was because they are, as the prophets said, a "stiff-necked people."

In the case of the Greeks, it was philosophical or metaphysical truth that was considered good in itself. As Socrates was dying from the hemlock, he rejoiced that he would have discussions with wiser people on the other side of the Great Divide than could be found on earth. Clearly, wisdom had its own virtue that did not depend at all on its popularity. With the Romans, it was the development of law, a concern that is present in all of Western civilization to this day. In the case of the United States, the division of powers in government represents the recognition of the necessity for some men to possess power in combination with an awareness of the perennial tendency of power holders to abuse that power. Just *this* awareness was thought to have inherent value. People were to approve of it because it had value; it did not have value because people approved of it.

In previous historical periods, top down authority in this sense has enjoyed a great deal of respect. Regardless of whether the standards of value are philosophical truth, scientific veracity, legal rectitude, or aesthetic integrity, the general view within the community was that these are good or, indeed, are the Good. If they enjoy a measure of respect within the multitudes, they do so because the multitudes see the value that is inherent in these qualities. But the value is in the qualities whether or not it is recognized by large numbers.

THE RISE OF THE MEGA-CHURCH

The mega-church arises from the confluence of three cultural streams in which this intrinsic value of the Good is in eclipse. The first of these is the tradition of frontier evangelism, which we have discussed. The second is American *commercial civilization*. Within the framework of this culture, goods and services are manufactured and offered for sale. The enterprise that offers them is considered to be good to the extent that it does indeed sell them and, in so doing, realizes a profit. With the exception of the cases of a few bad products, such as illicit drugs and tobacco, there is only one standard for measuring how an enterprise fares: whether its products *sell*. In this sense, the "bottom up" reigns supreme. Competition for customers is the name of the game, and there is no other standard by which business activity can be measured. The third stream is *celebrity culture*. Here we have performers of various kinds. They are actors, singers, or speakers who perform for, and who please, large numbers of people. There are limited numbers of such performers; their most distinctive attribute is that they are *known*. They may be regarded as important, but if they are so regarded, it is because they are first known. Elsewhere on the social scene, certain persons become important in various spheres of activity. And because they are important, they are known. With the celebrity, it is the known that comes first. Fame is a beginning point, not a result or a reward for being worthy. Importance derives from being famous.

True, the celebrity is celebrated because vast crowds admire her. Also true, the crowds admire her because she is a celebrity. There is a circle that has no beginning point and no ending point. It just goes around and around.

THE MEGA-CHURCH
AND THE CULTURAL STREAMS

Religion in America clearly has its origin in the evangelical wing of Protestantism. Its message, its assumptions, and much of its atmosphere are those of the frontier evangelist. It differs from its evangelistic origins, however, in that it makes rather few demands of its attendees or members other than that they should be active, in or supportive of, the enterprise. Where it does make a clarion call for morality, it is likely to be the other guy's failings that are condemned. Some mega-church preachers will rail against abortion, homosexuality or homosexual marriage, and the like. But these are standardized views on issues, not demands made of the attendees themselves.

Commercial civilization is evident in the mega-church project of becoming ever larger and of measuring how well it is doing entirely by its growth in numbers. Lyle Schaller made this point in his *From Cooperation to Competition*. In that book, he made it clear that, as he sees it, there are winners and there are losers in the coming competition among churches. The winners are those who pull in the largest numbers of people; the losers are those who do not succeed in the numbers game. He even suggests that the winners are likely to be people with business experience rather than people with theological education. It would be hard to conceive of a more explicit hegemony of commercial civilization. There is no place for excellence or faithfulness that has value in itself and apart from the extent to which it sells.

Celebrity culture is evident in how the mega-church develops after it leaves its evangelical base. The preaching, music, and all aspects of the worship events resemble the performances in which one or a few people are on stage and hold forth in front of vast seas of adoring fans. For this reason, the music is almost entirely new and unfamiliar, and it is also repetitious and trite. The performers pride themselves on their ability to reach those whom other churches fail to reach. They claim that they are being *relevant* to people for whom hymns such as "Abide with Me" do not evoke fond memories. But what they do not say is that there is no standard by which their performance can be evaluated *other* than whether people respond in large numbers.

THE MEGA-CHURCH AND TOP DOWN AND BOTTOM UP AUTHORITY

As the three streams of frontier evangelism, commercial civilization, and celebrity culture converge, they produce special ways in which top down and bottom up concerns relate to each other. There certainly is a top. The pastor is king in the mega-church more than elsewhere, especially when the elsewhere is a church of congregational polity such as the Baptist. His staff is entirely beholden to him and the staff—with him—is entirely in charge of the whole operation. But this top of the organization has no quality of its own apart from its appeal to the bottom. In whatever way its status as a top may be pictured, it is entirely eaten up by having appeal to the rank and file. Unlike a Catholic, Lutheran, Anglican, or Calvinist who may admire clergy or other church leaders because those leaders are learned, pious, or otherwise worthy of admiration, the participant in the mega-church has an admiration for the preacher that is entirely self-authenticating. The preacher's being *admirable* is entirely contained—or exhausted—in the fact that he is *admired*.

We see, then, that the mega-church is an entirely new actor on the stage of Christian history. Its major characteristic is its project of growing to an ever-larger size measured by the number of attendees or the number of members. In adopting this project, the mega-church crosses a line that separates it from other Christian churches, and perhaps even from Christianity itself. In authentic Christianity, there is always a dialectic or back and forth between top down and bottom up authority. There is always some space in which the question, what is involved in being a Christian, can be asked with seriousness and answered the same way. There must be a concern for Truth because it is the Truth, regardless whether it wins votes. This concern must have its own reality and value that does not bow down before the project of drawing in ever-larger numbers of people. We must be able to ask whether something is true or good without glancing to each side to see how many people are following.

CONFRONTING THE MEGA-CHURCH

Among the tasks that are urgent for the Christian churches today, that of confronting the mega-church would certainly have a prominent place. This is the case for a number of reasons. The decline of many mainline congregations is one of these. There is little question that mega-churches draw many people who would otherwise be active in authentic Christian churches. One might conclude that this criticism merely reflects simple envy. If I were a pastor in a mainline church, I might wish I had more people in my church and therefore take a dim view of the admittedly great drawing power of the mega-churches; however, there is no need to apologize for this concern. It is arguably a concern for the Gospel itself. If there is a dialectic between top down and bottom up authority, space must be made for both. A church that is concerned about the truth of the gospel must clear space for the activity of seeking that Truth for its own sake.

Beginning with the Lutheran Reformation, the concept of the *Word of God* was given a place of first importance. This Word is, above all, that which is proclaimed from a pulpit by a minister who has the Scriptures open in front of her. And it is of the essence of the Word that it is *unexpected*. It is from elsewhere and cannot be anticipated either by those who proclaim it or those who hear it. For this reason, there is an inevitable top down feature that needs to be noted without embarrassment or equivocation. The bottom up feature, however, should also be affirmed. The same congregation that hears the Word also responds, and this response is, in turn, the Word that is proclaimed to the minister who preaches. There is always an interaction between the top down and the bottom up. This simple fact forms a major part of the Christian Church's response to the mega-church.

THE IDEAL TYPE AS AN ANALYTICAL TOOL

To understand this new kind of religious organization, we need to describe the mega-church as an *ideal type*. This term comes from Max Weber's sociological works of about a century ago. By this term, we refer to a way of talking about complex entities such as human societies or human organizations. In these entities, there are many parts or features. These parts exist in a structured relationship with one another. A given set of parts having a certain structure is then what we wish to understand. To do so, we form an idea in our minds of the parts and the structure. This idea is called an *ideal type*. It properly exists only in our minds, but entities in the real world resemble this "type" to a greater or lesser degree. We may have in our minds an idea of a "type" of human society. Actual societies may then be like this idea or different from it. We can then see different societies as being contrasted to one another in terms of the degrees to which they resemble the "types."

We could think, for example, of a close-knit New England community of two or three centuries ago and contrast it to a modern industrial city of today. We could call the one a "traditional" or "agricultural" community and the other a "modern" or "industrial" community. We might note that in the first, people knew each other intimately. Any two of them who formed a pair were linked not by one but by several relationships. One man was another's neighbor *and* his grocer *and* a fellow member of his church *and* of his community club. The dealings that they had with one another were well structured by family, kinship, and neighborhood, and perhaps also by church. In the other type of society, the modern industrial society, people constantly deal with strangers. Their relations are necessarily *specific*. Each individual generally has only one kind of relationship, or one kind of business, with any other person. Each knows of, and is concerned about, only those attributes of the other person that have to do with the business at hand. And the whole pattern of relations is structured in turn by what is a still more highly structured world of administration and commerce.

In speaking of these "ideal types," we are *thinking* of the earlier close-knit community, and we are *thinking* of the later industrial city. We have these as ideas in our minds. And as ideas, they can be "pure," or "ideal" or simply "idea," even perhaps with a capital "I"—"Idea." The small town expresses the image of "small town." All of the personal relationships within it are precisely personal. The modern city, on the other hand, is absolutely commercial or industrial. All of its objects and events and all of its human relationships proceed from the idea of *business*. All dealings of one person with another have a business nature and all are structured by business. This perfection of the two types as "ideal" or basic "idea" exists only in the mind. What is actually "out there" in the world is always messier and deviates from these basic types or ideas of types in one or another way and to one or another degree.

This untidiness is true of everything that has actual existence in the world around us. And this untidiness shows itself in the fact that features of so-called modern business behavior can be found even in the most so-called traditional village. Business intrudes, we may say, into the presumed traditional warmth of kinship and neighborhood. And, on the other side, aspects of warm, personal bonding can be found in the industrial commercial city. Human beings insist on finding or establishing warm relations with each other, even in the midst of the structures of business. We human beings, being *human,* insist on *humanizing* the things that we do in various ways. So, while there have been traditional communities, and while the modern city is to be found everywhere in the world, the pure form of each is to be found nowhere, except in the mind. Hence, the ideas of these pure forms are, in themselves, merely ideas.

Yet although mixtures of all kinds of human relationships are found in all communities, there are real and significant differences in the *incidence* of these relationships in different communities. One sort of human aggregate is characterized by a preponderance of one form of relating, and a different form looms largest in another aggregate. For this reason, the idea, or ideal type, that we have in our minds is *useful* in understanding the communities and the differences between them. We may label one community "traditional" and then note ways in which it deviates from that type. Another we may call "modern" and then consider certain particulars in which it veers from the image of such a community that we have in our minds.

This, then, is how we will approach the following discussion of the mega-church. We have the idea of such a church in our minds. Hence, mega-church is a mental construct or image. And armed with this image, we look at actual churches that have been called "mega-churches" by those who participate in their church lives and/or by observers. We note how they fit the concept that we have in our minds. And we then also observe how they deviate from that concept. In theory, we assume that no actual church will fit the ideal type perfectly. In practice, we assume that some will come close to doing so, and others will deviate in greater or lesser degree.

We use the concept of ideal type because it is *useful* for the task that we have set for ourselves, namely the task of understanding. We use it for that reason and only for that reason. There is nothing that is either "correct" or "good" about the type itself. As a concept, it is only useful or not useful. If it is useful, it is so because it helps us to understand the material at hand. It *happens,* we must emphasize, to help us in this way. It simply turns out that the very complicated objects and events that we observe assume some form and pattern and become intelligible by the use of the concept. By noting that some churches come close to exemplifying the type, while others do so only imperfectly and still others are not churches of that type at all, we make the world of churches understandable.

This discussion has an evaluative as well as a descriptive nature. At each point, we see the characteristics of the mega-church as being defined by the way it compares to what we consider to be good and true and authentically Christian. It is in this comparison that mega-church characteristics assume their true and proper nature and reveal their significance.

THE MEGA-CHURCH AS A TYPE

The Regal Pastor

Distinctive about the mega-church is that it exists as a church that is *of* and *by* a certain pastor. The personality and the *charisma* of a person are at the center of the church's life. In many cases, the current pastor of the church is also the founder. He (rarely she) is often referred to as the "founding pastor." This was certainly true in the case of Bill Hybels at the Willow Creek Community Church near Chicago. This is also true of the Saddleback Church (in southern California) founded and still led by Rick Warren. In other cases, a pastor was called to a small congregation and then, under his leadership, this congregation grew to a very large size. And as it grew, the pastor assumed a position in the church very much like that of a founder. It became *his* church; its life was centered entirely around him. His preaching gave form and focus to everything that happened within the organization.

His position, in contrast to that of a pastor of a conventional church, let us say a Baptist church, is absolutely secure. Such security is not typical in Baptist and in (other) Protestant churches. Commonly, a church has a congregation. Indeed, the church (not the pastor) *is* the congregation. And just how secure the pastor's position will be is determined by the "standing" he has in that group of people and its leaders. The congregation and pastor are independent of one another and can make independent decisions and judgments, but the pastor of the "normal" church serves at the pleasure of the congregation.

The congregation "calls" a pastor, and it can also dismiss or "fire" him. Indeed, it does so rather frequently. In a certain year, it was reported that in the churches of the Southern Baptist Convention 1 congregation in 20 had "fired" its pastor. If we spoke of a span of time longer than one year, that figure would of course be much larger. Whether such dismissals occur because of something wrong with the pastor or something amiss in the congregation (or both) is open for discussion, but it is not our concern here. What is important to note is that the congregation and the pastor are two distinct entities and are capable of having varying relations with each other.

Matters are very different in the mega-church. Technically, there is a "congregation" that has "members." But this membership—this collection of people—does not have the nature of a group that can determine who the pastor will be and whether the pastor will be retained or dismissed. The pastor (also called "minister") has a firm grip on the membership, and there is very little possibility that it would act independently of him. Not everyone who attends (patronizes) the church is a member. Actually, only a minority of the church's constituency, or clientele, forms the body of members. And those who are members become so in a process that is governed and controlled by the pastor. Properly speaking, then, there is no mega-church congregation that can fire the mega-church pastor. The collection of members does not have the reality or substance that would enable it to take such actions.

In some mega-churches, there exists a technical possibility that the group of members could be mobilized by certain leaders to threaten the minister's position. In these instances, there is a "congregation" as a legal entity that has charge of property, finances, and personnel. And it could act. But in the actual case, there is virtually no possibility that it will do so. The members are people who have been "let in" by the pastor. They form a personal following that, in effect, belongs to the pastor, and in actual fact they are certain to remain loyal to him. If someone is disgruntled by what the pastor says or does, that person can withdraw. Indeed, many do, but their withdrawal is hardly noticed. The pastor has the membership, so to say, in his grip. If the pastor were involved in a scandal that was publicized nationally, it might be possible that a congregation or committees might be mobilized, but that would be very rare. And even then it would probably be only with the minister's consent.

A basic feature of the mega-church is that people in very large numbers are flowing into it all of the time. It would not be a mega-church if this were not the case. The coming-in of large numbers of people then becomes a factor that sustains the pastor's position. It is presumably because of him—because of his preaching and because of the church program he oversees—that the flow continues. Any one member of the church, then, perceives this to be the case. The constant flowing-in of attendees occurs because of the minister, and in this sense it belongs to him. This flow-in is *his* just as is the congregation itself. The awareness of this is then a constraint on voting members, a force constraining them to conform their judgments to his.

We may, then, refer to the mega-church as having what we will call a *regal pastor*. The mega-minister is king in the mega-church. In a certain First Baptist Church in a southern city, the minister was clearly approaching the end of his career and knew he would soon need to retire. He had served for more than 40 years and was in his late seventies. The question of replacing him was mentioned in the local newspaper. In that article, the minister was quoted as saying that the process of finding a replacement for him would begin with candidates having an interview *with him*. He would of course not have the authority to hire his replacement. But clearly, he would play an important role in the selection of the new pastor. Actually, he would play the decisive role. The congregation would technically "call" a new minister, but this would be a rubber stamping operation. There would be no possibility that anyone would challenge or even question the senior minister's judgment. In a standard Baptist church, the selection of a replacement for a retiring pastor would not involve the retiring pastor. Actually, it would not be any of his business! He would have no "say" in it at all. Or at the very most, he would respond to specific questions from members or leaders of the congregation. But he would not in any way or to any degree choose the person who would replace him.

Further, in the standard procedure of churches that have a congregational polity, once a new pastor has arrived on the scene, a retiring pastor who remains in the community is expected to move quickly to the sidelines and to allow the new minister to assume full responsibility for all aspects of church life. He is to refrain from performing funerals, weddings, and baptisms, and from seeking to influence the congregation's decisions. Because pastors usually have a personal relationship with the members of the church, this is often an issue. The people feel "bonded" with the retiring pastor, and they want him to bury their dead and marry their sons and daughters. This is especially the case with infrequent attendees who may scarcely know the new pastor, even after a period of several months or longer. For this reason, it is a matter of agreed upon ethics that the old pastor should leave special services to his younger replacement. Some ministers make their acceptance contingent on the retiring pastor's agreement to accept a call to a new church. In the Presbyterian Church, there are presbytery regulations establishing these rules.

Against the backdrop of these traditions and practices, it is remarkable that in the mega-church a retiring pastor remains active in the congregation. In some cases, he does so to such a degree that the new minister finds himself pushed to the margins of church life. His role may be reduced to that of giving sermons, and even that may be limited by the old minister's wish to continue his preaching. A newspaper advertisement for one Baptist mega-church even lists the older pastor as "senior pastor" while calling the younger man "pastor." The manner in which the new pastor is selected and the relationship between the new pastor and the retired pastor are in great degree inconsistent with the Baptist tradition, or more generally with the traditions of the religious groups that have a congregational polity. Clearly, we see here that the mega-church is a new kind of church and not just a church that has a larger congregation than those of other churches.

More Attenders Than Members

In the mega-church, the number of people attending services on Sunday (or the weekend) is greater than the number of members, commonly by a factor of three or four. There may be 2,000 people attending services, but only 500 members. This may be understandable, considering that people in large numbers are coming and going all the time, while membership is granted to those who go through certain processes and procedures and display the right characteristics and qualifications.

This is in sharp contrast to what is usually seen in Protestant churches. The common pattern is for the names on the membership rolls to exceed by a large margin the numbers present in Sunday services. The number present at a Sunday service, or the combined numbers at two or more services, is equal to between 20 and 60 percent of those on the membership rolls. The figure will be near either the bottom or the top of that range depending on a number of factors including the sorts of people who make up the congregation, with its corporate "personality," the frequency with which the names of nonattenders are deleted from the membership rolls, the nature of the community surrounding it, and the number of nonmember visitors who flow in and out. In the case of small congregations, it may even be a matter of "survival of the fittest." That is, only those churches that have a large percentage of their members present for Sunday services stay in operation.

To understand why these figures are turned upside down in the case of the mega-church, it is important to remember that there is a large number of people flowing into the mega-operation all the time. Whatever the explanation may be, many people appear at the mega-church's doors.

Certainly some may leave, that is, cease attending. But the number arriving is so large that some hemorrhaging can occur without being noticed. It is likely that many of these people have little interest in being actual "members," just as they are not "members" of the stores in which they shop or the concerts they attend. They see no need for such a status in a church to which they visit. What is key here is that they "go to church" just as they go to stores or concerts. Some even waltz between large churches just as they move about in the shopping malls. In contrast to the regular church in which a visitor is likely to find himself warmly welcomed or even pulled vehemently into the life of the congregation, the mega-church wishes to allow a visitor the ability to remain anonymous.

Further, it is not easy to become a member of the mega-church. There is a "gate-keeping" operation that ensures that the names of only the right people will be added to the membership rolls. This may consist of attending a class that meets for some substantial number of hours during a period of several weeks. This will be required even of people transferring from other churches that are, it is supposed, of the same denomination. For many people, the abandonment of their anonymity and the possible scrutiny of who they are may prove obstacles to jumping through the necessary hoops. And while the outsider cannot know just how decisions are made about accepting people, it is likely that the minister controls who may or may not become members. He has the position of gatekeeper. If his charisma were not sufficient to maintain control over the operation, his gate-keeping ability would certainly do so. Those who are members may be well aware of having been admitted by the pastor and of being part of his personal following.

For the many people who attend the mega-church, whether frequently or infrequently, the operation has a meaning very different from that of the usual congregation to which a person may belong. These people who only attend are not part of a congregation or community. Rather, they are individuals who choose to "tune in," perhaps regularly, to a presentation. It is, for them, like a television program they watch every week without any involvement other than the act of watching. For some, this is the way they like it: anonymous, free to come and go, and only tuning in at will.

Some others, fewer in number but a distinct set of people, choose to be more involved and to be more "connected" with a few attendees—a manageable number of persons—who attend or who are members. These people participate in small groups or classes that are similar to the Sunday school classes (for all ages) found elsewhere in American churches. By meeting with these few others for study and discussion, these people find the church to be a site of belonging and participation, as well as allowing them to be part of an audience listening to a performance. For them, the small group gives the church a more "family" nature than it would otherwise have. When two of them greet each other in the "auditorium" where the musicians and preacher hold forth, they feel they are *part* of something personal even in the midst of large masses of people. We will consider this group and its activities further in Chapter 5.

Alongside these "others" (those who only watch or attend such groups) are those who are actual *members*. These people make up a kind of elite corps mainly as a chorus singing and taking action under the direction of the head pastor. They are those who have been "let in" through the "gate." Basically, they have been admitted by the mega-pastor. And just as the church belongs to the pastor, for the most part so do they. They are his personal following, those who we may gently describe as his admirers and supporters.

THE "MEGA" IN "MEGA-CHURCH"

A prudent observer will exercise some caution about explaining why so many people seem to flow toward the mega-church. Is it because Americans have learned to trust entities that are big, as with large department stores, large universities, and large branches of government? Is it because mega-church worship resembles a rock concert? Is it because it offers a rich program that smaller churches could not provide? These and other possibilities may be considered. There is no question, however, that the multitudes *do* indeed move toward this kind of church. So numerous are those who enter the mega-church scene that the character of the operation is shaped by the sheer abundance of its attendees. The church "campus" takes on a shopping-mall appearance, as various booths or counters appear and have people to answer questions and otherwise deal with the ebb and flow of the crowds. A quantitative difference is transformed into a contrast of a qualitative sort as the numbers overwhelm and transform the usual meaning of "congregation."

When something takes place, there must be a reason why. How do we account for this tremendous popularity? Bill Hybels thought that the mega-crowds consist of those people who find the traditional church service dull and something of a "turn-off." When he was young, someone spoke of a man who had not been to church in years but who now expressed an interest in giving it a try. Hybel's internal reaction was, "Oh don't take him to a regular church service. It would seem very strange to him, and he would not find it to be at all appealing." In viewing it this way, he was seeing matters very differently from the way the frontier evangelist saw them. That "revival" preacher clearly thought that the whole point was to *remind* his listeners (the *sinners*) of the religion that they had rubbed up against as children.

In line with his perception of the task at hand, Hybles arranged for the worship event to be drastically different. It would be what this seeker is familiar with, rather like a rock concert or other entertainment event. The music would be jazzy and loud and vigorous. There would of course be an apparent "Christian" nature and content. For a person accustomed to rock concerts, the change would be minimal. He could ease his way into the religion of his ancestors or of his neighbors. The nature of the lyrics would remain very much the same; only the content would change.

In the past, people lived in small communities. They treasured the identity, warmth, and mutual affection found in their very own "our town." Much of the entertainment they enjoyed was home-grown; local performers provided music and song, while traditions such as that of the square-dance abounded. Religion was constructed on the same pattern. A local preacher teamed up with singers and organ-players to draw congregations into a vigorous church life. There was a congruency between the realm of entertainment and the sphere of religion.

That congruency remains, but both the entertainment and the religion have changed. Now the realm of entertainment is dominated by the *celebrity*. An individual or small group of individuals is "well known" within a large collection of people and to its multitude. The individual or small group is the *performer*. The large collection makes up an *audience*. The two take on interdependent natures or qualities with each other. To be a celebrity, the performer has to have the admiring attention of a very large group of people. To be an audience rather than just an aggregate, the people have to be mesmerized by a performer. It is a two-way relationship in which each side depends for its identity on its encounter with the other.

The celebrity depends, then, on the audience for his celebrity status. Without the audience, he might be attractive, interesting, or even "sexy." But these qualities would have a quantitative and therefore limited nature;

he would have a certain amount of the qualities and only that amount. He would be as attractive as he is, but *only* as attractive as he is. The degree of attractiveness would be multiplied by the number of people in his audience, thereby producing a magnification effect. Without witnesses to perceive and magnify his celebrity status, this celebrity would be something like a little mound of dirt that is alright as a mound of dirt but would never resemble a mountain. Only if he could become a celebrity might his appeal and allure take on a seemingly special character. His appeal would be bestowed on him by a seemingly limitless mass of fans. And the seemingly limitless extent of the mass audience can be transferred to the performer and can thereby become the measure of his importance, stature, and glory. This glory is then an illusion—*the* illusion—that fuels the ever-growing mega-church.

Further, any one person in the mass audience becomes significant and real in her own eyes by virtue of being one who shares the audience's interest in the performer. She could talk about the performer with any one else within the mass. Each would understand the other's estimate of the importance of the performer. The two would see themselves as participants in the great ocean of enthusiastically interested witnesses or "fans." So they could thus talk *with* each other *about* the performer to share their shared interest.

If the performer acquires "celebrity" status from the mass audience, the reverse is also true. To be such a mass or a mass audience, this oceanic expanse of people has to have the celebrity. It is by responding together and simultaneously to this celebrity performer that they are transformed from an aggregate form—people who share nothing except the space they occupy—to a "mass" or an "audience." There is an electricity surging back and forth among them that gives them character. This current is derived from their shared devotion to (or at least interest in) the performer. The importance of being part of an audience that has such a symbiotic relation with the performer is dramatized by what people will pay to attend. In some cases, they pay upward of 100 dollars apiece per event to be part of a group that idolizes the performer. Clearly, they get something for their money. And what they get is not the pleasure inherent in hearing the music. They can do that for a far smaller expenditure. The return they get for what they spend has a metaphysical character: They are part of the Great Celebrity's Audience. And each of them owns a piece of the glory that arises from the union of celebrity-performer and audience.

The mega-church is constructed on the same model. There is the preacher who is the "star" of the operation. He is backed up by one or two stand-ins who can take his place when necessary. He is also supported by a collection of performers, both vocal and instrumental. The instrumentalists will be mainly performers on the piano, guitar, and percussion instruments. Once the preacher has become a religious celebrity, even if just a local celebrity, his status is secure. For now he has a "place" bestowed on him by the audience. But it is bestowed by an audience, which is, in its turn, dependent on him for its reality as an audience. And to the extent that they treasure being a part of something big and unified, they are all dependent on him. The interdependence of performer (preacher) and audience is established and becomes fixed and secure.

LARGE SIZE BEGETS LARGER SIZE

Here we see another characteristic of the mega-church. *Because the organization is big, it becomes bigger.* We start here by accepting the statement that the church somehow managed to emerge as a big operation. We do not know what gave it its initial boost; we note only that it did indeed have that boost. Then once it has become big, its being big is the factor that enables it to become bigger still. Its increase in size is self-perpetuating. Once it passes a threshold, it will move on to ever-greater numbers. People perceive it to be a massive operation and they are, for this reason, attracted to it. And their being attracted to it causes it to become bigger still and so the snowball grows and grows.

We can see here why some efforts to imitate the mega-church do not prove successful. Some ordinary churches have had "contemporary" or "folk" (a misnomer) services in addition to their traditional events. They have had the music, the words projected on a screen, and all the rest of it. But these events often attract fewer people than the regular services. This occurs because these churches do not have the large size to begin with and so cannot attract more people. And because they have not attracted more, they cannot attract still more. The snowball effect simply does not get started.

The attraction to entities that are the "big" that results in their becoming bigger still is not true only of churches. It holds for schools, hospitals, entertainment, and, most notably, businesses. From an early age and throughout their lives, Americans are socialized to trust operations that are *large*. If it is big, people think, it is something you can depend on. A drugstore with vast size and many aisles will take care of people. Mr. Jones's pharmacy with less to offer and fewer people working, or even just Mr. Jones himself working, apparently cannot be trusted as much. Indeed, few such pharmacies are still in business, and those that are are likely to serve a clientele that is the personal following of a pharmacist who went into business a long time ago. When he retires, his store probably will also. Although a century or so ago, people trusted individuals who had names like "Mr. Jones," they now have confidence in large organizations with elaborate administrative structures. If this is true in business, it can also be true in churches and religion.

The Music Is New

An important part of any religious tradition is the forms of worship that have developed over time, and a basic part of worship is the music. In the cases of both Protestant and Catholic Christianity, there are rich treasures of music. Some is the performance kind. The worshiper hears it presented in the form of preludes and postludes played by an organist and as anthems sung by a soloist or duet or by a choir. She may also hear it in musical performances taking place outside of church. Other parts of the musical heritage consist of hymns that are to be sung by congregations. These hymns are extremely numerous, filling books and then more books. Some are majestic and awesome such as "A Mighty Fortress is Our God." Others combine a sense of the pathos of the world with a sense of the mystery of God. Among these, "Thou Who Almighty Art, Earth Hath Forsaken" is a good example. Still others are meditative and penitent such as "Amazing Grace," which is probably the best known and most frequently sung of all Protestant hymns. It is significant that these pieces of vocal music are called *hymns* and not just *songs*.

Some congregations sing better than others. Wandering among churches, a visitor will attend a few where people seem mainly to listen to the organ (or piano) or to a lead singer. In others, the singing is lusty and makes the "rafters ring." In some Mexican Protestant churches, a congregation of a half dozen can cause the widows to vibrate. In the Churches of Christ, in which instrumental music is ruled out as a matter of principle, the congregation often sings in four-part harmony, in effect performing like a choir.

For Protestant churchgoers, including those who have always been active in church, as well as those who return after an absence, this rich heritage of hymns plays an important role. The sound of an organ playing or people singing hymns congers up memories of Christianity as experienced in the church life of one's youth or, as they say, at one's mother's knee. By singing, humming, whistling, or otherwise "doing" hymns, a person claims or *reclaims* the church life of his youth or, for that matter, of his parents or grandparents. He once more stands in a long line that reaches way back, certainly to faith traditions of generations ago and ultimately to the New Testament period itself (although not with these hymns). The faith in a Lord crucified and risen from the dead echoes with a sound that never grows dimmer as one generation gives way to another. The worshiper locates himself in a sequence of generations that reaches back and goes forward. By singing the hymns, he claims his place amidst a "great crowd of witnesses" (Heb. 12:1).

Considering this, it is significant that in the ideal type of the mega-church and in many actual mega-churches, the regular attendee or visitor *never* hears a familiar hymn. She never even hears a familiar *type* of hymn. The music, although much emphasized, is music she has never heard before. And it is music that is not even *like* the church music she is familiar with. It is altogether new and different. Not only does she not know the particular song, but the songs do not remind her of the kinds of hymns she has known previously. They do not seem to be hymnlike. Indeed, they are not even called *hymns*. They are called *songs*.

The Christmas season affords special opportunity for observing this novelty. In Ocean Tide Church (not its real name), the guitar players and singers on the stage sang one traditional Christmas carol and then launched into a few special Christmas songs that were totally unfamiliar. A soloist appeared on the stage and did an artful rendition of another equally novel piece. A choir that had been on stage early in the Christmas season was missing on the Sunday before Christmas (Christmas being on a Sunday that year).

The insistence on novelty and uniqueness here is especially telling. Elsewhere in the mega-church program the leaders could assert that the unchurched person in America is "turned off" by traditional worship, which can only seem strange and unfamiliar to him. "Amazing Grace" may seem alien to people whose entire entertainment consists of rock concerts. But is the same true of Christmas carols? Are these not songs that are familiar to almost all Americans just as are secular Christmas songs? The popular singer who delivers odes to love and romance the rest of the year puts on a pious face and comes forth with "O Little Town of Bethlehem" as though it were his normal offering. *All* are familiar with the carols. The rejection of them in favor of novel songs would therefore seem to have a basis different from that of appealing to those for whom the worship services of most churches would seem strange and unfamiliar.

It is not clear whether the worship leaders expect the people present to sing. The words are presented on a screen, possibly on two screens to make viewing easy. But there are no notes, so the person in the congregation who wants to sing has to somehow "get" the tune from the leaders up in front who are singing into microphones. And this is a neat trick if he can do it. If a visitor looks around, he will see some people singing or trying to sing, while many more are just listening to the performers up in front. And not only are the songs not familiar, but chances are that a person attending will never learn the songs just by being present when they are sung. He will not find himself whistling or humming them later in the day. He will not learn them through repetition. There is no haunting tune to become familiar with. This absence of a tune is a feature of popular "rock" music of the sort that is presented on MTV. It seems to express an emotionality that is entirely diffuse and has neither form nor content. Perhaps it also expresses a *life* that explodes with outbursts of feeling but in which there is no effort to shape either a present or a future.

It is hard to exaggerate how remarkable this is. The evangelization of the frontier in the United States was accomplished in great measure by events that we called *revivals*. And they were precisely *re*vivals (bring-to-life again). The preacher assumed that his listeners had religion somewhere in their past (at "mother's knee"), and he then undertook to evoke the memory of that earlier contact with the Christian faith. His preaching and singing were intended to be *evocative*. The link with the past was, for those who had drifted far from that past, the passport to the faith itself. The "old familiar hymns" would play a big part in establishing this link.

If this was the case with the rough and ready folk of frontier society in an America moving ever westward, why is it not at all the case with their urban-industrial descendants? Why is the road back to faith in Christ no longer adorned with familiar hymns or, for that matter, with anything familiar? Why does it all have to be new, unfamiliar, and uncharted?

To answer this question, we must notice that there is a difference between the frontiersmen of an earlier era and the denizen of the modern industrial city. Some of the men who wondered out to the frontier came from fractured family-neighborhood backgrounds. Their place of origin held little promise or even appeal for them, so they wondered westward and took up the life of the cowboy, or, being even more extreme, of the "desperado." They had few norms or rules to live by other than "the code of the West." Yet they had bubbling under the surface of their minds and hearts some notion of what they would tell you was a "better life." The life they were living was not, even in their own estimation, the "good life." They often felt themselves closed off from this life, as though their departure from it took them past a point of no return—a barrier that would block their way if they tried to reverse course and go back to where they started. Even so, some of them managed to build farms or businesses, find wives, sometimes by "mail order" in which the mail went east and the prospective wives came west, and having families. Yet even with this possibility, there was the problem of *guilt*. They felt they had become "bad" and could not or did not have the right to go back.

Enter the revival preacher. He might be a Methodist circuit rider. Or he might be a gifted Baptist farmer who took up preaching as an avocation. Or he might be a traveling evangelist who wanted only to convert people, not to establish churches. To this preacher, the sinner or *ex*-sinner, once "saved," was expected to betake himself to a church that was available in his town or county. But whichever of these the revival preacher was, he could easily gain an audience, for once he set up his tent, he was presenting the "only show in town." Hard-working frontier farmers, tavern-keepers, and blacksmiths had little other entertainment available.

In social-psychological terms, the revival preacher's message was a masterpiece. He told the frontiersmen that they were indeed sinners, a status that they had generally assumed about themselves all along. He might have said that they were even worse sinners than they thought, although what they thought they were was bad enough. Hearing this, they sank into despair. But the preacher went further. He declared that Jesus, by his crucifixion, had paid the debt for their sins that they could never pay themselves. And by doing so, he had wiped the slate clean for them. Their sins were, in effect, written on a sheet of paper, and a rubber stamp with ink had been applied to the paper. The stamp was the Cross of Christ, and it said, "paid in full." The sins were *gone*. The slate was wiped *clean*. Their past had become totally *irrelevant.* Their lives as Christians began *then,* with no debt to pay.

In sociology, "labeling theory" asserts that one major reason people engage in undesirable behavior is that they think they have to. They think they have to because, as they see it, they are the *kind* of people who do those things. They think that they are this kind of person because they think that *people think* they are *this kind* of person. In their eyes, then, they have no choice. The revival, however, gave them a choice. It was an intense social process in which the label was lifted up and then removed completely. It was removed by "the blood of the lamb," and permission was granted to become whatever sort of person they chose *at that point* to be or to become.

Noteworthy here is that the person came out of a life centered on family, work (usually a farm or other family enterprise), and neighborhood (and maybe church). It was a structured life. And it was considered to be *good.* The person had departed from the structure and so felt guilty. With the guilt removed or rendered irrelevant, he could then return to the structure. The return was a process of guilt, repentance, forgiveness, renewal. The faith that brought him to it necessarily had that structure.

By contrast, in the modern urban setting, the concept of a family-neighborhood life as *structure* is replaced by a concept of life as *process.* It is a process in which the idea that life should be lived in the service of the *Good* gives way to the belief that *Success* and *Happiness* are the valued items to be sought. Of necessity, then, I am doing the right thing if I am successful, or happy, or both or in process of becoming successful and/or happy. Things are bad with me if I "fail" (at whatever I undertake) or am not happy or am moving in the direction of failure and unhappiness. In the earlier era, family and neighborhood were structures "out there" in the world that defined what was good for me. Nowadays, the important things might be *in* me—in the subjective or mental-emotional state of being *happy.* Or they might be in the realm of business and the professions, a very *public* realm, in which a person climbs the mountain to success to fame and fortune.

The revival preacher of the mid-1800s offered people a way back that they feared had been closed off. His counterpart in the twenty-first century sees his task very differently. He sees his audience as consisting of people who are not looking back. They do not want to, nor do they wish that they could, return to something. Rather, they want to go forward. And what they want to go forward to is the pinnacle of "making it" in business, the professions, or in the world of entertainment. Or they want to move forward to happiness and peace of mind.

Success, of course, has something of an objective character. If I make a lot of money or achieve a high position, I am successful. Happiness, on the other hand, is subjective. I find myself to be happy inside of myself, or I do not. Or I may be partly happy while being beset by various kinds of malaise. And since this is my problem, I betake myself to religion and churches with the idea that they are to help me with my subjective problem. The task assigned to Jesus is to relieve my inner anxiety and distress and to embolden me as I face the difficulties and obstacles of personal and professional life. Or, more accurately, the task assigned to *singing about Jesus* is to accomplish these ends.

We can see, then, why the "old familiar hymns" have lost their appeal. The person attending a mega-church is not looking for a "way back" any more than she is looking for forgiveness for her sins. In fact, she does not think that she has sins. She may not even understand the concept of *sin*. She may, however, suffer from low "self-esteem." She may lack "self-confidence." She is therefore looking for a way forward in which she can feel good about herself (enjoy high "self-esteem") as she pursues success and happiness.

Although success and a happy, smiling self-concept may be at the center of attention, the idea of *goodness* is not altogether lacking. Indeed, it is never totally absent. Whatever their endeavors or projects may be, human beings always call down an aura of "the good" or "the noble" on what they do. The wish for the label of "to be approved of" seems to be as constant in human affairs as the wish for breakfast and supper. Thus it is not surprising that preachers and attendees in the mega-church lay claim to the label or aura of "the good." What is distinctive, however, is that this penumbra of goodness is not *serious*. It will not require people to veer from paths they would otherwise follow. The partisan of the mega-church who is pursuing happiness would never follow Martin Luther and declare "here I stand" about an issue she deems to be important. She would not even understand the "here I stand" feeling. To her, the aura of goodness is frosting on a cake. It is something added to that which is felt to be of crucial importance, which is not overarching goodness, but personal happiness and success.

De-emphasis on Denomination

The mega-church sees itself as, and indeed is, a new reality among the affairs of the world. Notably, the mega-church is not a "parish" of a particular denomination. In some cases, the mega-church has no affiliation. For example, the Willow Creek Church is called a "community church," which means it was established to be a specific congregation and not a parish of a denomination. Other mega-church operations are historically Baptist and retain some attributes of that pedigree. In these mega-churches believers (8, 10, or 12 or more years of age) must undergo baptism as a requirement for membership, and it is to be carried out by total immersion. But even here, the label "Baptist" is downplayed. In one such case, that of Ocean Tide, the name is printed in large letters on the sign in front of the building. And then "Baptist Church" is written in small letters. The person who attends is not encouraged to see himself as Baptist. He certainly may do so if he wishes, but he could forget entirely that he attends a Baptist church. He can, in his own eyes, see himself simply as attending Ocean Tide Church. Or it might be just "The Tide."

In explaining this phenomenon, we may note that the church set its task as that of growing to a large size. To do this, it needs to attract people of many different kinds. There may be a notion that the people should all be middle-class whites; indeed, some say this openly. But apart from that, the wish is for as many people as possible to attend the church's services. They are not supposed to be people of Baptist, Methodist, or Presbyterian background and identity. Rather, they are supposed to be *all* people, persons and families of every denominational background. In this sense, a denominational label might appear to be a fact that would push people away. And the church's wish is to pull people in, not to push them out.

More is involved, however, than just a strategy for maximizing the size of the gathered congregation. Of greater importance is the proclamation that what is going on in the church is being invented on the spot. We have here "church" in a new and special sense. This is not just one more Baptist, Presbyterian, or Methodist church. It is not just another *instance or individual case* of those species. It is a species unto itself! It is Ocean Tide Church, or just "The Tide," and that is its own reality and essence. A denominational label would seem to reduce its stature. It would bring "Ocean Tide" down to a category, and this is to be avoided! It is above the categories, all of them, including those of denomination.

When a church is identified in any way, perhaps as Baptist or Pentecostal, that identification then constrains the church. Its Baptist or Pentecost nature or identity is to give shape to the programs and activities that it carries out. Its Baptist nature shapes its life, or its Pentecostal essence determines the details and contours of what happens under its roof. The mega-church, however, is a mega-church *rather than* a Baptist, Pentecostal, or Methodist church. This does not mean that the church is *free*. It certainly is free of denominational attributes, but it too is constrained. It is constrained by its nature as a mega-church. It achieved that status by operating in certain ways (and having the right community around it), and it maintains that status by continuing to operate in those ways. It can no more decide to abandon basic features of the mega-church than an Episcopal church can decide not to be Episcopal. If questions arise as to why the head or *regal* minister acts in certain ways, why members of his staff conduct themselves in one or another manner, or the worship or programs assume a certain sound and nature, the answer will be that it is a mega-church. To be very large or "mega," it must do so.

The Life Adjustment Tradition

The history of Protestant Christianity in America is rich and includes many ongoing dramas that are rich in plots and subplots. There is, of course, the life that goes on in the churches, in their worship, their ministries, their Sunday schools, and much more. But in addition to this, there have been, and continue to be, other undertakings related or unrelated to the churches. Among these were the revivals and tent-meetings that occurred in the 1800s and beyond. There, the preacher spoke in thunder–and–lightning-like tones regarding the daunting prospect of hell awaiting the sinner and the sweet prospect of heaven open to those who have faith in the Gospel. Then, there were the preachers who took to the airwaves, first in radio and later on television. The sermonizing carried out in these mass communications media have become a prominent feature of the religious scene. Here, one person can preach to many thousands of listeners who receive the messages in the comfort of their own living rooms. The rich offerings of these oral homiletics (arts in themselves as the writing and preaching of sermons surely are) are supplemented by great mountains of written documents, books and pamphlets of all kinds and all sizes, most readily available through mail order.

The preacher using mass media is sometimes called entrepreneurial because he often starts out with nothing and then builds up an operation via his own persuasive powers and his ability to appeal to people in large numbers. He does not arise within the ranks of established institutions such as denominational organizations or in colleges or seminaries. He is, in this sense, a very different "breed of cat" from the leaders or officials of a Baptist convention, a Methodist district, an Episcopal diocese, a Presbyterian presbytery or synod, or any other "conference" or "general conference." He is also distinct from a scholar who arises within a college, university, or seminary, one who teaches classes, writes books and who may, in due course, be "in demand" as a speaker at denominational or school-related conferences of all sorts. Rather, the television speaker or "televangelist" is much more "his own man." He is, in effect, a freelance religious operator. Once he has gained a regular audience, the operation he carries out is *his,* purely and simply.

There are two distinct traditions among these enterprising religious virtuosos. The first we may call *evangelical.* This term, although somewhat overworked, refers to a religion in which the movement is from God to human beings rather than from people to God. It does not refer to any wisdom developed by noble and ingenious thinkers who may counsel people on how to achieve temporal or eternal bliss. It refers, rather, to an act of God in which the Lord reaches out to the sinner, first in accusation and judgment, and then in pardon and renewal. In this sense it is a proclamation or announcement. The sinner, that is, the listener, is given to understand that her situation is, as it stands, hopeless. But God has radically changed the way the sinner stands before God. God has done so in the Crucifixion and Resurrection of Jesus Christ. By faith, then, in what *God does,* the sinner is delivered from the realm of hopelessness to a sure hope of salvation in the Lord. There have been many preachers in this tradition stretching from John Wesley and George Whitefield of the 1700s to today, but the name Billy Graham stands out above all others in the period after World War II.

The second tradition is the life adjustment or positive thinking theme. Here, instead of being a sinner in need of redemption, the listener is taken to be a person suffering from *failure of nerve* who is in need of encouragement. He is beset by negativism or negative thoughts. Or he lacks a vision of the possibilities that lie before him. Accordingly, the listener needs to learn to entertain thoughts that are optimistic and "upbeat." He can induce himself to do this. Just as a house can be air-conditioned, so he can "condition" his mind to think positive or "can do" thoughts. He can, by an act of will, push away the dark shadows of pessimism and move himself toward the bright sunlight of a future wide open with wonder and achievement. The most famous name in this vein appeared a half-century ago—Norman Vincent Peale. His book, *The Power of Positive Thinking* was a best-seller for a long time. He was even taken by many to be a prominent *religious* leader and his books to be prime documents of Christianity.

Later, Robert Schuller became a well-known leader in this tradition. He coined the expression *possibility thinking.* He has been the pastor of the famous Crystal Cathedral of California. He, too, called for people to move themselves to an attitude in which they see all things, or at least many wonderful things, as *possible.* Once again, the dark, foreboding "can't do it" is to give way to a vibrant confidence that one can go out into the world of business, sports, entertainment, and the professions and, by dint of sheer determination and willpower, by cultivating a positive self-image, conquer all and stand tall!

The difference between the more historically based evangelical and the more breaking-from-tradition life adjustment perspectives is important. Certainly, the evangelical tradition has roots that extend much further back, back indeed, into the whole history of Christianity and Judaism, and most notably to the Middle Ages. It was in the Middle Ages, around l,000 years ago, that sin, guilt, and the prospect of damnation to hell were prominent motifs in which people envisioned their life situations. These were the problems for which the Gospel of Jesus Christ as proclaimed in the Word and celebrated in the Sacraments was the solution, a solution that human beings could not devise for themselves but that God gives as a gift. It is a stern and steely faced gift, however, for it involves an awareness of terrible guilt, an awareness that is *itself* a gift from God just as are the pardon and release that follow. Once pardoned and released, the sinner is indeed released; she is a "new creature."

By comparison, the life adjustment perspective assumes that the prime reality in human life is the world of commerce and industry. This world assumes a quasi-religious character. It is a place in which good and noble things happen. In it, a person achieves "success" or fails to do so. It is where all that actually *matters* in human life takes place. To *succeed* does not mean simply that one has been able to do what he set out to do. It does not mean only that he managed to engage in business, gain wealth for

himself, and enjoy material comforts while having the respect of his neighbors. Rather, success is *Success;* it is a holy grail that lifts a person above the
drab and dull world in which he lives and out of the opprobrium of being
a failure, or, for that matter, of being merely ordinary. On the basis of this
assumption, the life adjustment tradition then takes it to be the purpose
of religion to give people the necessary psychological and emotional resources they need to achieve this Success.

In the mega-church, these two approaches, the evangelical and the life
adjustment, are combined. True, the two approaches are radically different
in both concept and mood. But within much of popular culture, and in the
life of the mega-church in particular, the difference melts away into na-
iveté and then into oblivion. After all, historically, the mega-church arises
from the evangelical tradition, with its ancestry being in the preaching of
the forgiveness of sins on the cross of Jesus Christ. And in many ways, the
mega-church does continue this tradition. Most of the new mega-church
songs are songs about Jesus, how wonderful he is, how great is God's love
for us as expressed in his Crucifixion and Resurrection. The new lyrics say
just this in innumerable ways, with a great deal of repetition and with great
emphasis.

In the preaching, however, the life adjustment theme emerges clearly
into dominance. At Christmas time in Ocean Tide Church, a series of sermons was presented on the theme "handling holiday stress." Later in the
winter, the minister addressed problems of child-rearing and concluded
his sermon with a film clip in which a baseball player hit a home run while
the fans cheered wildly. The implication was that if you raise your children
in the right way, they will hit home runs, presumably in many more zones
of life than just baseball. In another sermon, the minister compared the
maintenance of the spiritual life to tune-ups in the routine maintenance
of automobiles. Here he interspersed film clips of his conferences with a
mechanic in the repair shop between parts of his oral presentations. In
the film clips, he chatted with the mechanic about how you keep a car
going, implying an analogy to keeping the spiritual life of a person in good
repair.

It is not an accident that Bill Hybels of the Willow Creek Community
Church, the original and model mega-church, conferred with Robert
Schuller of the Crystal Cathedral and of "possibility thinking" fame. Hybels recognized from the beginning that the life adjustment theme was
close to the heart of what he was doing. His stated intention was to appeal

to people who had no church background ("seekers") who would find traditional church services to be boring and irrelevant. In doing so, he was
making an assumption that was not stated; it was hidden and really just
taken for granted. He was assuming that the world "out there" holds out
prospects of success and warnings of failure, and it is the church's job to
give people the emotional-spiritual "tune-up" that will propel them toward success. Indeed, this is what religion is said to be "all about." In fact,
the emerging rejection of the concept of sin on the grounds that it does not
promote self-esteem is telling in this regard.

This is not to deny that there is wisdom in the life adjustment theme.
The preacher may indeed have had some useful counsel on "handling holiday stress." His remarks about being a good parent may have been well
taken. There might even be some point to comparing a person's emotional
life to an automobile engine in need of a tune-up. Such wisdom may have
its place if (a) we maintain our respect for the complexities of human emotional life, and (b) we are alert to moral and ethical problems that stand in
the way of an uninhibited pursuit of worldly success.

But two things are missing in this life adjustment approach. First, no
amount of such wise counsel addresses the situation of a person (that is,
of every person) who lives on the wrong side of a chasm that separates her
from God and who for that reason struggles to do for herself what only
God can do. She goes in quest of wealth, power, and honor. She may even
seek out a feeling of being "godly" for which she herself claims credit. All
of these are futile substitutes for the action of God that restores human
beings to his presence. This is a point where life adjustment council cannot help and where Robert Schuller's solicitude for people's self-esteem is
destructive rather than helpful.

And second, in life adjustment there is no call, nor can there be a
call, to righteousness as such. The possibility that a person would do
something because, and only because, it is *right* does not appear on the
horizon. That a person would refrain from doing something or from supporting something for the sole reason that the thing is *wrong* is nowhere
in sight. When the world "out there" in which we succeed or fail is taken
as "given," and as the one thing that is important is to succeed within
that world, there cannot be right and wrong. There can be only "works"
or "does not work." To make decisions on the basis of what is *right* is to
move into a strange and new place and to breathe an air that is radically
different.

Indeed, if one examines written works such as those by Bill Hybels and Rick Warren, she will find something approaching a total absence of the concept of right or righteousness. Martin Luther's "here I stand" would be unintelligible. The white man in Alabama in the 1930s who addresses an African American man as "sir" because he feels morally *obligated* to accord the man that respect would make no sense at all. It would neither be good public relations nor promote "adjustment." Rosa Parks's refusal to move from her seat on the bus would be something from another world. One could try to see these as instances of thinking that is "positive" or of the "possibility" kind, but these would be attempts to get a square peg into a round hole. We can keep trying, but the peg will not go in. Let it be noted: The concept of *right* is stubborn and recalcitrant; it refuses to be compressed into "that which works," or that which promotes a "positive self-image." It insists on being its own, unique self.

2

THE MEGA-CHURCH: WHAT HAPPENED TO RIGHTEOUSNESS AND TRUTH?

THE ESSENTIAL CONCEPT OF RIGHTEOUSNESS

In everyday speech, we often speak of actions that are "right" or "wrong." We make moral judgments about actions and possibly about the people who perform them. We also talk about actions that "work" or "do not work" in accomplishing the things that people intend. That is, we make judgments about strategy or effectiveness. These two are not the same. To do what is moral or right is not the same as doing what works, and doing what works is not the same as doing what is moral or right.

In this contrast of "right" and "that which works," we have another basic characteristic of the mega-church. It is a negative feature, something that is missing. And it is something that *must* be missing. The very nature of the mega-church rules it out in principle. This is the concept of *righteousness* or the *right*. It is a primary concept that cannot be reduced to other realities that are simply combined in certain ways. A person may understand it, or she may not. But if she does not understand it, if she has no idea of it in her mind, no one can tell her what it means. Someone speaking to her cannot cite ideas she does understand and then combine these ideas in different and varying ways. The person either "hears" the term and understands it, or she does not. Someone might say, for example, "the salesperson misled the customer about what the customer was buying. The salesperson *should* not have done that; it was just not *right*." If a person who hears that sentence does not understand the terms *should* and *right*, there is no way to explain them. Such a person might understand that the salesperson will suffer a loss of business in the future or may have to endure the wrath of the defrauded customer or even have legal problems. But the bare-bones meaning of "right" will escape her.

To say that a term is *primary* means that it cannot be defined as a combination of other terms. In the case of the *right*, we might think that it combines three ideas: (1) the person who does what is "right" will be happy; (2) he will be popular with people; and (3) he will succeed in what he undertakes. But his doing what is effective in the pursuit of these goals will not be doing what is *right*. His action will, instead, be based only on a *strategy*. It will be that which works in the effort to become happy, popular, and successful. By contrast, the concept of the *right* stoutly resists this subservience. It insists on standing all alone and by itself. It has its own and special meaning altogether apart from those other terms. The fact that certain things a person does will make him happy, popular, and successful does not mean that he does what is *right*; and if he does do what is *right*, there is no assurance that his doing so will make him happy, popular, or successful. His reward for doing what is right is that he has done what is *right* or is *the right*—*that* and nothing else. To someone who does not understand the concept, that assertion will make no sense. It might even seem silly. But to those who do understand it, it will make perfect sense. The sense that it makes will seem stern and uncompromising in the way it demands attention and obedience. But it will make sense.

While primary as a concept, the *right* is not without content. Paul Tillich has provided us a way of understanding this content in the third volume of his *Systematic Theology*. Reflecting on the biblical statement that human beings have "dominion" over the entire world, he said that by his powers of reason, the human being can control every object. He is surrounded by a vast collection of objects or "things." These things are all subject to his understanding and ultimately to his control. Although he does not in fact control them all, he has in his power of reasoning a potential ability to manipulate any of the innumerable objects that make up his world.

But there is one limit to this "dominion" over the plants, animals, and other objects that make up the human being's world. This limit is the *other person*. When she comes face-to-face with this other person, the human being confronts an inherent limit to her control over the things of the world. This is a limit in principle and not just in practice, for the human being depends on the other person for her own reality as a person. She becomes a person in and through her intercourse with *the other*. In this sense, she is dependent on that other. To be real herself, she must stand respectfully before the other person and before that other person's decision-making capacity. The other person must be a *person* and not a thing. If she tries to manipulate the other as she manipulates things, she makes the other into a thing. And if the other is transformed into a thing, without decision-making power, the first person is herself reduced to the status of a thing. A person can be human—we may say—only by meeting the other person as a fully *human* being. The other person is a "wall." The first person must stop and stand and wait before this wall. The wall will be opened only by the decision of the other person—the person behind it. The first person cannot break it down, for if she does, she breaks it down at the cost of her own reality and substance as a human being. This would be unconditional loss. The pictures of hell presented in thought and in art seek to capture the bottomless and unconditional nature of this loss.

This relationship of person to person is most easily seen in the man–woman encounter, which is the model or the paradigm of all human relations (Adam and Eve). Either the man or the woman can seek to control the other in a variety of ways. One can appeal to the other's need of gestures of approval or affection or the other's need of sexual attentions. Or he or she can take control of the other's access to things he or she needs, such as food and clothing and other necessities. Or the person could try to control the other's access to the approval and affection of others. The person could even do it by sheer bombast: "Do as I want you to do or else!"

If, however, the person succeeds in thus controlling the other, he or she does so at the cost of his or her own reality as a person. The man can be a man only by relating to the woman as a fully human being. He must be one who "stands at the door and knocks." A woman, similarly, can realize her substance as a woman only by relating to the man as one to whom she can appeal but whom she cannot control. If either controls the other, he or she becomes a thing. Both are bereft of human substance.

Here, then, we have the source and the nature of the concept of the *Right*. A person comes face-to-face with another person. In that encounter, there is a demand on him that he respect—indeed, that he stand in awe of—the other person's reality as a person. He may make supplication to that person; he may ask or beg for approval or affection. But he must do so as one who asks or begs. He cannot force or even cause the other to respond with acceptance or approval. He can say "please," but he cannot command. And in appealing to the other without making demands, he performs the model or paradigm of all moral action. He does what is *right*.

It is a matter of ultimate importance to her that she do so. In approaching the "wall" of the other person and with respect for the other as a decision-making being, she lays claim to her own reality as a person. Or, we could say, she becomes an *actual* human being. If there is question whether she will respect the other or will, instead, seek to manipulate him, it is an ultimate "up" and "down" issue. When she decides for respect, she is "up;" she becomes real as a person herself. When she opts for manipulation, she makes a "thing" of both the other and of herself and so loses her reality as a person. She descends into nonbeing, which is the ultimate terror. In pursuing her own being through the manipulation and control of the other, she loses her being. She descends into an ultimate loneliness that is an ultimate emptiness or nonbeing. Thus we see that moral judgments are always ultimate "up" and "down" judgments. Being and nonbeing always and by necessity stand in stark and total contrast with one another.

The content of moral judgments always derives from this paradigm. An individual stands before the "wall" of the other person, hat-in-hand and respectful. And he does so as a matter of ultimate importance. From this, then, as the model, there come all of the particulars that make up moral-ity as properly conceived. In line with the Ten Commandments, a person will neither do nor risk doing bodily harm to another (kill). He will not interfere with the other's cherished personal relationships—any of them (adultery). He will not deprive the other of access to goods and services (steal), and he will not damage the other's "good name" (false witness). He is also aware that the other persons who make up his world form a com-munity and that to live good and human lives, they need their community life to be ordered and structured. He therefore respects the patterns of life by which people who live together can have a life that is orderly and peace-ful. Yet because he cherishes individuals, she seeks to adjust or "stretch" the orders of community life to make room for special forms, as in the case of unions of gay couples.

In this sense, Jesus's saying, "inasmuch as you have done it unto the least of these my brethren you have done it unto me," is the emery wheel from which all moral assertions are the flying sparks. An issue is moral if, and only if, a person is in encounter with the "wall" of the other person. In that "wall," the person comes up against the limit to his ability to manipulate all of the things in his environment. He is, instead, constrained by the fact that the other person is a *person*. He is constrained from using that person to satisfy his appetites or as an instrument for acquiring that which will satisfy appetites or, for that matter, from ignoring the other person as irrelevant to his appetites. On the other hand, he is compelled to honor the other person, to rejoice in that person's presence and to assist that person in obtaining life's necessities, in avoiding life's dangers, and in acting on the basis of his own decisions. To say that he is constrained or compelled is to say that his own reality as a human being depends on his taking the other person seriously as a person. It is a *moral* matter.

THE CONCEPT OF RIGHT AND THE MEGA-CHURCH

In the mega-church, the concept of *right* is conspicuous by its absence. A careful reading of *The Purpose Driven Life* by Rick Warren will make this clear. There is a great deal of sentiment in this book, and more than a small air of piety. But the reader will look in vain for a call to righteousness. The church is seen as valuable itself. The "purpose" in the life driven by purpose is the construction of the church and its program. Apart from some charitable enterprises, there is no image of a larger human community that is made more truly human and communal by the "leaven" of a vital Christian church in its midst. The reader will not see in the book an upward draft holding family and neighborhood aloft above the whirlpools of divorce and family breakup that we see in our society. The unrestrained greed and aggressive tactics of many business corporations that do so much damage to people and communities will go unchallenged. In vain will the reader scan the horizon for a glimpse of the passion for justice that challenges the increasing gap between rich and poor in the United States today. Neither will she find questions about the abiding forms of racial, ethnic, and social class prejudice that continue to dull the American dream for many of the nation's people. Nor will the robust applause given to military adventures and the elaboration of the means of violence be brought into question. In general, there is no prophetic voice that will address the community *as* a community and challenge its injustices while calling it to an increase in equity and mercy.

True, other Christian churches in the United States have a very uneven record in these matters. The trumpet has not always given a clear sound! But there is always a possibility that churches will look beyond themselves and the society of which they are a part and will seek to promote peace and justice in that society. Whenever the church has a "looking beyond" ability, there is reason for hope.

By contrast, the mega-church is *by its nature* constrained from having a serious interest in society *as* society. Its project of becoming big, and ever bigger, is an integral part of its nature as the organization which it is. It is constrained by that project, and it is compelled to construct its entire life as a church around it. In the nature of the case, this makes the church itself the focus of attention. Its ever-increasing size is essential; it is what makes it authentic or valid as being what it claims to be. There is, for this reason, no room for maneuver. A preacher preaching or a teacher teaching cannot wander away from the enthusiasm that builds the church's clientele. She has to stay focused. To address, or try to address, social or economic problems would be to dampen the zeal that keeps the attendance constantly growing.

From time to time, a mega-church minister or other spokesman will be forced—or lured—into speaking about a community matter. When this happens, the minister will take the most simplistic position possible. He will not reason from basic principles to applications. The same urgency of growth that keeps him away from such issues will keep his treatment of them—when he cannot avoid the issues—simple. He will endorse whatever items in the culture's moral warehouse seem "obvious" and do not require reasoning. To reason—to think about principles and applications—would dampen the enthusiasm and dull the zeal. It would be like admitting that we are not on God's side always and by our very nature. It would offend the sensibilities of the mega-church leaders. For them, growing ever larger is a *sacred* undertaking. If, at some point, a person preaching in the mega-church were to begin to speak earnestly about a question of peace of justice, he would clearly clash with the abiding atmosphere of the operation. His doing so could cause trouble, but what is more likely is that it would just "fall flat."

To establish this sacred character, it is necessary to paint a moral halo over a church's project of growing ever larger. Lyle Schaller makes this clear in his book, *From Cooperation to Competition.* Schaller speaks of churches that grow in numbers of "constituents." He speaks of such growth as being good in every way. It is an indication that the church is vital and alive. Indeed, the growth of numbers of people is *identical with* being vital and alive. Without an increase in its numbers, a church is mired in mediocrity and does nothing but provide a comfort zone for its members. It is but a genial arena that supplements the social spheres of family and work—a "third place." When numbers increase, the church goes beyond such care-taking of long-term members and begins to *transform lives.* Schaller makes many references to "transforming lives," but he neither explains nor illustrates that expression. His readers are left with the impression that a *transformed life* is that of a person who participates in making the large church larger still. "Transformed life" and "growth in numbers" are mutually defining.

Schaller here performs a vital service to the mega-church movement. We might see such a church as an operation in which all Christian truth and all Christian values have been sacrificed to the goal of becoming ever larger. But as Schaller sees it, this is *not* a sacrifice at all. Even speaking of it as a "sacrifice" would be nonsensical. In actuality, for Schaller, there is no contradiction between Christian values and an unrestrained commitment to growth. To expand the size of the crowds in the church and to do so continuously is what Christianity is "all about." Growth *is* Christian value. Indeed, it is the one and only Christian value.

This may sound harsh, but it is not harsh enough. I have been reading books about Christianity all my life. I have read *From Cooperation to Competition* twice. I find that Schaller is quite innocent when it comes to Christian theology. Indeed, he knows neither theology nor the faith that theology articulates. *Indeed, so without understanding is he that he does not even know that he does not know.* We are all ignorant of many fields of knowledge. But we have enough of an inkling of these fields (say, Russian literature) so that we know that we do not know much about them. But when it comes to theology, Schaller does not have even an elementary sense of what Christian theology is. He has no "feel" for it. We might, of course, think that this is unimportant. Who, after all, is Lyle Schaller? In fact, Schaller is a major advocate and apologist for the mega-church movement. He and that movement have a basic compatibility. What is missing or shortchanged in his work is missing or shortchanged in the mega-churches he so energetically promotes.

TAKING DOCTRINE LIGHTLY—OR DOCTRINE LITE: DOCTRINE, THE CHURCH, AND SOCIETY

It is characteristic of the mega-church that doctrines or "beliefs" do not matter to any great degree. The tumultuous controversies that tore apart the churches of the past need not take place in the mega-church. These could not occur because it does not matter whether one or another of the competing beliefs is affirmed. As a rule, if an issue arises, the denizens of the mega-church will affirm whatever doctrines are thought to be most popular. This is what "everyone" thinks and therefore what "we" think. They do not do this out of having a passionate wish to declare "here I stand" on whatever is at the core of the Christian faith. Rather, they affirm what they affirm precisely because *it does not matter* whether a certain belief is affirmed or denied. It is because beliefs as such have so little *salience* that they can readily betake themselves to whatever views seem to be at the center of the cultural whirlpool. These are the beliefs that can be affirmed without thinking. Not a single moment of uncertainty and contemplation is required.

That we are "saved" by Jesus's death and resurrection is the item most frequently mentioned, including in the songs sung every Sunday. The classic fundamentals, such as verbal inerrancy of scripture, virgin birth, and physical resurrection and coming again, will be affirmed if the question of their validity comes up, but the question is not likely to come up.

These are the doctrines that are, so to speak, lying around in the living room of the household of faith. Like pieces of clothing that careless members of the family did not pick up, they are simply *there*. And if someone wants just a certain item of clothing, or simply a piece of cloth, she may pick up one of these pieces hurriedly and without examination or discrimination. She will not be "picky." She will just grab something that is good enough! Similarly, a person may take hold of an opinion about something. It may be any opinion about anything. And we then have a belief that is good enough; by holding it, a person can be declared to be on the side of whatever is good and right. Some vague and general assumption that this is a correct belief, or, better stated, a correct *Christian* belief is all that it takes.

Central to these occasional affirmations is that no process of reasoning is involved. No one declares to the gathered multitudes that these multitudes could consider, think through, a major premise or even a minor premise and then reach a conclusion. Even a simple logical process such as this one would be too much: All human beings are equal; both white and black people are human beings; *therefore* white people and black people are equal. The moment required to say "therefore" slows down the rapid, even immediate, pace of automatic affirmation that is expected to proceed without a shred of hesitation. Reasoning with its inevitable moment of hesitation cannot happen. There can be only instant declaration. Any delay is inconsistent with the spirit of the occasion. (Paul's letter to the *Romans* could not be taken seriously as the letter that it is.)

Strangely, Schaller asserts that the mega-church makes a clear doctrinal statement. He gives no examples of what such doctrinal statements would consist of. Indeed, he cannot, for to set up actual doctrines would open up the possibility of disagreement. Whatever is assumed but not actually stated cannot be an object of disagreement or controversy. The truth of the matter is that the mega-church can achieve a degree of doctrinal unity precisely because the truth or falsity of doctrines *does not matter.* For Schaller, what is good is having a clear doctrinal statement; thus, it is the clarity that is good, not the content of the statement. And even that clarity exists only because someone says it does. Here, as elsewhere in the mega-church, "aspiration equals achievement." We *wish* to be "clear" on matters of doctrine; therefore we *are.* That's all it takes. No thinking.

But what is doctrine? To answer this question, we need to assume the essential *encounter of faith,* which goes as follows: There is an individual who has an experience, but it is not just an experience. It is not, that is, simply an event in the subjective life of the individual. It is, rather, a meeting of the individual with that which is *other* than he, with that which is "out there." The objective referent of the experience is integral to the nature of the experience itself. Just as a man who is in love with "Laura" who is "only a dream" has an experience that is different from that of a man who is enamored of, and therefore in encounter with, a "Laura" who is a real and living woman, so the man of faith has an experience that is not properly understood unless we assume that the experience has an objective referent. Rudolf Otto makes this point in his *The Idea of the Holy.*

With this characteristic assumed, we can then say that a doctrine is an intelligible statement of what the encounter is and what it means. It is a statement that takes note of the person who is in an encounter (has an experience), of the objective referent of that encounter, and of the relation between the two. The encounter comes first, and then there is the effort to explain or make sense of it. It is an effort to refer beyond the encounter to what the encounter *means.* A person may say, for example, that he found himself in an encounter in which he was convicted of unworthiness and sin by a pure and righteous Man from God. He was then forgiven his sin in that same encounter and was given a new life. In this new life, he continued to be a sinner, but a sinner who was made righteous by his union with the Man from God. We could think of this simply as encounter (or experience), but we cannot speak of it without making appeal to concepts and ideas. Just as the man who is in love with a real Laura must have concepts such as "being in love" in order to make sense of what he experiences and to act on the basis of that sense-making, so the man of faith must have ideas and mental constructs to deal with the encounter with the objects of his faith.

Once the intelligible accounting of an encounter of faith has been made, it may then be used to ensure that the encounter is what it is and not another and an alien encounter. The faith has integrity. To be the faith that it is, it must avoid being "swept up" into a different vortex. It must steer clear, for example, of a dualistic faith in which the visible world is rejected as evil and another, purely spiritual realm, sought. It must keep itself aloof, that is, from Platonic, neo-Platonic, and Buddhist ways of understanding suffering and deliverance from it. It must also put distance between itself and a modern liberal faith in which a person simply "awakens" to the joys of a world of community among diverse peoples who live in peace and justice. This does not mean that the Christian must deprecate these other faiths. She needs only to preserve the integrity of Christianity as it is. And she must preserve the distinction between the faith of the Gospel and other faiths and philosophies. A way to say this is that doctrine sets up *guardrails* by which the Christian remains within the vortex of her faith.

Further, when a faith becomes the basis of a community—a *church*—it inevitably gets tied up with the rifts and divisions within human community. As long as we are in the "world" and not in the Kingdom of God, people will divide themselves into social, ethnic, and ideological groups. They then use doctrines as banners by which to exalt their groups, the "in-groups" and to set them apart from the others, the "out-groups." That doctrines and their liturgical practices have served as guardrails of the faith is then used to lend legitimacy and even holiness to what are really just worldly and social divisions. On the one hand, there is the guardrail function of doctrines in preserving the Faith. And, on the other, there is the service that doctrines perform as chauvinistic or "snob" symbols by which people who are "high up" set themselves apart from those who are "low down," or by which people who form an "in-group" distinguish themselves from "the others" or "the foreigners." These two functions are then mixed up in bewildering ways and are commonly difficult to disentangle. It is hard to know when we are dealing with a guardrail by which

Christian faith is set apart from other and alien faiths and when we are coming up against a symbol system by which social groups set themselves apart from each other.

DOCTRINE AND THE MEGA-CHURCH

What *is* clear is that Christian groups in the past have had a passionate interest in the doctrines and the liturgical and moral practices by which they are distinguished from each other. We could think here of the dispute between the Arian and Athenasian (Catholic) communities in the first centuries of Christianity, of the split between Eastern (Greek) and Western (Latin) forms of Catholicism, of the divide between Catholics and Protestants, of the sharp differences between American Protestantism's fundamentalists (evangelicals) and American liberals (mainline) on the other. And, of course, there are many other divisions.

Why, we may now wonder, does the mega-church appear on the scene as a group of Christians who are profoundly indifferent to doctrines or even to doctrine as such? As a first consideration in answering this question, we may note that the mega-church is *mega*. It is very large and constantly growing. The number of people who attend its events becomes larger by the week. And it is the intention of the leaders, notably the intention of the head pastor, that this growth should take place. Many of these pastors decided at the beginning that they wanted their church to be large, and they calculated how to bring about such an increase in size. They then acted to make the "mega" of their church a reality. Even if some would-be mega-churches fail to achieve this tumultuous growth, it remains a feature of the mega-church as an *ideal type*.

Of the innumerable religious movements of the past, most had certain features of doctrine, polity, or liturgics that set them apart from others. In many cases, these features distinguished them from the majority and gave them a distinctive raison d'être. The people who adhered to them felt that they were a group apart, and this separation from the majority was important to them. They formed a religious *sect*. In other cases, the distinctive features qualified those who adopted them as the majority or center-of-gravity members of a larger society. These made up an *establishment* or a *church*. But in both cases, the features of doctrine, polity, or liturgics that qualify their adherents as a group apart or as a majority coalition also serve to limit the group. Much as the people who hold these views and practices may feel that they are right, there will inevitably be some who do not share that view. There will be opponents. The larger community will be split. This limitation of a group's ability to attract adherents is a price that it pays for the features that attracted the people it has. If these features arouse enthusiasm in some quarters, it will give rise to opposition in others.

If we can think of these distinctive features as *religious baggage* that attracts some but repels others, we could say that the mega-church lightens its load by throwing all this baggage overboard. It does not have items of doctrine that attract a few enthusiastic followers. But neither does it have, in these items, a feature that repels others. Like an airplane that has little to weigh it down, the mega-church can fly high and fast. Nothing holds it back. Or, to turn the matter around, if the leaders of the mega-church want to grow fast and furiously, they do well to jettison unnecessary theological, ecclesiastical, and liturgical baggage. Thus unhindered, they can grow. And once that growth is underway, *this growth itself* becomes the distinctive feature that facilitates further growth.

True, certain core beliefs remain, notably the belief that we are saved by Christ's sacrifice of himself on the cross. And also true, it is hard to imagine a mega-church without an affirmation of this core, even if this core is emphasized more in song than in preaching. But we may note that within American Protestantism, and even beyond Protestantism, this is definitely a core that occasions little dispute. The people who do dispute the sacrifice of Christ are those who are of a modernist persuasion and want to see Jesus as above all a teacher or who wish to equate Christianity with a general, enlightened humanitarianism. These people are part of an intelligentsia who consider points of view to be important. They have reasoned their way to a rejection of the evangelical first principles. As far as the mega-church is concerned, these people are not candidates for their operation or their church as they call it and can in any case be viewed as expendable. Actually, many people are expendable, including those who come into the mega-church and then leave it. What is important is that the flow *into* the organization continues, not that it includes everyone. That is all.

Actually, the people who reject the core beliefs of the Crucifixion and Resurrection make up a small proportion of even the unchurched. According to survey evidence, most people who are not affiliated with churches and do not attend are simply indifferent. Few are principled modernists or atheists. With the rest—those who see little point in church—the act of accepting the evangelical core poses no great problem. If they continue in their Sunday morning golf routine, the core beliefs are only *unimportant* or lacking in salience. The beliefs are not, to them, wrong. They do not care enough about them to find them wrong. And if they decide at some point to "give church a try," the affirmation of the evangelical point of view readily commends itself. These beliefs are, we may note, part of the cultural heritage that has always been hovering in the background. They have a certain aura of goodness about them, even when they are not important enough to get someone off the golf course and into a church. Once a decision to "check out" church has been made, the belief that Jesus saves us from our sins by his sacrifice is affirmed as readily as the belief that there is a God who created the world. Having little interest in doctrines as such, this new candidate for involvement in church life has scant difficulty affirming belief in a core that does little, after all, to set him apart from others.

To affirm belief in salvation by the Cross of Christ is, for an American, quite natural. It is what results when items of belief are tossed into the air and allowed to fall where they will. To affirm something different, perhaps that Jesus is above all a teacher of ethics, that there is no God (atheism), or that ethics is actually all there is, will prove difficult. This requires thinking or doing. A person has to stand up, pay attention, take thought, make decisions, utter statements, and, possibly, take action. The sequence is *deliberate*. This is the set of steps a person goes through when she does not settle for what is "natural" or the steps that simply fall into place. In the mega-church, such a decision-making sequence, or any decision-delineating at all, would be a serious dampening of the enthusiasm that is essential for the operation. Things must be allowed to occur without contemplation or question.

In the 1950s, Will Herberg published a book entitled *Protestant, Catholic, Jew*. Although it is a half-century old, it is still relevant. Herberg's argument was that "the religion of Americans is the religion of America." The national community, with its values of freedom of speech and of religion, is the true focus of devotion. But people can be devoted to America *as* Catholics, *as* Protestants, or *as* Jews. (The devotion of American Moslems to America did not come up in the 1950s as it would today. But this is not our concern here.) What we need to note is that, in the mega-church, this devotion to the values of the national community is cut loose from all limitation. The restraining bars of the mainline churches, ineffectual as they often are, are removed. The mega-church is free to affirm all that "we" (i.e., "we Americans") hold dear. Thus it is little wonder that mega-church spokesmen are little bothered by traditional doctrinal disputes or, for that matter, by doctrine as such.

CONFIDENCE IN DIVINE DIRECTION

Another characteristic of the mega-church is the apparent *confidence* that its leaders are acting on the explicit directives of God. In this viewpoint, God gives the leaders point-by-point instructions concerning what they are to do and how they are to do it. They harbor little doubt that the details of what they undertake, how people are to be involved, and the nature of programs to be undertaken are under higher directive. Indeed, all that they do is specifically and in detail directed by God.

We could, of course, say that this is characteristic of churches and of their people in general. But I suggest here that it is far from being true. In more than 50 years of observing church life, I have rarely seen people make the kind of claims to specific direction by God as we see in the mega-church. What I do see, rather, is people saying that they *feel* inspired by God, or that they feel a presence of God that *seems* to be leading them to speak or act in certain ways. It is a case of what "feels" and "seems." There is a hesitancy, a remaining open to a guidance that is not yet received, that inhibits claims to be acting on specific directions from on high. It is a case of "wait and see" and of being ready to be inspired differently the next day. Or, there is a feeling that God has set only a very general task, and it is our job to think about the best way to carry out that task. And when we do, we are aware that our thinking may be flawed by our finitude—by the limitations of our understanding—and by our continuing pride and self-seeking that may corrupt our judgment. I may think it is God's will for me to do something, but then I cannot see around the corner, and if I could, I might arrive at a different conclusion about God's will. And I have a subterranean wish to exalt and glorify myself, and *this* may corrupt my judgment and interpretation of what God's will is.

In saying this about utterances of church people of the past, I am trying to read backward from what I see in the mega-church now to what I have observed in a past that stretches over a very long time. While those 50 years were going by, it seemed natural that people *sought* guidance from God and *hoped* that they had correctly assessed where the hand of God was leading them. It is only after being jolted by the pretensions of mega-church leaders to know exactly what God is directing them to do that I see the greater humility and the constant "seeking" of church people and church leaders over a span of many decades. Christians in general did not think that they were God's lieutenants acting on the basis of orders from above. They assumed that assessing the will of God was an on-going process, one requiring struggle and adaptability.

In addition to feeling that they act on the explicit instructions of God, the mega-church people also have a "chummy" attitude toward the Lord. He is their "best friend." Rick Warren of the Saddleback Church says as much. What is missing from their view of God is any sense of God as *holy*. The God who "looks upon the earth and it trembles and on the mountains and they quake" (Ps. 104:32) is unknown to them. The God who is a mystery and who remains a mystery even when He reveals himself is outside of their purview. It would seem that these two things are connected: confidence in a step-by-step divine directive and, being on familiar terms with God.

OCEAN TIDE CHURCH AND THE IDEAL TYPE

Although we assume that no entity in the "real world" perfectly exemplifies any ideal type, Ocean Tide Church certainly comes close to being the pure mega-church. It has the regal pastor, "Brother Jim," as he is affectionately called. He has a central place in the operation that is secure and would never be questioned. The auditorium is filled in its three Sunday morning events with many more people than are actually members. Its attendance is high indeed, with perhaps 600 people attending each of its three Sunday morning events. The music is altogether new. Aside from a rare occasion in which a Christmas anthem is sung by a youth choir, the people attending will not hear any familiar hymns. Nor is it likely that they will ever learn one of the songs. The denomination is certainly deemphasized. The sign outside says in large letters OCEAN TIDE. Then in tiny letters the passerby is informed that it is a "Baptist Church." Nor will he be reminded by anything else other than an occasional baptism by immersion that the operation is, historically at least, a Baptist church.

The content of sermons over a period of many months is for the most part of the life adjustment kind. There is virtually no call to righteousness at any point. Indeed, the very idea of a concern for the morally *right* seems strangely out of place. What call to *goodness* is to be found in the church turns out to be a call to be busy within the Church's own program. And on the rare occasion when a moral issue does arise, the pastor will take a position that is highly standardized and taken for granted. This will be a position that does not, and indeed cannot, require steps of thinking, premise-to-conclusion reasoning. Such reasoning and the inevitable moment of hesitation it involves are alien and even treasonous. It is not congruent with the "good guy" or "God's own man" image that is being projected. In one sermon concerned with forgiveness, the pastor commented that the wife of an unfaithful husband may forgive him, but she does not have to live with him! Thus the pastor made his praise of forgiveness, but did a dutiful bow to morality. It was a gesture that involved no complexities, no effort to apply principles to cases, and no "ifs, ands, or buts."

Nor will there be a concern about particular beliefs or doctrines. Apart from affirming the central place assigned to the crucifixion and resurrection of Jesus, the preacher will say little that informs the curious as to just what he believes. And if he is backed into a corner, he will affirm the most rudimentary of doctrines. He will affirm, let us say, "creationism" over evolution. He will call for restatement of biblical literalism or "inerrancy" over a scholarly treatment of the scriptures. He does not want to be busy making any of these affirmations, for they by their nature tend to exclude or "cut off" those who do not accept the affirmation. They might even "cut off" some of his own following. He can make them when he must exactly because doctrines as such do not matter to him.

On the other hand, if we go to First Baptist Church in the same city, we find much of the mega-church character, but not all of it. The minister certainly is regal, as indicated by the fact that he played a major role in choosing his successor. On the other hand, he is rather scholarly in his demeanor, and he preaches from a pulpit, albeit with his face projected on a screen for those who are some distance from him and so do not see well. He also bestirred himself when it turned out that a restaurant was serving liquor less than 200 feet from the church building, a practice that was forbidden by local law. (This zeal for moral rectitude is not truly "in character" for the mega-church on the other side of town.) The First Baptist Church has a choir of about 100 singers, giving a far more "congregational" mood to the event than will be found elsewhere. So we see here some of the character of the mega-church, but not all of it. The idea of the mega-church is just that—an idea. Real operations or churches can approximate the mega-church in varying degrees.

THE MEGA-CHURCH AND "RELIGION"

Over time in any society certain things come to be taken for granted. The people assume certain things so completely and without question that it does not occur to them to question those items. Only when a challenge to these bits of "conventional wisdom" is made do the items become objects of conscious decision making. We may imagine, for example, that a visitor is present at the meeting of the school board of a small city. The visitor has something to say about the sports programs of the local schools. Her proposal is that the sport called *football* be deleted from the agenda. She argues that it is a dangerous sport, that it has been the occasion of many injuries, some of them permanent. She also argues that football is par excellence a spectator sport. People do not expect to play it; they expect only to watch it. And because a school is supposed to prepare people for life, says the visitor, the sports it sponsors should be those that people will play and not just watch, and, further, play when they are 50 and not just when they are 18 or 20. Perhaps tennis, golf, shuffleboard, or hiking would be better.

Put this scene in front of any group of Americans. Put it in front of people who are football fans and in front of those who are not football fans. Am I not correct that most will respond in the same way? They will agree that the visitor to the school board has lost her mind! Nothing could be more absurd! Such a proposal will not even be considered! Even the few who are inclined to agree will think that everyone else will consider it unthinkable. And yet it is quite sensible, is it not? The fact that it is both sensible *and* unthinkable is an indication that we are dealing here with an item of culture that *"floats"*—it is always present and hovers over all that we do. And being something that "floats" or hovers, it belongs to all of us. It is, as we say, in the air.

Similarly, religion is something that floats and belongs to all of us. Perhaps we could say "spirituality" or "the spiritual" has this nature. And because it is there hovering in the background, it affords opportunities for one or another enterpriser to set up shop—or a television program—and offer services to the public that pertain to their religious proclivities. Just as musicians can get busy and provide music that will appeal because it is a genre of music that "floats," so people engaged in religious enterprise can appeal to people's interest in a diffuse "religion." Their relation to "religion" is much the same as the musical performer's relation to "music."

Alongside the performers who bring music down from "floating" and actually perform it, there are promoters who arrange actual performances. These are agents or organizations that arrange, support, and publicize performances. They train musicians in the arts of looking good and appealing to audiences. And they arrange the facilities and the publicity that are necessary if performances are to take place. But they can do those things because the music "floats." It already has standing in the assumptions and fashions that have currency in the larger community. What the promoters then do is to capture the "floating" musical styles and instrumentations and bring them down to appreciative audiences.

Again, the case is similar with religion. In addition to the performers who perform "religion" for all who will listen, there are also *churches*. There are the church buildings that we see on the street corners. There are the congregations that meet in those buildings. And there are the denominational organizations that assist, promote, and sometimes govern these local congregations. There are also schools of religion and theological seminaries. But like the music conservatory, these come *after* the "floating" of religion and *after* the performers who make it audible. They exist to endorse, clarify, and promote the religion or spirituality that "floats."

Churches, church organizations, and church schools, however, are not the only agents who capture the diffuse religion that "floats." There are also the entrepreneurial promoters of "spirituality." There are the peripatetic evangelists who appear in different places holding "revivals" and making conversions. These have been around for a very long time. And there are the people who carry out radio and television "ministries." These speakers are heard and seen by vast multitudes of television viewers. For them, even a small percentage of potential viewers can be a large absolute number. These religions spokespersons differ from the denominational–academic leaders in that their operations are their own. They initiate the operations and, in effect, own them. This is why we (and others) call them "entrepreneurial." And they, like pulpit ministers, capture the diffuse religion and spirituality that "float."

In a news commentary recently, a writer said that people used to think the term *religious leader* referred to televangelists like Jerry Falwell. But nowadays, it is different, said the writer. Now the religious leaders of greatest importance are likely to be certain bloggers (Web-loggers). It is people whom one can meet on the Internet! But whether it is the one or the other, the church leader is conspicuous by her absence from that commentary and from the roster of religious leaders. She is not mentioned. Among these are denominational executives, pastors of leading churches, scholars in the theological seminaries, and executives of the denominational and supradenominations organizations (e.g., Church World Service) that carry out tasks deemed to be important to the churches. Why, then, we may ask, are these not the religious leaders of our time and our country?

The answer has to do with the "floating" nature of religion in American society. It is there as something that hovers over all that takes place. And it is present in the individual mind as a religious or spiritual feeling. And this has precedence over the churches. It is what comes first. The churches then appear as organizations that may or may not assist with it. Even a Catholic who has gone to Catholic schools and attended Mass all his life may feel that way. The Catholic Church, in his mind, exists to assist him with his "spirituality." That is its role, and that role defines the Church's territory and also its limits. This is a state of affairs that is taken for granted, and, unless challenged, serves as the basis on which decisions are made and judgments rendered.

Is this inconsistent with Christianity as traditionally understood? Yes it is, and for good reason. The churches have traditionally assumed and asserted that *faith* (there is reason now to use that word) arises within and from the churches. It does not just "float." Rather, it emerges from the bosom of the church—the church as armed with constituted church order or government, with proclamation, and with the sacraments. More basically, faith emerges from the Church as an assembly within which the action of God in Jesus Christ is remembered and is therefore continually effective as present occurrence. It is grounded on God's action in Jesus Christ and not on a religious proclivity of thought to reside in the human mind and heart. Nor does it "float" in the air as something that "everybody knows." For this reason, it depends on *knowledge*. Those who proclaim it must have an understanding of the relation of God to human beings, of the call to righteousness, of the human being's alienation from God (sin), of God's redemptive action in Jesus Christ, and of the coming of the Kingdom of God. Whoever will proclaim this Gospel, as opposed to vague "spirituality," must have some understanding of these parts of the Gospel message and of how they go together to form "The Gospel."

The distinction between the Christian Gospel and generalized religion is crucial. In the Christian understanding, human beings are alienated from God—they are sinners—and this alienation touches and takes control of all they do. No realm of activity, no philosophy, and no assertions of feeling or "heart" are outside the domain of the human separation from God. Most notably, religion as a special way in which people express their humanness, is corrupted just as much as is any other expression. We see this in the long history of intolerance, bigotry, and violence carried out in the name of religion. Indeed, these negatives are even sanctified by religion in many of its forms. Far from alerting people to the demand for justice and to instances in which injustices are perpetrated, religion frequently blinds its proponents to those offenses against decency. Often, religion even appears to sanctify them. We could think here of the genocide in Jericho described in the book of Judges. We could also think of the present-day approval of Israel (the strongest power) and its atrocities perpetrated on the Palestinians. If someone wants to flee from "man's inhumanity to man," therefore, he cannot find refuge in religion or in spirituality. There would be no resting place there!

If there is a refuge to which the lover of human beings can flee, it is the Gospel of Jesus Christ in all its fullness and its insistence that Jesus alone is Lord. And the Jesus who is Lord is one who cares nothing about all of our fine and noble sentiments, our human loyalties, our heartfelt loves of tribe and country and, in general, everything we assert with great emotion to be *good*. He is a Lord who gives us a choice. He brings us to a place of decision that we cannot avoid. Either we follow our fine human sentiments, or we can submit to his lordship. We cannot combine or compromise these divergent loyalties. Either Jesus is our Lord or He is not. And if He is Lord, then Church is and must remain an object of our loyalty, for it is here that Jesus is remembered and therefore present. Our loyalty is not to the Church as the Church. It is, rather, to the Church as a finger pointed away from itself, that is, from itself as a human group and to its Lord.

We can now see how the mega-church fits in where the Christian Gospel is pitted against a religion that "floats." We see the mega-church as occupying a mid-point between the television preacher viewed as entrepreneur and the church. The mega-church leader is like the television preacher in that he seeks to take hold of the religion that "floats" and bring it down to people where they are, just as the musician performs items that arise from the musical tradition. The "floating" religion is there, and the televangelist does something with it. He markets it to television viewers. The mega-church preacher does much the same thing. He, too, is a performer above all else. He, too, brings the religion down from where it is "floating" so that it becomes something people can see and hear. He, too, gives people what they *want*. And he measures his performance by no standard other than that it is what people flock to hear and see.

Unfortunately, unlike the man who performs only on television, the mega-church preacher asserts that he is founding and leading a *church*. Instead of giving people a *supplement* to church, as television preachers have commonly done, he presents his performance as *being* church. It is intended to take the place in people's lives that was formerly occupied by actual churches. Note that there is among Christians a long tradition of people "going to church" on Sunday. This attendance at Sunday worship has defined, in great degree, what it means to be Christian. Much else is and has traditionally been involved in the Christian life, of course. All along, the Christian was supposed to live as a Christian in all zones of his life. Betaking himself to the place where a worshiping congregation prayed, sang hymns, heard the proclamation of the Word, and celebrated the sacraments, was a hub around which the rest of the Christian life revolved. But today, the mega-church movement arises and puts on display a style of church life that is in sharp contrast to the traditional Christian church life. In this deviating form, people feel that they can discharge the "church" part of Christians' responsibility by attending the mega-performances.

If the mega-church founder-leader is aware that there is something lacking in his operation, he covers himself by *assertion*. He *asserts* that he does superior preaching. He *asserts* that his ministry is biblically based and doctrinally clear. He *asserts* that his church "transforms lives." He *asserts* that people find in his operation the "family life" that they are missing at home and, presumably, in other churches. And since, as we have said, the mega-church believes that "aspiration equals achievement," once these things are asserted, they are taken to be what actually takes place. Simply by saying that *lives transform here,* they do. They transform to believing they transform just by being in the mega-church.

3

WORSHIP IN
THE MEGA-CHURCH:
THE CHURCH AND ITS MUSIC

Ocean Tide Church (not its real name) is located in a southern city, about seven miles from the city's center. The area is partly upper-middle class and partly upper class. It is on a street that is very wide and well traveled by commuters traveling back and forth between the center of the city to the prosperous outer fringes. Just a little farther in toward the city there is the Lake View "development" in which the wealthy live and in which the not-so-wealthy either aspire to live or do live, albeit at great sacrifice. Its apartments, condominiums, and houses are new and shiny—and prestigious. A short distance from the church is a major north–south thoroughfare. It is lined with restaurants, clothing stores, and a nursery. At one end of that street is a large and very popular shopping mall. Although this mall would seem to have everything, its abundance has not prevented Wall-Mart and other large businesses from appearing to its north and south.

COMING TO AND LEAVING THE CHURCH

As the visitor approaches the church, she sees little or nothing that has the appearance of a church. The buildings could be those that house either a school or corporate offices. Because this is a modern American city, the visitor is of course approaching by private automobile. As she enters the parking lot, she sees that the area in front of the building is already full of cars, so she moves to her right and enters a large zone in which she notices many empty spaces. She then parks her car, gets out of it, and walks past a large one-story building called the Ministry Center. If it is raining or if the sun is too strong, she will feel relieved to find herself walking under a sheltered walkway. Once she gets past the Ministry Center, she faces the main Church building.

As she walks into that building, she finds herself in a large vestibule that contains little more than an information desk and tables with brochures. She does well to go out where she came in and then walk past the "auditorium," as it is called, to a lobby on the other side. Once she is inside this zone, she encounters a scene in which people are walking around, talking with one another in pairs and small groups, and, in general, appearing to be acting purposively. On the walls are announcements of events and programs. In the middle and to one side are counters with people behind them ready to deal with one or another aspect of the church's life. The counter in the middle is open on all sides. It has pamphlets laid out in neat piles. These provide the visitor with information about compass groups and other program offerings of the church. The compass groups are divided into those that are for men, women, both men and women, and different age groups. The time and place of their meetings are given. Other pamphlets explain how a person can become a member of "The Tide." They inform the reader that a prospective member must meet with the pastor on a number of Sunday afternoons for three-hour sessions, from about 4:00 to 7:00 P.M. This is true for people transferring from other Baptist churches, as well as for those coming from churches of other traditions and those seeking to enter from the "no church" category. Those who have not been baptized as older children or adults and by immersion will need to undergo that procedure, although in fact most baptisms in the church are of adolescents.

To her right, the visitor will see a large counter divided into sections. Three or four women are stationed there and are quite busy. Overhead, the section announces itself as the "Pre-School Center." It has separate places for "Visitor's Registration" and other categories. Moving back from that counter, restrooms and water fountains are handy. In general, this area looks more like the administration building of a university than like the usual church. With large numbers of people walking around, there are only small circles of those who speak to one another. The main impression is one of people moving rapidly about, much as a visitor might see in a university's administration building.

To the visitor's left as she enters the building are two doors that lead into the auditorium. There have been three services on Sunday morning, at 8:30, 9:45 and 11:00 A.M. Although the auditorium is quite large, it is well filled for all three services. Just recently, the number of services has been reduced to two, perhaps because there were too many empty seats in the 8:30 service. When a service is in progress, the doors leading into the auditorium from the lobbies to its right and left are closed. Latecomers are requested to enter from two doors to the rear. This is quite important, as the auditorium is often darkened, and open side doors let in annoying spurts of bright light. As soon as a service is over, the side doors are opened and people go out in streams. To the right of the exit door is a box into which people now put their offerings and visitors put a card on which they have written their names and other information. At this time it is clear to visitors waiting in the lobby that they can attend the next service.

Once inside the auditorium, the visitor surveys a scene much like that of a large concert hall or a facility in which dramas are presented. To her right and at the front of the large room is a stage. On left side of the stage is a raised area that serves as a choir loft for the rare occasions when a group of people sing. To the right and rear is the place where musicians sit and perform. For the most part, there are just three kinds of instruments: guitars of various kinds, percussion instruments, and a piano. The music they produce is amplified, almost to the point that a person might feel his ears are in danger, especially if he is close to the front. The near part of the stage is the area in which singers and the preacher put on their performances. There is a podium in the middle-front of the stage, although it is used for very little. If the minister ever looks at the notes he has put on it, his listeners have very little occasion to be aware of his doing so. If the visitor looks to the rear of the auditorium, she sees a raised booth with abundant projecting equipment. The scenes projecting onto the screens at the front of the room and above and to the left and right of the stage emanate from this booth. The booth also holds a large digital clock that keeps everyone informed of the time.

There are two doors entering the auditorium, one on each of the two sides. One door faces another door that enters the area from the front lobby. There is a wide path or aisle leading from one of these side doors to the other side door, often containing people walking in one direction or the other. On the side of the aisle close to the stage at the front of the room is a large number of seats, certainly in the hundreds. On the side of the aisle away from the stage is a much smaller number of seats, about four rows with about 30 seats each. The seats in all parts of the auditorium bear no resemblance to the "pews" to which churchgoers are accustomed. They are more like theater seats, padded and comfortable. The three services (now two) are intended to be identical, and each lasts exactly one hour. With just 15 minutes between the conclusion of the 8:30 service at 9:30 and the beginning of the second service at 9:45, and between its ending at 10:45 and the beginning of the third at 11:00, we might think there would be great difficulty in moving cars in and out of the parking lot and people in and out of the buildings. In fact, these movements seem to take place without either traffic jams or long, frustrating periods of waiting. Sometimes cars are lined up at an exit awaiting a chance to leave. This can be especially difficult if someone is determined to turn left onto a busy street. But what is remarkable is how little trouble there is in moving people in and out of the church during these 15-minute periods between the early and the middle services and between the middle and late services. Even so, it is puzzling why those in charge of the church set their early service at 8:30 rather than 8:00, as the earlier time would allow a half-hour rather than 15 minutes between services and would serve the people who want a truly early service. Also, given that many more Americans work on weekends than was the case in the middle of the twentieth century, it would be interesting to ask why the services are not more spread out in time. A very large church would certainly have the resources for doing this.

Up above the stage and to the right and the left are the two images coming from the projectors in the rear. These are identical images. In the 15-minute period before a service begins, the images on the screens shift from one item to another. As the images change, each appears to be moving away like a page turning. These images appear professional and well done, much as we might expect to see on a major television channel or in a motion picture theater. Sometimes the images pertain to the theme of the day and the day's sermon. On one Sunday in the spring of 2006, the image was that of a red heart-shaped object with decorations of the same color above and below it. In the middle of the heart was the word HOPE. Under it, there appeared the words "for failures." The theme was "hope for failures." At other moments, one or another of the programs of the Church was featured on the screen. As this continued, people were walking around, chatting in small groups, and slowly filling up the auditorium.

As a rule, five minutes before the time when the service is to begin, a digital timekeeper appears on the screen announcing the time remaining before the beginning of the event. The countdown is given in minutes, seconds, and tenths and hundredths of seconds. At one point, for example, the screen will read "04–38–52." Then while the four will, of course, remain for a minute, the three-column will change every 10 seconds, the eight-column every second. The five column will appear for such a short time that it will be difficult to see it, and the two is part of a blur that the viewer cannot really see at all. As the page-turning continues, this countdown appears in different parts of the screen and in different size numbers, but it is always there during the last five-minute period. The stage is dark during this time, and someone watching can barely make out the figures of people coming or going.

THE WORSHIP SERVICE OR WORSHIP EVENT

When the countdown reaches the exciting "00–00–00," the service begins. The precision with which this beginning takes place is equal to that of a radio or television program. Abruptly, the stage lights come on, and the people on the stage come clearly into view. Now we see a man (or woman) with a guitar and a microphone held up by a rod. Or this person may have no guitar and just hold the microphone. To his left and to his right, there are about four others holding portable microphones in their hands. Typically, two of the four are men and two are women; however, this varies. Behind them are several other people playing guitars and percussion instruments. Only the man in the middle of the group in the front might both play the guitar and sing. The other four just sing. The man in the middle also serves as a master of ceremonies. He is the only one who also speaks. He comments that it is a very good day to "worship the Lord," and elaborates on this theme a bit. The person doing this, incidentally, has always been the same man at all of the services that I have attended. No one else, not even the preacher, has been so regular.

After his opening remarks, this master of ceremonies asks the people on stage to stand and begin a series of religious songs. It is not clear whether he and the people to his left and right are leading the congregation in singing or are making a presentation. The words for the songs appear on the screen. But there are no musical notations, so the people present could sing the words, but they have no help in knowing whether any particular word should be at the same pitch as the word just before it or should be to a certain degree higher or lower. For this reason, it would be difficult for the people to sing. One assumes that the five people on the stage have seen the musical score itself and so can sing it. Indeed, we have the impression that they have memorized the songs, although they can see the words written on a screen in the rear of the auditorium. If a visitor looks around, he sees that a few people are singing or trying to sing. Some do so with their hands raised, but most of the people are just listening. Whether trying to sing or not, the people in the audience cannot compete with those on the stage in making themselves heard. In this sense, the songs with which the service begins are more like a presentation than like a participatory event.

The songs themselves are songs of "praise." The words of the songs praise God, Jesus Christ, and Jesus Christ as the one who died for us and for our sins. The songs are not familiar; not a single traditional hymn is going to be heard. They are not even traditional *types* of hymns. Even in a normal Baptist church, I may find that I am not familiar with some of the hymns being sung, but these hymns are familiar to me as *types* of hymns. In contrast, the songs sung at "The Tide" are totally different, even as *types* of songs. This may be why they call them "songs" rather than "hymns." The word *songs* seems correct. Further, the songs of the mega-church repertoire do not as a rule present a tune a person can recognize or mimic. The listener cannot hear the songs and then whistle the tunes later, as there is little in the way of a recognizable melody.

The mega-church singing is accompanied by a combination of guitars and percussion instruments being played at the back of the stage. This instrumental background is very well done; it is much like what we would expect to hear in professional rock or popular music concerts put on by professional popular singers and instrumentalists. In short, mega-church is more a production than a worship experience!

SONGS OF PRAISE AND THEIR UNIFORMITY

To know more about the culture of the mega-church, we can consider further the nature of the music that is presented. I say "presented" deliberately, for what takes place in the mega-church is not much like the congregational singing that may be heard in (many) more traditional churches. In "The Tide" the songs are far more uniform, both in their content and in the tunes. We do not find in them any of the variety of themes that are found in the traditional collection of hymns such as "A Mighty Fortress is Our God," "Amazing Grace," "Glorious Things of Thee Are Spoken, Zion, City of our God," "Holy, Holy, Holy, Lord God Almighty," and "Thou Who Almighty Art, Earth Hath Forsaken." There are hundreds more, but these few titles indicate that the traditional repertoire of hymns contains a variety of themes, moods, and contents. It also contains a variety of tunes and styles of music. The Christian faith is rich and many-sided. It is therefore to be expected that the content and messages of the music that is sung and heard in the usual gathered congregation would be varied as well. We may note that a Christian has moments when she is pensive and thoughtful, triumphant and ready to march, humble and contrite, compassionate and giving, or awestruck and "trembling" at the presence of the Lord. Similarly the music she sings will be varied in style and mood.

By comparison, the songs of the mega-church are surprisingly uniform in content and in musical style. There is little change from one song to another. We could compare this uniformity to the greater difference that divides "Arise O Men of God, Have Done with Lesser Things" and "O Jesus I Have Promised." The difference between these two hymns, both favorites in Protestant churches, is far greater than any difference in the songs heard in the mega-church. And it is not only that there is variety in the contents of traditional hymns. It is also that there is *content* in these traditional hymns. Critics have sometimes called many Protestant hymns "trite," but in so doing they were comparing them to such items as the "cosmic ecstasy" of Medieval Plain Chant and Gregorian Chant, not to the flat and relatively meaningless offerings of the mega-church.

PRAISE PRODUCED AND PRAISE EVOKED

Hymns praise the Lord and in so doing evoke a state of mind and spirit. The concept of *praise* itself requires examination. When we say that a person praises another person, the statement can have two rather different meanings. In the first meaning, a person "pulls up" the praise from within himself, from his own mind and heart. In the second meaning, the praise is a response to something that is "out there." A person sees a person, group, or principle that appears to be praise*worthy*. The object of the praise pulls the praise out of the person who does the praising.

In the first case, a person reaches down inside of himself and "pulls up" the praise. And having pulled it up, he then directs it toward an appropriate object. We may think here of a man who is gong to love a woman. To do so, he reaches into himself and "pulls up" the *presumed love*. He then finds the right woman and directs his love to her. She is the *appropriate target* for a love, which, like an arrow, he *already has in his quiver*. He could of course do the same with any object of love, another person, group, or even an abstraction. Further, he could love an object because he wants to *or because he thinks he should*. If he is told that a good person is one who loves his parents (or his country or anything else), he could decide that he is such a good person. He therefore pulls up from within himself that love and he directs it toward his parents or his country. He becomes the loving son or daughter or the patriotic American. He could then extend this to God. "Because I am godly," he could say, "I love God. I decree that I am someone who loves God. I find the love in me and I pull it up from my mind and heart, and I then direct it toward God." In so doing, the person sees himself as a good and godly person because he loves the Lord. This is an idea of himself that he has in his mind. In this sense, his praise of God could even be seen as a praise of himself. "Look at me," he says to the world, "I am a godly person because I love God."

Distinctive about this praise-of-another that is pulled up from within the self is that this praise allows the object of the praise, perhaps an admired person, little *freedom* to say or do anything other than what is expected by those who do the praising. She cannot move in one direction or another and still receive the praise. The people engaging in giving honor are, in effect, giving it to an *idea* they have of the object of their admiration, and not to the object itself. They *expect* God or their bishop, pope, or faith leader—or king or president—to desire or to approve of certain actions or programs. And God is the object who is presumed to be wanting and approving those actions that they praise in song and in speech. The object, whether a lay person, a faith leader, or a God, has *no freedom to deviate* from the expectations of those who do him honor. If he does speak in ways that do not fit with these expectations, the chances are that those who praise him will just not take notice of the deviations. They will simply not see these deviations. For example, some American Catholics may give great honor to the pope. Their praise of him may seem to be without limit. But if these same Catholics also approve a war, say the American war in Iraq (or any other war), while the pope disapproves of it, they may simply *ignore* that disapproval. So while they honor him greatly, they do not allow him the freedom to say or do anything that does not fit with their expectations of him, that is, that deviates from the *idea* they have of him. (They may also quietly ignore the pope's disapproval of birth control in an ever-more crowded and homeless world.)

When this is the case, the person who praises another *maintains control over that which he praises*. The god whom she praises is a god who is just what she wants that god to be. The same would be true of praise for her country, of an ideology such as free enterprise or socialism, or of an honored person. In truth, she is the author and creator of that which she praises. Where the object is God, the technical word for such praise is *idolatry*. A person may praise God with great energy, a loud voice, and an air of sincerity. But the god whom she thus praises is a product of her own imagination, an artifact of her own wishes and ambitions. Whatever the "god" may be in himself, he is effectively *that which* the worshiper imagines him to be, at best an artifact or construction of a presumed or invented reality.

The second reason a person may praise a man or woman (or a group or an idea) is that he actually admires the man himself; that is, he admires the *object* of his praises. Where this object is a man, a person sings the praises of the man himself, viewing him as the Great Man. It is the man just as he is, clothed in his greatness, who *evokes* the attitude of praise. The person who does the praising learns about this Great Man (or Woman). He contemplates the man's qualities and characteristics, together with his actions, his achievements, his sufferings, and his sacrifices. He is then *struck* with how great the Man who has these qualities truly is. The Great Man's nobility and worthiness grasp him and *evoke* in him an attitude of awe and admiration. The object of a person's praise is, in this case, outside of himself. He is beyond the reach of the admirer's imagination, and takes hold of that person from his position "out there." Here, when the person praises the Great Man, it is indeed the Great Man whom he praises.

He may admire and praise the Great Man because the Man exemplifies qualities that the person admires. The Great Man appears as the Great Philosopher or the Great Humanitarian. Or it could be that the person is first struck by the greatness of the man and *then* discovers *what* it is that he admires in the person. Here, the encounter with the Admired Person and the admired characteristic are parts of the same epiphany. The biblical confrontation of Paul with the risen Christ on the road to Damascus would likely be a case of this epiphany.

Where this is the case, the admired person or group has a great degree of *freedom*. She can assert beliefs about what is real and true; she can make statements about what is right and wrong; she can give directives that tell her personal following what they should do. Because the focus of attention is on the Great Woman herself and not just on an idea the devotees have of her, those devotees will pay attention to what she says. They will take note of it, and quite frequently they will change their views to fit it or alter their courses of action to be in line with her words. Their acts of devotion, such as their singing and praying, have a character somewhat different from those who praise the idea they have of the object of their praising. Those who honor the Great Woman herself will do so in a way that is more somber and alert, more quiet and attentive. There is an air of waiting or expectancy. Any minute now, the word will come. We do not know now what that word will be. But we will hear it, and then we will know, for it does not derive from our expectations, but from the heart of the Great Woman Herself.

In the first case, a person performs an act of *self*-presentation; he presents himself to the world as one who offers praises and is, for that reason, praiseworthy himself. In the second case, he sings songs and makes speeches in order to bear testimony to a greatness that has come to him from outside of his own mind and heart. We may then ask whether the "praise teams" (as they are called) of the mega-church are the one or the other. Are they presenting themselves as good and worthy because of their praising? Or are they expressing awe and wonder in response to a word coming from one who is other than they and who is, in his basic nature, praise*worthy*. In the first case, people are praising for the sake of praising. They are, in effect, praising themselves. In the second, they are, in the proper meaning of the expression, praising God. They are *witnessing*, to use the classical Protestant expression. Here we may recall Karl Barth's image of a person who looks out of a window at an airplane that is flying overhead. He does not see the airplane because the eave of the building is in the way. But he looks down and sees people *seeing* the airplane. He perceives the airplane, so to say, through the witness of those who do see it. Concerning the "praise teams," then, we can ask whether they are putting on a good performance or are, instead, bearing testimony to a reality that is outside of themselves and to which they can only respond with awe.

To answer this question, we need to inquire into what it is that impresses someone who listens to the praises of the "praise teams." If the person listening is impressed with how great the praise "teams" are, these teams are praising themselves. If the person listening is awestruck by how great and mysterious and wonderful God is, the praise teams are praising God. Commonly, the former will be more enthusiastic and "spirit-filled," while the latter will be more subdued and attentive. Those who praise are subdued when they are praising the Lord, so to say, with their ears as well as with their voices. They *wait* for the Lord (Ps. 62).

THE MUSIC: CIVILIZATION AND THE FAITH

We may also wonder why the music and songs that are to be heard in the mega-church worship events are *new*. Why do we not hear a single familiar hymn or even type of hymn? This question is more important than is immediately apparent. If we go into a traditional church, whether evangelical or mainline, we will hear certain music being presented as preludes and postludes at certain points in the service, such as the time when the offering is being brought forward. We will also hear certain traditional hymns being sung by the congregation and anthems presented by the choir. Quite naturally, we will hear only a tiny proportion of the repertory of music that is available in hymnbooks and other musical publications. It does not seem strange, therefore, that we hear the particular items that we hear and do not hear any of the much larger number of possible such items.

We could also hear the quite novel songs in the mega-church this way, but in doing so, we do not notice the extent of the novelty in the musical offerings. Nor are we aware of the length and breadth of the musical legacies that we inherit from the past that have been jettisoned to make room for the novel musical items. We would do well to put this brash novelty out on a table so that we can get a good look at it. Just what is the novelty? What is the reason for it? Why should the rich musical heritage brought forth *and preserved* by men and women of faith in previous decades and centuries now be purely and simply *gone*? Is there some reason why the mega-church should treat that heritage as of no value? We might take a look at the hymnbook of any of the major Christian traditions. It contains in excess of 500 hymns. Among these hundreds of tunes and lyrics is a rich variety of musical expressions of faith. We may then imagine that the book vanishes, as if by magic. All those old and not-so-old favorites (and not-so-favorites) are purely and simply *gone*. They have vanished into thin air. Why have they been thrown overboard? Why have they been deported from the land of faith by the mega-church? And what are the consequences of the wholesale abandonment of the traditions of our grandparents? We cannot understand the mega-church without answering these questions.

We want to know the reason for the abandonment of traditional hymns, and we want to note the consequences of this change. We want, in particular, to perceive the consequences of the change for society and for civilization. A civilization is not just a large community that possesses advanced technology and the apparatus that uses that technology. It is, in addition, a community that is bound by a host of moral assumptions and principles. These principles form and structure the lives of individuals, families, and larger organizations of many kinds. They also clear space for the individual so that she is not altogether sacrificed for the "good" of the community as a whole. In both the structuring and the clearing of space, there is a body of taken-for-granted moral assumptions or ideas about what is good and right. These assumptions were not invented by individuals; nor were they the work of committees. They arose, rather, through a give-and-take between people that took place over a long time. They are, in a word, *traditions.* They are gifts, we could say, that the communities of the past present to those who live in the present. The people who live in a "today" are indebted to the long parade of those who went before the traditions, for they do not have either the moral sensitivity nor the intelligence to invent them on the spot, in the "now," without the benefit of history and time. They have these traditions the only way they can, as an inheritance from the past.

The traditions, and the moral assumptions that both drive these assumptions and are at the same time embedded within them, are the beliefs we inherit, the time-honed beliefs about what is right and decent. These are, as we may put it, "in the air." They seem to be external to individuals, yet they exist only in the minds of individuals. Each person holds the beliefs and has the ideas. Yet they are essentially something outside of each person who holds them. When a person wants to do something, but her conscience will not let her do it, a moral principle seems to direct or to *have* the person—to command her. Yet it also seems correct to say that the person herself has the principle. This is a dialectic that we all understand.

Quite commonly, we are unaware of these assumptions, and their workings are just taken for granted. They are, so to say, part of the air that we breathe. They are background for all that we say and do. But when the assumptions are violated, something else happens. Now we are "shocked." This state of being "shocked" wakes us up; it is the indication that something sacred has been violated. Quite possibly, this sacredness is something that we were not consciously fully aware of because we had so thoroughly taken its directive for granted. Once we have been "shocked," then, we can examine what it was that was "in the air," that was violated, and so become aware of the principle *as* a principle.

What marks a principle as being "in the air" of a certain society or community is that it is *shared*. For example, there exists the principle that a person accused of a crime is "innocent until proven guilty." This principle is shared in much of Western civilization. In Spanish-language countries the expression is "doubt favors the accused." In the Bible, it takes the form of a requirement that there be no charge without two or three witnesses (Deut. 19:14). I believe this, and I further assume that others around me make that same assumption. And I assume that each of those others assumes that all "others" make the same assumption. I assume everybody thinks that any and all accused persons are innocent until proven guilty. And the confidence that each person has actually taken in and holds this principle depends on his actually believing that everyone else, almost everyone else, holds this belief. To wit, if one person thought that accused persons *should* be presumed innocent, but did not think that others shared that opinion, the presumption of innocence would not be "in the air." In effect, it would not *be*. It would not exist.

The fact that an assumption is "in the air" is manifest in the response of "shock" that occurs when the principle is violated. Let's say that a person accused of murder or rape is being "railroaded" toward a guilty verdict. When we perceive this to be happening, we are then "shocked." We exclaim, "but he did not have a fair trial!" In so doing, we expect people to take our remark seriously. We do so because the belief that a trial should be fair is "in the air." It is shared within the community.

But if this belief is indeed *there,* it is there because we inherit it from the past. It comes to us from our fathers and grandfathers going way, way back. We did not invent, compose, or develop this belief via our own intelligence. Our intelligence and creativity are not equal to such a massive task. Rather, it is a *gift* to us from our ancestors. It comes to us from the back-and-forth of people over many generations; in effect, it comes to us from history.

What happens, then, when there is no past, or when we receive nothing from the past, is that a lot of this cultural equipment on which we depend for civilized living just disappears. It is there no more. Whatever is to be considered right or wrong is thought up or invented "on the spot." It is a "right now" thing. The immediate present is, then, all we have, so what is to be invented has to be brought into being in this current moment. Thus when a person is accused of a crime and the "railroading" begins, the accused person is without recourse. He (or for that matter *we*) may say, "but the trial was not fair," but no one hearing that assertion will pay any attention. They will not expect others to be "shocked" at the unfairness of the trial. And because each person does not expect others to be "shocked," he feels no "shock" himself. If, someone does cry "foul," that cry will meet only silence from those gathered around. No one will pay attention, for the assumption behind the cry of "foul" is not there. The state of mind we call "shock" and the cry of "foul" are dependent on the assumption that the dismay is *shared*. If it is not shared, it does not exist. People are not "shocked." Therefore the shrug of the shoulder is all that can be expected.

Add to this "presumption of innocence" many other moral assumptions like it. Let there be many other principles that are taken for granted, that are "in the air." Let the violations of these principles produce a "shock" that reverberates within a community and is its common property. And we have something very important. We have *tradition,* which is, in turn, an essential ingredient of *civilization.*

When tradition is gone, so are the assumptions. And with this evaporation goes a great deal of what makes life humane and good and sweet. Civilization itself is in jeopardy. Now we can be accused of a crime and "railroaded" into prison without a fair trial. This happens because no one cares or, better stated, because no one *can* care. The useful function of shock is no longer in the air. Now all sorts of things can happen, all sorts of brutalities and injustices can be perpetrated, and there is no help from the assumptions and from the "shocked" responses that are based on them. The cultural barriers generated over the centuries have been knocked down.

Even worse, in events such as the "worship" process of the mega-church, an aura of the sacred is produced and maintained. All present at the events feel that they are being good and godly. This is a feeling that they have pulled up from within themselves as individuals and as a crowd. Once this feeling of "good" is generated, it will add force to notions in which basic principles are ignored. Not only will a person accused of a crime not get his "fair trial," but those who deny him that favor will feel that they are being "good," "godly," or "patriotic" while they take on these behaviors and beliefs in the "now." That sacral feeling will make the way back to civilization even more difficult to travel.

Now there is a wind that blows, and it does so unimpeded. None of us can stand in these gale-force winds. It is to prevent that storm that the mandates of law, and specifically of "due process," are carried out (when they are) consistently and sometimes ferociously. When a woman who is held in little esteem in a community is accused of a crime of which she is, in fact, not guilty, that woman is to be defended in a court of law with all of the resources the law gives her. If the community indulges its disdain for her by denying her that defense, the winds will blow in which no one can stand upright.

Further, many of the bodies of principle that are "in the air" and taken for granted are quite *esoteric*. That is, the depth and history of such principles are not readily understood by people in general. Only a cadre of people who have studied these in great depth, or who have taken a special interest in them, understand these bodies of principle and have full command of their details. These people can be physicians, lawyers, theologians, other kinds of scholars, or others who have studied on their own or just taken a vigorous interest these matters. These people acquire their understandings by extended periods of study, contemplation, and extensive experience.

To say that ordinary people do not command this high level of knowledge of cultural schemes (like law) does not mean, however, that they are totally ignorant of them. They may know the bodies of principle only from afar and vaguely. But they know them, at least, this way. They have an idea of what it is that they know little about, and they sense that for which they are dependent on experts. The average citizen of the United States, for example, has an image in his mind of the criminal courts, of such processes as the examination and the cross-examination of witnesses. He may not be able to explain this in detail. And he tends not to want to serve as his own lawyer. But he knows that there is this field of knowledge "out there," and that it is to be respected and honored. He knows its place in his life and in the things that might happen to him.

As these lines are being written, there is a lot of attention in the news to the wiretapping of telephones "without warrant." The news media accounts normally report these occurrences with a note of "shock." Yet it is likely that the average citizen does not readily share this "shock." She does not know why a warrant is needed, what a warrant is, or what difference it makes whether a warrant is or is not obtained. Yet she senses that she should be "shocked." She may think that if she were to go back to school, she would learn more about the system of "checks and balances," more about the courts that grant warrants, more about there being part of an independent branch of government, more about how this independence is important in a government in which the power of government to act is held in tension with a "check" on a possibly dictatorial exercise of its power. (Or she may not know, or have the opportunity to know, that education can provide this information.)

We have, then, bodies of principle, and we have esoteric principle. All of these, the more simple, manifest, and obvious, and the more esoteric principles, are in the realm of the taken for granted. They are "in the air." They depend on *everyone* believing that everyone *else* treasures the principles. They are, for this reason, vulnerable. When people violate the principles, and the sky does not then fall in, that is, there is no "shock," everyone ceases to see the principles as being "in the air." The principles appear to have evaporated, if they appear to have ever existed at all. They just are *not there* anymore! And with their disappearance, there is the loss of much of what makes civilization civilized. Fundamental principles of justice and fair play are gone from view. They disappear into the dustbin of history. This occurs in the case of governments based on extremist politics, such as fascism or communism, and it can occur in seemingly less extreme circumstances as well.

We need to be wary, then, of a great deal, including signs such as the triumphant march of novelty in the musical offerings of the mega-church. They certainly can have new songs, which they may or may not call hymns, just as any church can and most churches do. But the wholesale jettisoning of the corpus of traditional hymns is another matter. It is one of those things where something done consistently or a great deal has a different meaning from that same thing done sparingly or only from time to time. The difference is qualitative and not just quantitative. In presenting an entirely new collection of religious songs, and I must add, songs of monumental triteness, the mega-church has made an announcement to the world. It has announced that as far as it is concerned, the traditions of Christian worship, especially worship in song, do not exist. In effect, *there is no tradition.* There is only the "right now" and the ingenuity with which we can improvise expressions of faith in this "right now." The traditions of the past have been covered with grease and are slipping out of our hands. We are hardly alert to what is slipping away.

TRADITION AND "REAL PRESENCE" OF JESUS CHRIST

The full-blown dedication to countertradition novelty that we see in mega-church worship, and quite specifically evidenced in mega-church music, has a consequence. The consequence is that the teachings of the Crucifixion and Resurrection of Jesus are reduced to something less than teachings; they are reduced to novelty ideas, slide shows based on picture book stories. These once potent teachings are reduced to cheapened and relatively disconnected projections on a screen and then celebrated for whatever they may seem to be by an audience. But no matter how much they are celebrated, they are projected as ideas with little depth of meaning, and, as such, they are basically impotent. They are without power to influence morality when they come up against the pride and greed that reside in the human heart and against the massive injustice and violence that afflict our world. We would be hard-pressed to find in the piety of mega-church worshipers a point where the pitfalls of moral decay that infect human individual and social life are cast out by the mere *idea* that someone named Jesus gave his life on the cross to win forgiveness for the sins of humans. What we find instead is blind, ungrounded, coreless enthusiasm that is produced in the now—"on the spot"—and is an enthusiasm of the mega-church itself.

What does have power is not just a simple idea but a full and potent reality—the *reality* of Jesus's Life, Death, and Resurrection. The essence and meaning of Jesus are really present where Christians gather to remember him and to worship him "in spirit and in truth." In this sense, the memory of Jesus is more than a memory; it is a *presence.* His Death and Resurrection are not just history, but are effective in concepts as well as events *in the present.* Like the Frisbee that, when thrown, does not go down but seems to float on the air, so the memory of Jesus does not fade. This memory is more than a memory, it is a reality, and it continues on indefinitely. It is, for many, just as vivid today as it was in the first century. The teachings and the spirit and the reality of Jesus, even Jesus himself, do not fade. They *live on. In this, He lives on.* And it is then, in the Word that the Real Presence of Christ is central and is "what it is all about."

But this ongoing, living and very Real Presence depends, in turn, on the church and the congregation that come to us through time, travels to us from the past, and then includes us. We do not invent this or create this; rather, *we receive this from the past and then become part of it.* We receive this real presence from those who went before us and who lived and died in the faith and who passed the faith on to us.

One does not have to be a member of this congregation traveling through time to grasp the character of the Faith, the Real Presence itself, that is being generated and regenerated. This Faith is perceived by onlookers as well as those who experience it, the latter being those for whom it is preserved. Those who remember do so for all of us, whether we are members of the Church or outsiders, in their very remembering. They remember the events of the Gospel, and they do so in many forms such as speaking and singing hymns. Once such hymns are sung, they become integral to the *remembering* of the events recorded in the Gospels. Today, when we sing hymns about these events, we continue the remembering that our ancestors in the faith did, and we extend this remembering into the present and into the future. We become carriers of the faith and of the presence. It is true that we are always creating our worship even as we continue what others created before us, but we do so *in continuity* with what went before. It is through this continuity that Jesus is really present and the events of the Gospel are really effective in our own day.

4

———◆◆◆◆◆———

THE SERMON IN
THE MEGA-CHURCH

The Ocean Tide Church service is usually divided into three parts, some-what like a theatrical play production in three acts. There is the opening with several songs and a prayer. Then there is the special music. And, finally, there is the sermon, a discourse that takes up more that half of the hour-long event. The division between these three acts or parts is dramatic. The lights are dimmed and the room becomes dark. When the lights come on again, the scene has changed. With the first dimming of the lights, the five people at the front and the equal number of instru-mentalists behind them disappear, and then there suddenly appear the persons or the group that will perform the special music. Then the lights dim again, and when they are turned back on, the minister is there stand-ing in front of the audience. He appears as though from nowhere. The people in the audience have a definite feeling that the *main event* is now about to take place. All that went before is a buildup to what happens now. There has been the music. On a certain Sunday morning, a "Hope" symbol has appeared many times. Now something great will happen. The theater of the mega-church is in full play.

The sermon or speech that follows gives a major indication of the nature of the mega-church. For this reason, I will analyze a particular sermon and will view it from the standpoint of what I see as authentic Christian proc-lamation. Basically, I will contrast the earnest and traditional-in-nature proclamation of the "good news" of the Christian Gospels to the life adjustment lecture that we hear in the mega-church. It may seem unfair to consider just one, or even a few, sermons in this way. The addresses delivered by the minister of First Presbyterian or any of other churches in an American town may not represent all of the sermon-giving of even that one minister. But this is at least a way to begin the analysis and understanding of the mega-church. I will then discuss briefly other sermons and their distinctive characteristics.

The mega-church sermon was presented on a certain Sunday in spring, 2006. Two concepts were central to this address: *failure* and *hope*. How they go together is indicated in a small pamphlet that ushers handed to people as they entered the auditorium. The statement in that document read:

> Americans don't have much patience for losers. A team starts having a losing season and ticket sales plummet. In our country we hate losers and love winners. We adore and worship winners. We adulate achievers. We canonize champions. Everybody wants to be a success and nobody wants to be considered a failure. Failure is seen as the unpardonable sin, and you can't be labeled a failure. For some, failure is seen as a death spiral from which they cannot recover. No matter how many strikes you have against you, there is hope for your future. Even though your life is a mess and miserable, we will see how Jesus offers hope.

The speaker here talks about opposing realities. Something good is set against something bad. The intent is to provide counsel that will help people arrive at the "good" side of the divide and to steer clear of the "bad" side. The "good" side is called *Success (capital S intentional here)*, and it appears under a number of different headings. One of these is "making it" in business or a profession. This kind of success ranks well above failure in those same pursuits. Another is *victory,* as in a baseball game or other sporting event or, for that matter, any competitive undertaking. Its opposite is *defeat* in sports or in any competition. Here, the desirable and the undesirable stand in stark contrast to one another. In both cases, there are two features, one objective and the other subjective. The objective feature appears as something in the factual realm. A person or group succeeds or fails; it wins or loses in a measurable way. The subjective feature appears alongside these matters of "fact." It is an event in the mental-emotional life of those involved. They *feel* themselves to be successful or unsuccessful. They *experience* themselves as being victors or losers.

When we are in the factual realm, fear and hope can be rational appraisals of a situation. For example, a person who is stuck in a traffic jam may be concerned, or fear, that he will not arrive at his destination on time. On the other hand, his memory that traffic usually thins out after the next intersection may give him a quite rational hope. These are cases of the perception of fear and the reasoned calculation of hope. A quite different fear and hope, however, may arise from a person's emotional condition. His fear may be greater than circumstances warrant because of a mood of pessimism he carries with him into all of the situations he confronts. He just *feels* certain that the traffic jam is terrible, even if what he sees does not justify so dark an assessment. At the same time, this person may have a hope that is expressive of his general outlook about matters and thus may expect outcomes better than those indicated by the signals he receives from his environment. No matter how bad the traffic jam actually is, he thinks he will arrive at his destination on time. These inner emotional-mental conditions of fear or hope may then affect how the person performs. Emotional-mental fear can even paralyze a person and thereby bring about the very thing he fears. The emotional-mental hope may spur him on and so he achieves what he hoped for. These would be cases of what sociologist Robert K. Merton called the *self-fulfilling prophecy:* the very *act of believing* can bring about the condition in which a person believes. This self-fulfilling prophecy concept is the basis for much life adjustment writing and preaching.

The people who write and speak in this genre use a great variety of terms and phrases to convey their message. Those who come to this genre later frequently invent new ways of saying things that earlier arrivals used. For example, the earlier "positive thinking" approach explained by Norman Vincent Peal yielded its place to the later Robert Schuller's "possibility thinking." In this way, second-generation writers can appear to be coming up with fresh and new ways of dealing with life's problems, although the message remains much the same: People fail because they have pessimistic attitudes. They therefore need to condition their outlook so that they expect to succeed. In so doing, they will certainly move forward and, it is to be hoped, will actually succeed.

The pursuit of success in business, sports, or other worldly projects is a major feature of this positive approach, but there is a troublingly subjective side to it. This is the quest for a positive or rosy outlook as something to be treasured for its own sake, not for what its results are. A person wants to feel good about herself and about her world. She wants to be, as we say, "happy." To the end of achieving that state, she meditates, reflects, and studies. She also may attend conferences, or read books, or, in some cases, consult a counselor, one that is either secular or religion-based, say Christian (where she is a Christian). Or, she goes to church. In all of these endeavors, she goes to work on her own attitude about life and the world. She is seeking to become more positive and life-affirming. She undertakes to banish dark, brooding thoughts from her mind and to generate from within herself a cheerful and "happy" outlook. She goes to church with a hope that its music, prayers, and sermons will help her in this endeavor. As she would put it, she hopes the church will "meet her needs." She hopes that the church will help her achieve the desired state of mind.

Among the terms and expressions available for this state of mind are those that come from the Christian theological tradition. Such a person can have this "positive attitude" simply because he sees that "God loves him," or "Jesus loves him," or that Jesus died for him and forgives him, and so on. These ideas can be worked and reworked in various combinations. But, in all of this use of Christian vocabulary and this reiteration of "saved by the blood of Christ," the actual message conveyed has only to do with assuming a more positive attitude toward life's challenges. Here, the call to righteousness in word and in deed is disturbingly conspicuous by its absence.

This righteousness is slipping away virtually unnoticed, and in its mounting absence is a key to what the oh-so-modern mega-church means to modern people. But let me be clear here: Certainly, in the sermon given on the date of which we are speaking, the vocabulary of evangelical Christianity was more in evidence than it is in many of this minister's sermons. It was present, however, with a profound (yet elusive to the uninformed onlooker) difference. The vision propounded by this minister says that the sinner (who in traditional evangelicalism stands in need of forgiveness) withdraws into the background, and his place is taken by the person who has *failed,* is depressed, and needs encouragement and hope. And just as the sinner sinks to the depths of despair and then right there—in those depths—finds himself to be a *forgiven sinner,* so people who have experienced failure are told that they can find "in Jesus" (that is, *in what they are told is Jesus*) the encouragement they need to put the past behind them and surge forward into a better future. Just as the sinner is forgiven, so the person who fails learns to stand tall and do better in the years ahead. Because the deceptive packaging appears relatively similar to many people, the core values within it are thought to be the same. *This is the central flaw and peril in the emergence of the mega-church, disguising itself as religion, and its values as religious.*

Precisely because there is such an analogy between this mega-preacher's failure-and-then success motif and the sinner-redemption image of more traditional evangelical Protestantism, the major differences between the two can come all the more clearly into view. In the failure-success image, we have something that has been important in American popular culture for a long time. Innumerable writers and public speakers have appeared claiming to be able to instruct people on how to get whatever it is that is good in human life. Some of these have presented themselves as religious leaders. Others put on the mantel of psychology or social science and present themselves as experts on motivation or healing or the like. Still others claim greater identity with business itself and claim to tell people how to work themselves into a "success" attitude that they say is sure to produce what is so earnestly believed in. Although there may be differences among these writers, they do share the belief that failure results from what may be called a "failure of nerve," and that success takes place whenever the fear of failure is replaced by an attitude of self-confidence.

In contrast, in the sinner-redemption (saved by the Blood of Christ) imagery, we have a moral or a good versus evil manner of thinking. Here the negative feature is a failure to do the will of God, or a failure to do the Good. A person could have willed to do right, but instead she willed to do wrong. Either a high-powered wish or a high-voltage anxiety moved her to decide to do wrong. Yet she still had the power to make a *decision* and therefore *could* have decided for the right, even in the face of, or in spite of, the wish or anxiety (temptation). As she sees herself, therefore, it appears to her that she has done *wrong*. Even when she intends to do what is right, she yields to temptation and ends up doing wrong.

Thus in many churches, the people confess their sins and are declared forgiven every Sunday. It seemed inevitable that they would sin, yet as they look back at their misdeeds, it appears that they could have done right. They had the ability—the freedom—to choose the right rather than the wrong that they in fact chose. It would not have been easy to walk the right path, which is why they did not choose it. But they *could* have. And for this reason they are responsible; they are and feel *guilty*. The possibility of doing right was there and available. It is the very presence of this possibility that leaves them without excuse. Therefore they pray for forgiveness and pardon.

So, in the sinner-redemption model, the problem lies in the *will*. Forgiveness lifts the sinner up to a place where she can once again *will* the Good. As in the beginning of Psalm 32, being "forgiven" and being someone "in whose spirit there is no deceit" go together. When a person is forgiven, she is repositioned so that she has freedom to choose the right and will do so next time. The contrast between these two motifs is most instructive. In the case of the former, the Success-Failure image, the content of *doing well* is provided by the cultural environment. A set of taken-for-granted motifs define and describe what it is. In these descriptions, the content of "Success" consists of such items as prospering in business or having a very busy law or medical practice. These motifs are "in the air." They have the nature of the self-evident or obvious. No one questions where they came from or whether they are right, for they are simply *there*. They just *are*; they have the nature and texture of the easily seen. The exact contents are different for people in different occupations. They are different for those who manufacture and sell products, for lawyers, for doctors, and even for ministers of churches. Yet "Success" is always the same *thing*.

In common usage, to *succeed* is to accomplish and to acquire certain things that are recognized by people –in general as "to be desired." To *fail* is to be unable to accomplish or acquire these things. Various factors may determine whether a person experiences Success or Failure. He may or may not have the required knowledge and skill. He may or may not have the determination and "motivation" to use the resources he has to their best advantage. He may or may not have "contacts" or "connections." But whatever he does or does not do or have, the *content* of Success is given by the larger culture. A person does not in any way determine what that content is. He determines only how much energy and ingenuity he will devote to achieving it.

Success is a symbol and an emblem and has the character of being a *thing* in American culture. In its basic meaning; the word *success* refers to the occurrence in which a person sets out to acquire or to change something and then actually does so. She succeeds in her endeavor, whatever it is. But in American society and culture, Success is separated from the various forms it may take and made into a reality in its own right: Success with a capital S. This "Success" is now the central theme and actual essence—the hypostasis of mega-religion; it has arisen from the mundane particulars that make up our world and assumed a godlike character. True, this Success takes on differing forms, as in the cases of, let us say, a doctor, a lawyer, a salesman, a scholar, or, yes, a clergyman. But it nevertheless is and remains the same *thing.* And as a thing, it is something that everyone understands. If a speaker in a high school assembly tells students that they can, with hard work and a positive attitude, achieve Success, all present know what she has said. And they know that the Success of which she speaks has a substance altogether different from the supposedly more mundane success, in let us say, getting a stalled automobile started. It is part of the mental imaging of reality that is shared within our society. For the minister of "The Tide," the baseball player who hits a home run and the football player who runs 80 yards for a touchdown serve as examples and symbols of Success.

Significant about this failure-success motif is that the contents of success arise from the common life of people in a national community. They are, as previously noted, *given.* They exist within a particular culture, and it is this culture that determines what they will be. In this sense, they exist before the question of whether people have whatever it takes to acquire or achieve them. People may or may not have the knowledge and skill, the determination and "will" to do what it takes to achieve success. But what Success consists of or "is" exists prior to and apart from whatever it is that people set out to do.

A few more notes on this Success motif. The contents of success arise within networks of interaction called communities or nations. After they arise, *religion,* then, is invited to enter this honored space and to help people with the motivational or emotional problems that impede their progress toward Success. Religion here is a resource in the realm of means and has nothing to do with ends, which are provided from a different quarter, from the culture at large. If a person succeeds as a shoe salesperson, let us say, the definition of Success consists of selling many shoes and making a great deal of money. This definition is out there and "on the stage" to begin with. It is part of the background, and religion then enters to provide the emotional support or "gumption" necessary for achieving that culturally defined Success.

In sharp contrast, the sinner-redemption image does *not* say that the problem is failure to achieve Success as opposed to Failure. Rather, the problem is a *moral* matter. It pertains to doing what is *wrong* or failing to do what is *right.* There are things that a person has a wish to do. And there are things that she may do to get whatever it is that she wants, whether fame or fortune, or whatever. But there is a moral Good that imposes limits on her pursuit of the objects of her wishes and desires. There are actions that she could perform that might win fame and fortune for her. But these possible actions fail the moral test. They are not Good; they cheat her employees, her customers, or the general public, or they involve dishonesty and telling lies. She therefore pulls back from some actions that hold out prospect of Success because she thinks that certain of these actions are *wrong.* Yet these actions are not wrong because they fail to achieve an objective. They are wrong because doing them is not consistent with love of God and neighbor or with Truth.

Significant about this image is that the content of the Good—just what it is that is good to pursue—is *not* given by the culture. It comes from elsewhere; it is given by God, and it is from God. An action is, as the saying has it, "the Will of God." It is not given by culture, but from a realm outside of and beyond culture. Culture mediates but does not produce it. It is the Truly Good. In some cases, it will be consistent with the pursuit of success in worldly terms. A businessman earns a reputation for honesty. And because he is viewed that way in the community, people flock to his business, and he prospers. Yet he was not honest because that would get him business. If he were, his honesty would be a matter of strategy rather than morality. He is honest, rather, because it is *good* to be honest. It is good and right and to be approved of for its own wake, not because it facilitates his movement toward some worldly objective.

This congruency of the Good and what "works" holds in some cases, but in others it does not. Here, a businessman loses in the competition because she is truthful. In speaking the truth, she passes up chances to increase her sales and to fare well in competition with others because these others are not being held back by such weighty and burdensome scruples. Her being truthful remains *good* in this case just as it is in the other. From a moral standpoint, it does not matter whether doing what is right does or does not move a person toward Success. (Or were we to take this to the next level of moral judgment, now actual Success with this capital "S" would actually be—and often is—achieved by doing what is right *no matter what this costs.*)

In the light of this contrast between the Success and the Righteousness images, it is interesting that the mega-church preacher so completely aligns himself with the former—with the Success motif. True, as we read the statement in the brochure just cited, we might not be sure of this. He said, "Americans do not have much patience with losers." We might think that this is a statement about Americans rather than about losers. We might even think it is a critical statement to the effect that Americans are overly preoccupied with achieving worldly Success. But as we go on, we see that this is *not* what he means. What the preacher intends, rather, is to give "Americans" great authority, indeed *moral sovereignty*. If they do not have "patience" with something, it is because the thing is *bad*. If they stop buying tickets to events, the events are thereby proven to be deficient. There can be no criticism *of* Americans. There can be only criticism *by* Americans.

Of course, the preacher's intention is to announce that there is "hope." As a matter of fact, hope is his basic theme. And this hope is "in Jesus." He asserts that even people who have experienced great Failure or multiple Failures can find "in Jesus" hope that they may do better in the future. We have here a picture of a man who has failed in business or in a profession and who then puts all that failure behind him, takes a deep breath, rolls up his sleeves, gets to work, and moves on to great Success in the future, in whatever worldly pursuit he undertakes.

As the preacher sees it, it is a crucified and risen Jesus who provides the motivation to get busy and succeed. To wit, there is a definite parallel between the mega-church preacher's discussion of failure and hope for success, on the one hand, and the Christian proclamation of the forgiveness of the sinner in Jesus Christ, on the other. Here, the concept of *failure* melts into, or merges with, the concept of *sinner*. The former is treated as though it were the same as the latter. Being a failure and being a sinner are the same thing in the mega-church's new economy of salvation.

But of course these are *not* the same thing. A failure is a person who has set out to do or to accomplish something but has not been able to complete this action. He has *failed* at what he was trying to do. In American culture, however, the concept of failing or Failure takes on a metaphysical nature. To fail in business, sports, or a profession is a cosmic event. It is something that occurs in the core of being itself. If a man fails, he *is* a Failure. Having failed defines who and what he is. The man is "he who has failed." This is his name or identity, and it assigns him a place of ignominy in reality. In this observation about how many Americans think, the preacher is correct.

A sinner, on the other hand, is something very different. She is someone who does not do what is *Right*. Or she does what is *Wrong*. It does not matter whether she does or does not succeed in her worldly endeavors. She may fail. Or she may succeed. Yet she achieves her success by doing something that is wrong. On the other hand, the good woman may have failed because she limited the means she used to those that her conscience would allow. She was truthful, or she was fair, or she was compassionate. And it was just these qualities that limited her success or prevented her from succeeding at all. From the moral standpoint, that is, whether the woman who does what is right subsequently enjoys Success or suffers Failure is irrelevant. She is neither better because she succeeds nor worse because she fails. If she does what is right, she succeeds morally or with God. *That* is what matters. She may have failed; however, she is not a sinner.

ESCHATOLOGY AND LIFE ADJUSTMENT IN JOHN, CHAPTER FOUR

As the sermon continued, the minister spoke about the account in the Gospel of John, Chapter Four, in which Jesus spoke with the Samaritan woman by the well of Jacob. The Samaritans were an offshoot of the Hebrew faith that arose in the postexilic period. They were rejected by orthodox Jews whom they, in turn, rejected. In the account, Jesus was weary and was sitting by the well when the woman came to draw water. He asked her for a drink, an act that surprised the woman because Jews usually did not speak with Samaritans at all, especially not with Samaritan women. The conversation then goes through two eschatological (end-of-time) phases. In the first, Jesus responds to her surprise by saying that if she knew who he was, she would have asked him for *living water*. That living water would then satisfy the thirst of anyone who drinks it and would do so in eternity. In the contrast between the mundane water from the well that satisfies, but only temporarily, and the divine water provided by Jesus, we have the messianic or end-of-time proclamation. In it, Jesus proclaims himself as the one in whom God speaks the Word that decisively overcomes death and nothingness and the anxiety and despair of death and nothingness— the One who gives "living water."

In the second eschatological proclamation, the woman speaks of the contrasts between "this mountain" where Samaritans worship and the temple in Jerusalem where Jews worship. Jesus confirms that "salvation is from the Jews," but then puts both beliefs about the right place to worship to one side with the assertion that the time has come when people will worship the Father "in spirit and in truth" rather than in one place or another. To this the woman remarks that the Messiah is due to bring that into effect, and Jesus confirms that he is the Messiah. The woman had already perceived that Jesus was "a prophet" because he knew that she had been the wife of five husbands. So it was a movement from prophet to Messiah.

In both eschatological statements, Jesus confirms that there now dawns a whole new order of things. And this new order comes in and through him. The *new order* is one in which eternal life becomes a reality within reach of those who will have faith in him, faith in the *living water*. There is in him a possibility of worshiping God "in spirit and in truth" and therefore of not needing special and defined places or ways of worship. Both statements bristle with an "end of time" or eschatological awareness.

With this testimony to the stunning blow of the decisive action of God in human history, the special nature of this and all accounts in the fourth gospel comes clearly into view. It takes us to a place where all of the details of human activity together with the ups and downs of worldly fortune fade into insignificance before the ultimate yes and no that confront us as we stand before the decisive action of God in Jesus Christ. It is a place in which the world, all of us and all of Creation, stands judged before the True Righteousness and is redeemed by faith in him in whom that Righteousness is present.

With this understanding of the eschatological nature of the Gospel of John and of the account of the woman at the well, we may see how the mega-church preacher handles this text. We will see that he transforms the end-of-time vision of Jesus of Nazareth being "the resurrection and the life" (John 11:25) into a source of the mega-church's life adjustment wisdom.

To Brother Jim, it was of great significance that the woman had been married to five different men. It seemed clear to him that the woman had been involved in "troubled relationships." He pursued the matter further by suggesting that whenever a person is involved in such an unhappy marriage, he develops a set of unfortunate expectations or ways of coping. He refers to these as "baggage." A person, that is, leaves a stressful marriage with certain expectations about married life and certain ways of coping that are based on these expectations. These expectations and ways of coping are well honed. When the person enters a new marriage, he will then take this baggage into that new relationship. And if he is married several times, the baggage will accumulate and the whole collection of "baggage" will then disrupt and erode at or even destroy any new marriage.

The issue here is not whether this analysis of troubled marriages is correct. A sociologist, psychologist, or simply an insightful person could make this the basis for a lecture, or even a series of lectures, on marital problems or "the state of marriage today." With research studies at hand, he could undertake to explain the high divorce rates of the last few decades and to suggest what, if anything, could be done about it, or, at least, what married people could do about their own marriages. It is quite likely that she will make major use of the concept of "baggage"—coping devices—in her analysis.

The issue, rather, is twofold. First, there is the question whether the woman's checkered marital history is a subject of concern at all. Certainly the account does not itself suggest that it is. The matter that does seem to be of concern is that Jesus *knew* that she had been married five times. His knowledge of a matter about which he did not have information suggests that he is "a prophet," or even "the Messiah." The woman told the people of her village that "He told me everything I ever did." His knowledge of her past seems to have eschatological significance. Knowing something that he had no way to learn about suggests that a New Order has come into the world. And it has come in Jesus.

Given the highly symbolic character of much that is in the Gospels and specifically of the Gospel of John, the "five husbands" could have another meaning. Some scholars think that it might refer to the belief that the Samaritans had lived under five emperors or rulers.

In his sermon on "hope," the minister is taking the five failed marriages of the woman at the well to be a special case of *failing.* The woman had been stuck in unhealthy relationships, in unhealthy romances, and in unhealthy religion. Her life had been riddled, that is, with Failure. And in this, she was not at all unusual. Most of us have experienced failure at one time or another. Indeed, many of us have been through it one time *and* another! These failures need not have all been in marriage. They can be in any realm of life, but in every case, they are failures.

The message of *hope,* according to the preacher, is that we do not need to be stuck in Failure. The failures we have experienced in the past can be deprived of power. They can be neutralized or offset. We can refuse to allow the past to control our future. Problems can be conquered. Personalities can be changed. We can admit our failures, and we can then quit whatever it was that brought us to the point of failure. It is not just a second chance that we seek or may find, it is, rather, a change. If we quit the failing routines and practices, that is, coping devices, in which we had been mired, we will have no more of whatever brought it about and therefore no more of Failure itself.

It is Jesus who helps us to move along this path. In the Cross of Jesus, all of our failures are canceled. The "forgiveness" spoken of in the Bible has to do with this. Whatever our failures may have been, they are canceled in the Cross of Christ. True, God does not remove the consequences. Whatever happened in our failed efforts of the past continues to affect our present. Just as the prisoner who repents must nevertheless serve his prison sentence, and the businessman who "blew it," must live with the losses he has incurred, so the consequences of what we have done go with us into the future. But they do not need to dominate us or the course that our lives will take from the present moment. With the help of Jesus and a right spirit, we can move forward into a better future.

We may see this message in the light of two features of the Gospel of John (though not only John). First, there is the eschatological content in which the end-times have "beginning and power" (Tillich) in Jesus who *is* the Resurrection. And, second, there is the call to servanthood and righteousness that forms the actual content of the Christian life. In the light of these two features, the life adjustment nature of the message of the sermon being discussed comes clearly into view. The preacher is not concerned to call people to Dietrich Bonhoeffer's "costly discipleship" or to a righteousness that is greater than that of the Pharisees and Sadducees. He is concerned, rather, to speak to them in the midst of the aspirations, hopes, desires, and ambitions that are the content of their thinking and their living. And, speaking to them there, he addresses them about how to find *Success* within it. Religion, then, is a *help* for us. It helps us to do whatever it was that we were going to do anyway.

This "already given" nature of the goals to be pursued is implicit in the concept of *Failure*. For to fail is to experience a collapse in a person's projects. The person does not achieve what she set out to achieve. She either falls short or makes no progress at all toward the goal she had set for herself. There are several zones of life in which such Failure may occur. Most obviously for Americans, the contrast between Failure and its opposite, Success, occurs in the realm of career and money-making. To succeed here is to attain heights that are widely recognized as being admirable. The person who rises in this realm does not just succeed, nor does she simply enjoy Success. Rather, she *is* a Success. Her "making it" in her own business or her ascent in the hierarchy of a corporation define her basic identity. She stands tall before the whole world. And conversely, the person who does not make it not only fails, but *is* a Failure. This is her identity.

To this contrast of Failure and Success in the realm of job –and career may be added a person's experience or performance in personal relationships, as per the woman who had been married five times. The person who has "unhealthy relationships" has *failed* in marriage, family, and in other intimate circles. Regardless of what his experience in the economic realm may be, he feels himself to have "failed" if things have gone badly in his marriage, with his children, or in other personal bonds.

The preacher's message, then, has to do with these and related forms of Failure versus Success. He asserts that there is, in his church and in its proclamation, a resource for enabling a person to do what the preacher has said a person should do: to put the Failure behind him, to not allow Failure to dominate his thoughts and feelings, and so to go forward to a better future. But both the Failure of the past and the hoped-for Success of the future are those of the person himself or those of the cultural context in which he lives.

Clearly, what is missing here is the call to Righteousness that forms the very essence of the biblical and Christian message. This call tells us that the purposes to be pursued, and the associated contrast of Failure and Success, are those that God assigns, not those that are created in the human sphere. They are neither a person's own goals nor those that are honored in the community and its culture. We might ask, for example, what would happen if a person is busy making a success of a certain commercial enterprise and then hears a call from the Lord to abandon that enterprise as not being good and wholesome for people or the community. If this were to occur, then God would *not* be delivering a person *from* Failure. On the contrary, God would be calling her *to* Failure. God would be calling her to do what is right even if, or especially if, failing in a worldly endeavor could be reasonably expected. Such a failure would not be just a consequence of clumsiness in carrying out one's business affairs. Nor would it be the suffering of a bit of back luck. It would be, as Bonheoffer put it, a "cost of discipleship."

The call *to* Failure in this and other ways is a summons from an "elsewhere." If the goals that people pursue are set by culture and are well understood by everyone within a society (even by those who reject them), we can say that those goals are *right here*. The pursuit of wealth or of high position in a business, a government agency, or an educational or religious institution is widely recognized as *good*. They are "obviously" what people *want*. No one who pursues them feels a need to explain to others why he does so, although a person who does not pursue them may feel a need to account for his indifference and possibly to justify it. For if she does not, her Failures may be viewed as due to sloth or incompetence. But the call of God to righteousness, justice, or kindness is from *elsewhere*. It is not from here but from somewhere else.

This "elsewhere" nature of the call of God is suggested by the expression that occurs throughout the Bible that God is *Holy*. God is *Other*. He is not contained in our personal aspirations or in the accepted, "taken for granted" goals of our society. In this view, God is seen as awesome, as holy, and as one who "makes the mountains quake" (Ps. 104:32). This view is altogether missing from the preacher's discourses. Not only is it not present and emphasized, but one senses as he surveys the preacher's comments that any view of God as holy would be incongruous and strangely out of place. It would not "fit." Basically, there is little room for God in the mega-church.

THE SERMON: SERVE THE CHURCH

Alongside the life adjustment theme is that of *serving the church*. Here the theme is that we respond to the Gospel by serving. We do this, as in the classic rhetoric of Protestantism, with both our efforts and our money. The preacher devoted two sermons to this theme, one focusing on our activities and efforts, the other on *what we do with our money*.

With these matters put before us, we might expect the preacher to devote his remarks to any or all of a number of themes. We could get busy seeking to promote wholesome education in our communities, or attending to the needs of the emotionally distressed or victims of abuse. We could get active in organizations seeking to protect our liberties, or to promote racial and ethnic equality, or to make a "better deal" possible for the unemployed, the underpaid, and the poor in general. We could undertake to establish peace on earth, or to call a halt to global warming and to other environmental disasters. It is quite a list, this collection of things many people *are* busy at, and therefore that we *could also be* busy at, to make a better world (or prevent a worse one).

And if this is true of ways in which we could spend our time and causes to which we could devote our efforts, it is true also of what we do with our money. In this case, we could seek the welfare of our fellow human beings "at a distance." as we may put it. Others are out there in the trenches, while we write checks and so provide the needed financial support. Compared to what they do first hand, what we support financially can be far more diffuse or spread out. Someone who devotes his efforts to a cause must choose one among many. She is, after all, just one person. But the individual who donates money can spread that resource among many highly varied causes.

So, then, as the preacher warms up to this discourse on serving the Lord with our efforts and our money, we are "all ears" to hear what of the many good, human, and humane causes he is going to mention. But we are in for a surprise, although by now it should not be much of a surprise, for what he speaks of is service *within* or support *of* the church itself. The community, the nation, and the world "out there" are left waiting for their share of this mega-church service. Is it ever coming? The mega-church tells us we need to be busy in the work of the church and that we need to be donating our money to the church. One might think that the devotions and activities of the church exist for the purpose of "revving" up our motives and honing our spirits for service "out there" among our billions of neighbors. But those devotions turn out, instead, to be ends in themselves. There is a strange similarity here between the mega-church and the medieval monastery. In the monastery, the monk in his stall was not preparing for serving God in the world. Rather, what he did in his devotions was the sum and substance of that service. Devotions directed to God are the final good in the contemplative monastery. Similarly, being busy in the activities of the mega-church is the final good in that organization. The similarity is a pained one for those who can glimpse the profound contradiction within it.

Because the mega-church founders–leaders set rapid and continuous growth as their ultimate and only actual goal, everything they say, approve of, and do has to be *devoted* to that goal. Any concern to set to rights an injustice or to significantly relieve a suffering "out there" in the world would be a digression from this dominant imperative. Where the devotion of medieval monks *directly to God* was understood as direct and even pure service, the modern mega-church introduces (or imposes) between the would-be-devotee (the mega-congregant) and God a medium (or currency) of supposedly spiritual commitment and exchange—money. And this money is for service, yes, but service only to the mega-church and its ever growing body. A sort of nested no-exit, no-logic loop of seemingly God-driven spiritual purpose fueling itself drains the purpose from the spiritual endeavor and then even drains the spiritual from the spiritual endeavor.

We have, then, two features of mega-church preaching. There is the life adjustment theme in which the mission of the church is to motivate people to achieve Success in the goals that are set for them by the culture that surrounds them. And there is the promotion of activity within the church itself, aimed at feeding the mega-church rather than the souls of its congregants.

AN EVANGELICAL SERMON

Although most of the sermons are on life adjustment themes or focus on service within (which is actually service to) the church itself, there are occasional expressions of the Christian evangelical view. As Christmas 2006 was approaching, Brother Jim devoted a sermon to this theme. It was not what the listener would have expected on the basis of the brochure that was handed to worshipers as they entered the auditorium. That document spoke about the "Grinch who stole Christmas." It described a creature who had a heart that was too small and therefore could not love. But the heart then grew very large, producing an abundance of love and warmth. With that as introduction, we might have expected a discourse on loving, caring, and human warmth.

But what the sermon, the first in a series, actually did was to spell out the basic evangelical theme. The preacher spoke about all human beings having been made corrupt, rather like a nearby river that has been badly polluted. Then he described how Jesus had died to deliver us from our corruption, and that His doing so was—and is—a gift. We do nothing to earn or deserve this gift. Our salvation is entirely God's doing and is pure gift. This, as we may readily recognize, is the basic assertion of evangelical Christianity. This basic assertion was spelled out in varying ways by both backwoods Baptist lay preachers and by sophisticated theologians (by Karl Barth, for example). It is also asserted by Bill Hybels of the Willow Creek Church, one of the first and possibly the most famous of the mega-churches. Hybels proclaims frequently and with enthusiasm that salvation is a *gift*.

To this evangelical core, Brother Jim then laid out a three-way contrast among the non-Christian, and then the half-way Christian, and then of course the committed Christian. The non-Christian, he says, is self-centered. The half-way Christian is saved, but does not put Christ at the center of his life. The fully Christian person is fully Christ-centered in all he does.

Does all this move us toward a more Christian proclamation? The answer is both yes and no. It is yes in that we have moved into a theological as opposed to a life adjustment mode of speech. The lordship of Jesus Christ and His redemptive work have appeared in speech and not just in song. But something is missing—something rather basic. If we said that we see here some positive steps toward Christian proclamation, we would be right. But this is like saying that an airplane that is taxiing down the runway has "made progress" toward completing a flight to a distant city. The airplane certainly has done so. But the question as to whether the airplane can *take off* remains. If it turns out that the airplane cannot *take off*, then we have progress, but progress that is stalled. The airplane went a certain distance, but it did not take the next crucial step.

Similarly, the proclamation of the deliverance of the sinner by the Death and Resurrection of Jesus Christ is movement. But as an elucidation of the Christian message, some crucial steps remain. It is not at all certain that the proclamation can "take off." What can stand in the way of this needed next step in its journey is the concept of *righteousness*. Without a well-developed idea of what it means to love God and the neighbor, the assertion that we are "saved by the blood of Christ" remains mushy and without content. A person is "bad" and Christ makes him "good." But if "bad" just sits before us as an idea, it is indeed soggy. It cannot, on its own, stiffen and take on the quality of being something, or some thing. To arrive at that point, the term *bad* would have to embrace a persistent preoccupation of a person with himself, with his possessions, his honor, and his power. It would be a preoccupation that affects everything he does. It appears at one moment as his quest for pleasure, at another as his attempt to "lord over" his fellow human beings by appearing more virtuous than they, and at still another moment by wanting to control what the others do. This self-centeredness would affect and *infect* his every action and thought. It would affect even, and especially, his efforts to rise above his self-centeredness to become *good*. We see this in the unlovely self-righteousness in the name of religion that some "religious" people have displayed throughout the ages.

What is missing is a purer, more genuine, concept of *righteousness*. This genuine righteousness is symbolized by the simple command, "love your enemies." In this righteousness, we rise above our self-centered condition, an ascent that we cannot perform on our own because our selfishness infects even our efforts to rise above it. As long as we are without such a concept of what God's demand of us is, the proclamation "saved by the blood of Christ" will remain mushy and without content. The airplane may taxi most vigorously, but carrying the mush, it cannot rise up off of the ground.

True, this "mush" is more the rule than the exception in Christian churches of today (and perhaps in those of every day). This is so because of the limitations inherent in 20-minute sermons and because of the limited imaginations of preachers. This is also true because of the limited tolerance of today's congregations whose members are sound-byte oriented. Of course, this low tolerance is not unique to our modern times. Hence we have to ask: If people in Jesus's day could not tolerate the vision of True Righteousness when it appeared before them, should we expect anything different today? And have not many ministers "toned down" their remarks to fit what they think their congregations will tolerate and allow?

We are living with, and perhaps helping to expand and even perpetuate, a "mush" that is in no way the exclusive property of the mega-church. There is a challenge here for all of us, including those of us who think we have actually been brave and "spoken out." The prophet is no more free of sin than is anyone else. But here once more, the difference between authentic churches and mega-churches has to do with whether there is a *way back.* In churches that are not "mega," a concern with the True and the Right can be independent of the wish of the church to "do well" in worldly terms, in terms of numbers of people and finances. The ever-growing church, on the other hand, is *locked in* by its project of growing ever larger, a direction that by its very nature blocks a way back.

THE GOSPEL AND THE MEGA-CHURCH

In my critique of mega-church worship, I have thus far focused on several key matters. First is the basic matter of "praise," which may all too often be praise of one's self or of ourselves rather than true praise of God. Second is the jettisoning of tradition and, with it, the loss of taken-for-granted assumptions that are essential to our civilization and to any civilization. The third matter is the mega-sermon, which seems to be in the life adjustment vein rather than in the evangelical tradition. Fourth is that the mega-sermon seems to view the "Christian life" entirely in terms of service within and to the church itself. And last, the mega-sermon may often have evangelical content, but is all too often beset by a "mush" that saps the power of the proclamation.

Many objections could, of course, be made to these and other of my critical assertions. And among them would be the suggestion that these assertions are by no means unique to the mega-church. And certainly this is correct. We must be alert to the creeping in, to wider realms of religion, of the characteristics already apparent (that is if we are looking for these) in the mega-church. What I have said may apply to broad sections of American church life. The praise of God that "bounces" and so is really a praise of one's self can be found wherever people are busy pulling up "praise" from within themselves. Disrespect for tradition is a basic feature of our technological society, with its constant change and its adulation of the "new" and the "up-to-date." And worldly wisdom, if and when it is, indeed, wisdom, that is called on to do duty as a substitute for the Gospel is not uncommon. Such "wisdom" might even be epidemic. Nor is there anything uniquely "mega" about a proclamation of the Gospel that is "mushy." We could say that these items grow like weeds in the garden of the Lord.

But the mega-church is different from other expressions of Christian faith, both the profound and the shallow, in one important regard. The founding pastors of the mega-church *set out to build a very large church.* This is their project at the beginning of their endeavors and it remains their objective throughout. Alongside the project of "winning souls for Christ," or calling people to discipleship, is the goal of establishing a very large enterprise, or "church" as they call it. We might even say that the objective is establishing a large ever-growing church *instead* of winning souls or calling disciples. Here, winning souls is merely a *means to mega-church expansion,* with accumulating many "constituents" being the *end goal.* The goal of maximizing the size of the operation takes on a sovereignty. It displaces the objectives that are proper to the Gospel. So it is that we have arrived at the sharp edge of the painful distinction between the mega-church and the church. We witness the energies divide. The mega-church congregant is transformed to the "constituent" or even the "consumer" of a product, the mega-church experience. Label this as religion in order to sell it. What deceit is inherent here?

If the objective is to build a very large operation, as mega-church pastors have done (successfully), then other characteristics follow. Because they want the church to balloon in size, they praise the Lord in a way that boomerangs; they are really praising themselves, for everything that they do is an act of self-promotion. It is designed to attract and pull more people in. Its focus must therefore be on itself. "Come to us," is the message, "for we are a magnet pulling you toward us." When we "praise God," we are doing so to become such a magnet. "Praising God" is the means. Your coming into the operation is the end.

Because the mega-church wishes to draw in hordes of people, it preaches sermons on how to succeed in achieving personal goals or goals that are set for people by their society and its culture. Mega-church consumers buy experience of help or support for what they want to do, to carry out, or to acquire. The aspiration to grow very large *constrains* the promoters of the mega-church. It *compels* them to carry out certain forms of worship, to undertake certain kinds of singing, and to hold forth with a certain style and content of preaching. The forms and the content have to be as they are, given the eminence and majesty of the enterprise of growing ever larger.

In an interesting contrast, I attended a conventional Baptist church located geographically between "The Tide" and another very large church, which is "First Baptist." In this smaller version of the Baptist tradition, there are no more than about a hundred people in attendance. The congregation was small enough so that the minister could look over the group and recognize visitors easily (including me). There was a pulpit, and both an organ and a piano were being played, one on each side of the sanctuary (as it was called in this church). Many of the hymns were those that would be familiar to any Protestant churchgoer, and the others were familiar in type. In his sermon, the minister spoke, as did the mega-church speaker, about the woman at the well in John 4. But there was a difference. This regular Baptist minister emphasized that the expression, "worship the Lord in spirit and in truth" refers to a God who is sovereign and awesome and holy. He conveyed a strong sense of God as *Other*. What is interesting here is that the mega-church preacher *could not* do that. The project of growing indefinitely will not allow it. If it is true that the preacher has a big church, it is also true that, in a manner of speaking, the big church *has him*. The project of being big and becoming ever bigger dictates how ministry is to be carried out.

In all churches, both those that are smaller and those that are larger, there are things that "have" the minister, the congregation's leaders, and the people in the congregation. These things that "have" all the people involved in the church are factors other than the sovereign God who is holy. And they are other than Jesus Christ who is the Lord of the church. They are the need and wish for companionship, for people to joke with, for prestige (yes, I go to First Church), for "fun" things to do at Christmastime, and for an affirmation that one is a "good" person. The minister may aspire to be "the pastor" within the congregation who is respected by the men and adored by (some of) the women while being "the Reverend So-And-So" in the larger community.

But there is always the *way back* to the authentic Christian Gospel. Jesus may at any moment reassert His lordship within and over the congregation. Leaders and others in the congregation may at any time direct their faith, their trust, and their obedience, not to their congregation or their preacher, but to Jesus as Lord of the congregation. This can happen in a general way, or it can take place with regard to any particular issue or problem, as occurred in the case of the racial integration of churches and communities.

It is this *way back* that is missing in the case of the mega-church. The project of growing ever larger closes the door and locks it. If, by the grace of God, the minister and his staff took a trip to Damascus and wanted to return to faithfulness, they would have to break through that barrier. The large size of the church and the aspiration of growing larger in both membership and in income would have to be "up for grabs." They would have to be put into question. The possibility of shrinking rather than growing (both in membership and in "income") would have to become a real option. Indeed, it would have to be regarded as preferred over continuing to be inauthentic, even unfaithful.

5

THE MEGA-CHURCH PROGRAM: EDUCATION AND GROUPS

As the visitor goes into the right-hand lobby of the main building of the Ocean Tide Church, he sees a small space enclosed by counters on both sides. Much of the time, there is a person in the space. This person readily speaks with anyone who approaches her. A large number of brochures of various kinds are arrayed on the counters. Many of these are pamphlets announcing various concerns or programs of the church. Most are glossy and very well done. There are brochures on how to become a member of "The Tide." There are also pamphlets on why to become a member and on various aspects of this church and its program.

In addition, there are two printed sheets on that counter, one yellow and the other blue-green. The blue-green sheets have "Ocean Tide" printed in large letters at the top and then, in smaller letters, "Adult Compass Groups." Forty-two of the groups are listed with indication of topic, time of meeting, place, name of leader, class name, and class description. This last term refers to the categories of people the class is intended to include. Some classes are for men. Some are for women. Most are for both men and women. Of these, some are for one age group, some for another. Many are for "adults." Two are for "singles" and one is for the "college co-ed." The times of the meeting areas are set around the three worship services. Seven groups meet at 8:30 A.M.; 11 meet at 9:45 A.M.; 7 others meet at 11:00 A.M., and 17 at other times. Of the latter, 7 meet in church facilities, and 10 meet in homes, presumably those of the class leaders. One of these groups is located in a community about 10 miles away.

THE PROGRAM FOR PRESCHOOL CHILDREN

At the right-hand side of the lobby is a large counter with two or three people behind it. In large letters above the counter is written "PRE-SCHOOL CENTER." A smaller sign tells any visitor who has small children in tow that it is the place for "visitor registration." There are doors to the right and to the left of that counter. The right-hand door is designated as "entrance only," and the door to the left is for leaving. If the visitor enters this area, she will find a large multipurpose area. A number of smaller rooms surround the area on three sides. There are 16 of these rooms. Each of them is for preschool children of specific ages. To the left are two rooms for what are being called "Baby Birds," babies from birth to six months. Then there are "Sparrows" who are divided into an A and a B group. The A group is for ages six to nine months, and the B category is for ages nine to twelve months. To the left of this group are "Robins" A and B. The A group is for children 12 to 15 months, and the B group is for children 16 to 24 months. Older ages are designated as "Blue Birds," "Red Birds," "Canaries," and "Eagles." The latter category is A for younger and B for older five-year old children. To the rear of the large room there are several other small rooms. These are offices and utility rooms, together with one room that is called a "bride's room."

THE PROGRAM FOR SCHOOL-AGE CHILDREN

To find the programs for school-age children, we leave the main building and go to the building on its right. This is the Center for Ministries, a large edifice, with many large and small rooms spread out over a considerable distance. In the middle of the building is a large entrance area in which coffee is available throughout the morning on Sunday. People are normally gathered in small groups in this area.

In this building, we find a quite vigorous program for children as evidenced by the large number of young children of all sizes moving around and apparently having a good time. Adults are mixed in with them in most places, although from time to time a lineup of just children and teenagers appears. A map of the Center for Ministries designates which rooms in the building are for various categories of children. Those in grades 1 through

5 are active in the left-hand wing of the building. Two of the rooms are for the first grade. One is for second grade. One is for third grade boys and another for third grade girls. Then one is for fourth-grade girls and one for fifth-grade girls. The map does not tell where fourth- and fifth-grade boys would go. This, however, should be no problem, for as the visitor approaches the Center for Ministries, he sees a large door on the left-hand side of the building. When he enters that door, he sees a room on the right that is designated as "Kidsplace Checkin." There is a desk in that room and a person behind it who will direct parents and children to the right place for each child.

The children in these classes, presumably ages six through ten, also meet in a large room at the left-hand end of the building. This room is labeled "PraiseKid." The events that take place in this room are, for children, the equivalent of the church service for adults that is held in the auditorium. It is church, but *church* designed for their age group. All worship in the mega-church is intended to take forms that will appeal to people, and therefore certain categories of people, such as children. After this meeting, the children fan out to their various class-specific and sex-specific groups for the 9:45 hour. There is another gathering after the 9:45 hour; now children of this age group meet in the large room at 11:00. It would thus seem that most of these six- to ten-year olds are active in the church either from 8:30 until 10:45 or from 9:30 until 12:00. In this way, these children have an experience that in other churches would be "Sunday school," either preceded or followed by "church." Actually, there do not seem to be many children in attendance in the three main worship services that take place in the large auditorium. The children's program absorbs most of them, leaving the adults to their worship.

The older children, those in grades 6 through 12, presumably ages 11 through 18 meet in an area at the right-hand end of the building. The room is called the "Coffee Shop." From there they fan out to 14 small rooms housing groups for boys and girls in each of seven age categories. During the 9:45 period, one of the rooms is used by a college-age group.

ADULT COMPASS GROUPS

The adult compass groups also meet in the Center for Ministries. Their places of meeting are mainly in the center of the building, with the younger children to their left and the older children to their right. We may recall that the building is long enough from left to right to afford space for a long, brisk walk. With two large rooms at each end, the middle contains many small rooms of varying size. The smallest of these rooms are cozy little spaces for six or eight people, although it is clear that many more often fit in. The larger rooms could house a group of 30 or more people. Altogether, there are 34 of these spaces. In a traditional church, these rooms would be called *classrooms,* but here they are for *compass groups.*

Not all of the "constituents" of the mega-church participate in the groups. It is not possible to give an accurate figure on what the rate of participation is, but we may venture a guess. There are 42 compass groups. If they average 10 persons each, there would be 420 people participating. If the average is 20, that figure would of course double. How, we may now ask, does this compare to the people who attend the worship events? I have looked over the crowds and estimated their size, although I have never done well in this kind of demographic guessing. In fact, I usually overestimate the number of people present in any large auditorium. When I saw figures, they indicated that the *combined* attendance at the three Sunday morning services was in excess of 1,700. We may therefore estimate that participation in the groups is between one-forth and one-half of the number of people who "go to church" there. If we view this in the light of what happens in traditional Protestant churches, it is a remarkably good rate of participation. It is rare to find adults attending "adult Sunday school" in numbers equal to that proportion of attendance at worship services in the usual American church.

We may conclude, therefore, that the mega-church does well in inducing the people who attend its worship services to join themselves to small groups in which they can have personal and face-to-face contact with a modest number of others. We could say that it is a manageable number of others and that it personalizes the entire mega-church experience.

True, the person who attends the church is part of *audience* in the special sense of a mass that is electrified by its link to a celebrity (the pastor). The celebrity, in turn, is made to be a celebrity by his link to the audience. But being part of such an audience is also authenticated for those in it by each person's being part of a face-to-face group in which people know one another—in which they call each other by name. The audience or mass exists in a dialectical—a "back and forth"—relation, that is, a personal relationship. It is much like a family that enjoys an "outing" at the zoo. The people in the family are part of the hundreds of people milling about in the zoo. This, in fact, is what makes the occasion an "outing." Our understanding of what it is to go "out" means to go where there are many people. "Out" is a populated area. A lonely walk in the forest would be a very different experience. It would not be "out" in the same sense. But for each of the family members, the fact that the whole family is there in the crowd gives the occasion the personal substance and reality that would be missing if there were only the large mass.

I hasten to add, however, that strangers greet and talk with one another in the mega-church far more frequently than they do in such sites as movie theaters or grocery stores. Despite the massive numbers of people present, it is generally understood that it is church, and is, for this reason, a setting in which people may readily talk with strangers.

We could say, then, that the compass groups have a dual function. They create a small, intimate grouping within a large and largely anonymous mass. And they provide education of a sort that fits the proclivities of each person. They teach and discuss various matters of interest within the mega-church view of religious reality.

SMALL GROUPS AND THE MEGA-CHURCH

This program of multiple groups for adults together with the finely age-graded programs for preschool children and the programs for school-age children is remarkable. It clearly could be established and carried out only by a very large organization. Smaller churches cannot build programs of anything like this size and complexity. We could imagine a Presbyterian, Methodist, or Lutheran church having perhaps 350 members, with between 100 and 200 people in attendance at Sunday worship. If this congregation has an age distribution that is normal for such a congregation in an unchanging residential area, it would also have a sizable Sunday school, with classes for each age and grade. For adults, it might have one fair-sized class, or it might have two or three. It is likely that these include both sexes and pretty much all ages above about age 18.

We may now ask how it fares in this conventional church. Do the adults who attend that church and participate in those classes have a less vital experience of religious inquiry than those in the more sharply defined groups in the mega-church, or in some other large churches? There is clearly no definite answer to this question. On the side of saying that the mega-church *has* the advantage, we can state the obvious: There are people who are more comfortable or "alive" in a group that consists of just one of the two sexes or of certain ages; they can choose which group to participate in. Their group experience will be tailored to their needs, wants, or interests, along with the kinds of people with whom they are most "comfortable." On the other hand, we could suggest that a good class in Bible or related subjects is just that, a good class regardless of what the exact topic of the class is and of what its age–sex composition may be. Its benefit for those in it will be much the same whether or not the subjects are what its members would choose and whether or not the class's age and sex composition is what a participant would have chosen. It might be like comparing the experiences of two people who are going to read a good novel. The first person has his choice of 10. She will read just one. The second person has only one novel; she has no choice. Both will read one good novel. Does it really matter that the first person had a choice? It might be best to leave our question unanswered. Maybe the mega-church does have an advantage. Maybe the mega-church does not have an advantage.

There is one thing that cannot be said for the compass groups in the mega-church. They are *not* finely tailored to the interests, needs, or proclivities of those who participate. We may imagine a person who approaches the church and feels that part of his being "in" that church is to participate in one or another small group within it. He quickly learns that groups in that church are called compass groups, and he obtains a list of the groups, their leaders, their times of meetings, who may participate, and what subject is to be discussed. He approaches the collection of groups as an individual who necessarily has complex needs, interests, desires, and anxieties. He makes his living in a certain way. He has one or another kind of family life. Of course, having no family life at all is one of the possibilities. He has a personal history, including fortunes and misfortunes, and also including actions of which he is proud and actions of which he is ashamed. He has hopes and plans for the future. Now, does *this* person find a compass group that is suited to *all* that he is and does?

Most likely she does not. What she finds, rather, is a collection of groups that, at the time of their founding, seemed topically good to those who established them and who led them. These people conferred with the members of the church staff and arrangements were made for them to lead the groups. Certain requirements had to be met. These are indicated in brochures that are readily available in the church lobbies. So what the person approaching the groups finds is an array of options, not something designed to fit her in particular. It is, in this sense, like the menu at a restaurant. The diner's choice is made among the items that the restaurant offers, not just whatever the diner might want. Even less is it a combination of items that she might prefer.

WHAT IS MISSING IN THE COMPASS GROUPS

Critical Judgment and the Moment of Uncertainty

With this much said about the age–sex composition and the menu of subjects considered in the compass groups, we may now ask what, if anything, is missing. Is there something that we might have expected or wanted of such groups in view of their multiplicity? We are assuming, of course, that the church aspires to being a *Christian* church. What more, we may ask, might have been desired?

One such item would be the *moral dilemmas* that people face in their daily lives. Foremost among these, of course, would be the perplexities that arise in business and in the professions. One of the men in the men's group is employed by Wal-Mart. His position is a rather high one, the kind of position that pays a salary on which a person could live and pay his bills. He is employed by an organization that is said to be famous for (at least) two things. The first is its mistreatment of its employees in the matter of wages and benefits. The second is the obscene net worth of the major owners of the company. To be employed in a responsible position in such an organization is clearly to be presented with a moral and ethical quandary. Should he resign and try to make his living another way? Should he make vigorous protests on behalf of the poorly paid workers? Should he bide his time, waiting for a chance to do something that he cannot, at least at the moment, do? Is there something else that he could do for some of the underpaid employees ("associates")? There clearly are no definite answers to these questions. Whatever he does will likely be wrong in one way or another. But if every option is wrong, then, truthfully, none of them is fully wrong. There is only the "least worst" or the "best" choice among them. But it may be a matter of the utmost moral seriousness to make this *best possible choice* among them. Morally, it *matters* whether a person does something that is entirely wrong, rather than something that is the best of all less than desirable options.

Similar dilemmas await people who enter many other lines of business. Such quandaries are also certain to appear in the professions, such as medicine, education, social work, government service, the military, and—yes—religion. Nowhere are "good" and "evil" paths distinguished from one another with clear and absolute certainty. Nowhere is the obvious path that a person may take purely and simply "good." A person's moral sense always needs to be alert to the various levels of "more" and "less" good and bad that she confronts. True, if a woman contemplates stealing her neighbor's money or seducing her neighbor's husband, she certainly confronts a neat distinction between what she should do and what she should not do. But the forks in the road she comes to in business and the professions are rarely like that. Most commonly, the person who wants to do what is *right* has to make a decision without being certain that it is the correct decision. Rather, the decision is only her guess as to what is correct or right. Yet, even in the face of ambiguity, it may be a matter of unconditional moral seriousness that drives her to make her best guess.

Now here is the rub: So far as the observer can tell, these essential quandaries do not get discussed in the compass groups. Nor do they arise at any other point in the life of the mega-church. And, indeed, they cannot arise, for it is a basic feature of the mega-church that the contrast between right and wrong is made totally *simple*. The contrast comes with a "right now" certainty, a certainty that is free of any equivocation or waiting, with no independent rumination or deliberation necessary, entirely free of hesitancy.

Let's dig deeper into this phenomenon of absolute immediate right and wrong. As the mega-church grows, it struggles to keep that growth going. To accomplish this goal, it must maintain a high level of enthusiasm. Everybody involved must feel the excitement of the moment. This state of excitement rules out any hesitancy that may be involved in thinking. There must be no tentativeness. After all, thinking, by its very nature, requires a "moment" in which we do not know what we will conclude. If we are thinking about moral matters, there is at least a moment in which we do not know what is right and what is wrong—a moment while we think. Certainly, we believe it to be a serious matter that we find a way to know. We think we must go about the business of deciding, doing serious thinking about the alternatives of action before us, and then discerning which of these are right, good, and godly. But this sort of thinking, this waiting to see the outcome of thinking, does not fit with the enthusiasm required for the constant growth of the mega-church. The mega-church is supposed to grow and then grow some more, therefore, there cannot be any suspension of judgment while "thinking it over" proceeds. The necessary hesitation must be ruled out. There can be no moment of "wait and see," or of uncertainty. We have to just know what is right and what is wrong, and we have to know this *for sure,* and we have to know this *right now.*

Let's pause here to further examine the true nature of moral judgment. Notably, the *content* of actual moral judgment is affected by its process: There is no immediacy without time for examination because real judgment requires a process, not an instant knowing. Actual moral judgment does not proceed from a "right now" kind of thinking. Rather it involves a "think it through" mode of reflection. Now of course there will be a difference in what each of us thinks is right and wrong. Just as children display characteristics of the parents who precede them, so moral judgments bear the stamp of their origins. A judgment about right and wrong that comes "after thought" has a different texture from one that is immediate and "right now."

At this point, we may think of a person "supporting his country" in time of war out of a "right now" sort of judgment. It does not matter how the war got started or how it proceeds or who the enemy is. It is *his* country, and therefore he supports it in that war. If asked for a justification, a defender of the war may take offense at the question. As he sees it, we either are patriotic or we are not.

Now compare this form of a decision to support a war with that of a person who also supports her country in a war, but who does so after *thinking* about it. For this person, there was a real possibility that she would oppose her country's being in that war. As she began to think, the matter was "up for grabs." There was no telling which way she would go. And even if the person concludes that she should favor her country's action, her support for the war may be qualified. She supports it "because" of something, and her support is therefore limited by her reasons for taking that positive attitude. And she could cease to support the war if changes occurred in which her reasons for supporting it were no longer in force.

If, now, we compare the attitudes of these two supporters of the war, we find that there is a difference between the first person's support and that of the second person. Each has a family resemblance to its type. The first looks like the uncritical "right now" attitude that it both comes from and truly is. The other bears the marks of its origin in a *process* of thought. Its support depends on those stated reasons and for this reason could change if the reasons change; it has no sacredness in itself but is subject to the "ifs, ands, and buts" that all thinking involves.

Our assertion, then, is that the mega-church educational program will by its nature be restricted to the "right now" kind of moral judgments. To see whether this is true in fact, we would need to observe all of the compass groups and see whether the moral judgments they support are, in fact, of the "right now" kind. And even if we were able to do this, we would still have the problem of how we distinguish moral judgments that are "born of" uncritical judgment from those that derive from serious processes of thinking.

Concern for Community, Present and Future

Alongside the moral matters that, by their nature, require *critical reflection* about options, there are also those matters of right and wrong that are *communal* by their nature. These are issues that an individual cannot decide and deal with by himself and for himself. Rather, the good things that happen and the bad things that take place are the results of many people performing similar actions simultaneously. In these cases, an action by a single individual has no significant result. But when that one person's action "mixes" with the actions of others, the combined effect of the many actions is significant. For example, if one person refuses to buy a product because the producer has offended him in some way, the producer loses just one customer. It is not a "big deal." But if many refuse to buy the product, the producer is in trouble. We call this a *community action,* or a *boycott.*

Matters pertaining to the environment and pollution are certainly important in the world today. An individual who possesses an automobile may drive it around more, or she may do so less. And she can "pollute" either more or less. But regardless of whether she does maximum or minimum polluting, her contribution to "global warming" or other environmental outcomes is trivial. She would be correct if she thought that her decision to go on a pollution-causing trip or drive a car that pollutes more than is necessary will not really make a difference. The world will not be noticeably worse off if she pollutes nor better off if she refrains from doing so. But her decisions about driving *in combination with* those of millions of others like her will make a difference. This way of thinking is familiar to us from our reflections about voting in elections. Each of us votes even though we know that our vote, just by itself, will not determine the outcome of an election. We see ourselves as part of a mass voting in a certain way.

But are these community perplexities matters of *moral* concern? There is a long tradition in the branch of Protestantism called *Pietism* that claims they are not. In this genre of Christianity, *morality* has to do only with individual matters. Whether someone cheats his employer, has inappropriate sexual relations, or gives himself over to a life of "wine, women and song" is, in this view, a moral matter. Morality, as such, is concerned with how an individual manages his own life. These, and only these, come under the imprimatur of *morality*. Other matters may be important. A person may participate in community groups that are concerned with the welfare of the community as such. He may vote and otherwise involve himself in political processes. But these, even if "good," are outside of the sphere or arena of the *moral*. They are like matters of convenience or utility rather than of right and wrong, or godliness or ungodliness. They are secular or "this worldly."

In this belief, the Pietism of Europe was joined by the frontier evangelism in the United States. The target of the Methodist and Baptist preachers was the individual in frontier areas who was given to a life of adventure and of "fun and games." He was urged by the preachers to renounce his sinful ways, accept the Gospel, and take up a life of hard work and family responsibility. And, as an aid to doing so, he was to become active in his local church. Here, the story is much the same. To give up drinking and partying was a moral matter. To marry, "settle down," and raise a family were moral matters. And even though community organizations, community actions, and participation in politics were a major part of American life, they were somehow outside the sphere of *morality*.

With this tradition in the background, it is understandable that the compass groups in the mega-church would not be concerned with community matters as such. Whether they are studying the Bible and its "principles" or are addressing life adjustment issues, they will focus on marriage, child-rearing, and the like, and they will address matters of religion and religious belief. But they will not address community problems as such. To take a case in point, they are not likely to be concerned about pollution and global warming. It would not be in their nature to have compass groups that think of ways of dealing with it. It would not seem like a religious or Christian concern, even if they grant that it is a good thing for some people somewhere to be concerned about it.

And they may not always grant that it is a good thing. There is a certain and rather eerie suspicion of making a heavy commitment to resolving community problems like global warming. Such a concern seems to have an air of the "ungodly" about it, for it seems to require a preoccupation with "this world" that can only detract from devotion to God and Jesus Christ. For some, the coming "End of the World" or "Eschatological Event" may make things like global warming seem irrelevant. If there is to be no future of the World, why worry about it? Or even more, would not worrying about it bespeak a lack of faith in the coming Kingdom of God? (This view of community—global—issues is generally presented as a "right now" sort of judgment, not one with extensive thinking preceding it.)

THE MEN'S CLASS

While I was wandering in the Center for Ministries, a member of the Church staff asked me if she could help me. I asked her what compass groups she would recommend. She took me to a group entitled "MacArthur Bible Study Series." This was a group that, like all such groups, varied in size from one Sunday to another. Without me, it had anywhere from four to eight men present. When I first attended, the men were studying the book of Romans and were near the end of that book. I wished that I could have been with them from the beginning, for Romans is a document that is very inter-esting and quite demanding of its readers. In Romans, Paul does not make a great effort to be simple. The book of Romans is, in this sense, not congruent with the culture of the mega-church. As in other such adult groups in vari-ous churches, the group had a text that served as the basis for its study and its discussion. The book was by an author named John MacArthur. Also as in other groups, the leader asked the men to take turns reading aloud from the text. The leader would ask one man to read a few paragraphs, followed by the man to his left or right and so on around the room. This activity lim-ited the amount of discussion that could take place, although enough of it seemed to occur anyway.

If there is any difference from those other groups, one would be that the men in this compass group gathering are a bit clearer than are men in other churches about their conversions to the Faith. They are more likely to say that there was a definite moment in their lives when they aban-doned their previous lives and became Christians. I have not seen many instances in which this awareness was so clear and well marked. Nor have

I seen instances in which this moment, as the men see it, was followed by two stages: first, by a period of being new converts, and then by another moment of being more mature in the faith. Another difference is that the leader of the group is probably above average among the leaders of adult classes in non-Catholic churches in his willingness and ability to look into sources and inform the men of what he found.

For example, in the discussion of the last chapters of Romans, the men had an occasion to look back to the prophet Isaiah. As part of that treatment, I said that many scholars believe that there were two (or more) writers named Isaiah, and that Chapters 40–56 of the book of Isaiah are the work of Isaiah Number Two (called "DeuteroIsaiah"). One of the men had a refutation for that handy, one that emphasized the importance of prophecy in the specific sense of foretelling the future. The leader of the group looked into the matter the next week and had a report for the group. In his report he said that there are two points of view about the book. In one perspective, there are indeed two writers named Isaiah. In another, there was just one, the Isaiah who lived and spoke in the 700s B.C. The leader favored the latter view. In all of the statements favoring the view that one man is responsible for all 66 chapters of the book, the ability to "see" the future is critical, as Chapter 45 of the book speaks of Cyrus, emperor of Persia. The man named Isaiah knew in the 700s B.C. names and dates of future empires and rulers. And, among predictions of future events, the most important in Isaiah and in all of the prophets, as the men in the class saw it, was the anticipation of Jesus Christ.

With the study of Romans completed, the group then went on to consider the book of Daniel in the Old Testament. Here also, they had the help of a book by John MacArthur. And here also, there is question about when the book being studied was written. But I did not speak about the matter. I did not say that some textbooks on the Old Testament say (for example, the text by Bernard Anderson) that Daniel was written around 167 B.C. and is actually the latest of the Old Testament books, assuming that we do not include the "inter-testament-al" works. But I did not need to do so. MacArthur himself said that "some skeptical interpreters" who are unwilling to acknowledge "supernatural prophecy" suggest the later date. But he felt quite confident that all of the linguistic and other evidence confirms the earlier time of writing, that is, the 500s B.C.

Actually, it does not matter a great deal does it? Faith in God does not depend on having correct beliefs about authorship and dates of the books of the Bible. Christians lived for centuries without worrying about when and how the Pentateuch was composed. And theologians such as Thomas Aquinas and Martin Luther somehow got through their careers without considering that there might have been two or more prophets named Isaiah. There are some matters, however, about which there is more to regret. When we look at the prophets of the Old Testament, we see complex reactions to what was going on in the Israel of their day. We see men who felt called to denounce idolatry and oppression (Cf. Jer. 7:5–7). As Reinhold Niebuhr put it, we see men who judged the rules by which a society lived from a perspective of justice that transcended that set of rules. Given that this is what the prophets were and did, it is most unfortunate that their role as predictors of the future and of the coming of Jesus Christ could, so to say, *swallow up* their role as denouncers of the injustices and idolatries of their own day.

THE GROUP, THE CHURCH, AND THE BOOK

The 42 compass groups, and notably the men's group I have been describing, are part of the program of the mega-church. But they do not fully exemplify the nature of the mega-church. The defining feature of that nature, as I have seen repeatedly, is the imperative of growth. The mega-church wants to grow larger and then continue growing indefinitely. The project of expanding beyond any given level controls what it does and how it does it. That project tolerates no definitions of "success" other than that of perpetual growth. It allows no focus of attention on truth or justice or the plight of the poor or of people subjected to violence.

If this is the case with the mega-church itself, however, it is not so with the groups that make up its program. In collections of 5, 10, or 20 people, there is no imperative of growth. There is, instead, a gathering concerned with a subject to be taught or discussed, and there are the people who make up that gathering. The impulse, therefore, is to address areas of content (for example, the book of Daniel) and/or to mold the gathering of people into a kind of religious family. Whether the quality of the instruction-discussion is high or low is a matter about which I can make no authoritative statement. I have witnessed only one of the groups, and even here I hesitate to give that group a grade of A,B,C,D, or F. Actually, I think it is in many ways a very good group. I can say that the men's group is most captivating when the men talk about their own personal and family encounters with life's difficulties and tragedies and their own ability or inability to "trust in the Lord" as they cope with these difficulties. When they direct attention to these "existential" matters, questions about biblical scholarship have a way of fading into the background.

What we say about the men as they strive to see God in the midst of their worldly circumstances, however, cannot be said about the book on Daniel by John MacArthur on which the men rely. In addition to ignoring the best biblical scholarship, as, I suppose, the bulk of the evangelical movement does, the book is also exceedingly trite and unimaginative. It asks the men to write notes about their dreams, so that those dreams can be compared to the dreams we read about in Daniel. It assumes that God gave Daniel in the 500s B.C. information about what was to take place in the centuries following. And then, in "Summing Up" the author says:

> Scripture . . . declares that the end times will be characterized by great concern for world unity, world government, world economics, and world religion (see 2;7; Revelation 13; 17–18). The world is looking for stability and security and is ripe for the unifying role of a world leader who can stop wars and bring an end to political economic and social chaos—the role that one day will be filled by the anti-Christ.

(I assume that the biblical references are to Daniel Chapters 2 and 7 and to Revelation, Chapters 13, 17, and 18).

This is an extremely important passage. A reader may protest that he has never heard of this concern for world government, world economics, and world religion in all the public comment that we see in newspapers, magazines, and on television. We would look in vain, the reader might say, for books and articles that recommend such worldwide organization of human affairs. So where does this assertion about "great concern" come from? A possible answer is that MacArthur is referring to items that are more in evidence on the world scene. He may be speaking of the United Nations and of the many trade agreements that are now being enacted in the world. But, if so, how does it turn out that these are projects led by the "anti-Christ?" Or, what are we to say about the concern for peace and political stability? And what about the concern to bring about a viable world economic system that would make it possible for the peoples of the world to enjoy freedom from hunger and homelessness? Are these diabolical or evil? If a leader or group of leaders, or an organization such as the United Nations, should prove capable of bringing about such peace, stability, and well-distributed prosperity, would those leaders or organizations be the infamous anti-Christ or Satan in action? If so, we would be saying that the things that people want most are things they should not want, that peace and prosperity are satanic and evil. To want to live in harmony in communities in which everyone can work, earn a living, and raise a family is to have an inappropriate or evil wish. This could not be distinguished from any other vision we may have of an ungodly life, such as a total dedication to "wine women and song," to brutal quests for power and wealth, or to sloth and indolence.

It is likely that MacArthur does *not* intend the expressions "world government" and "world economics" to refer to the United Nations or to any other concrete occurrence that may be observed in our world today. He may speak, rather, of the general idea of world government and of a world economy. He speaks, that is, of what people might want, not of something they do want or that could actually come into existence. And, being what people want, it is something that would have to arise out of the creative activities of human beings, activities that are always beset by pride and greed. The imprint of Satan is, so to say, on these creative endeavors, and for this reason they have no chance of succeeding. World government and world economy can never be anything other than a hope that is never to be realized.

This being the case, what is the appropriate stance for the Christian to take? For MacArthur, it will be similar to that offered by the author of the book of Daniel. Whether that author was writing in the 500s B.C., or later, around 170 B.C., does not matter. MacArthur asserts the earlier date with great confidence. A very large body of critical scholarship developed over the last 200 years is equally confident in asserting the latter time. But we may note that in either case, the Jewish people were under a challenge to their faith. Foreigners may have wanted them to be absorbed into a society into which they had been exiled, as in the 500s B.C. Or conquerors wanted to supplant Hebrew symbols and practices with those designed to sanctify foreign rule, as with the various Greek kingdoms and, later, the Roman Empire. In either case, the apocalyptic writer was urging the Jews to stoutly resist efforts to make them give up their faith and to hold steadfastly to all that pertained to that faith: its practices, symbols, and concepts. MacArthur sees the Christians of today as being in a similar position. Their calling is pretty much to ignore the worlds of politics and economics and to hold steadfast to their Christian faith and to all of the practices, symbols, and beliefs that pertain to it.

But are Christians today in a similar position? The faith of the ancient Hebrews was based on a belief, or we could say a *memory,* that God acted to choose a special people to be his people. They would live under his law and they would live as a true human community. It would be a community in which there would be no oppression of the weak by the powerful. He, then, would be their God. He would go before them and keep their enemies at bay. And he would ensure that they would prosper. By his decree, the rains would fall, and the crops would grow.

When the people of Judah were in a foreign land, however, they were under a pressure or a temptation to adopt the sacred symbols, the religion, of the host society. This would be a symbol-system that would bestow sacredness on the social structures and relationship that existed in that society. The oppressions of the poor by the rich, or the structures that allow that oppression, would be considered good and even sacred. It would be seen as the will of the gods. There would be no court of appeal within the religion for those who are poor and powerless. Even to protest would be seen as sacrilegious. Special measures were, for this reason, necessary for maintaining the faith in the face of this kind of culture accommodation.

But, as usually happens in such circumstances, the religion itself, viewed as idea, as ritual, and as a set of practices, becomes the important thing. It is lifted out of its original context as a commitment to the establishment of a true community that embodies justice and made into the important reality itself. To respect the Sabbath, to observe the dietary restrictions, to marry within the religious community, and to be faithful in synagogue attendance become matters of critical importance. To refrain from worshiping any idol or other god is critical. Together, the positives (things to do) and the negatives (things to refuse to do) become the sum and substance of being a faithful Jew. These are the items that are in crisis, and they become ultimately important for that reason. The Jew may be in a setting (the Persian Empire) where he cannot establish the true covenant community and so all he can do is preserve his faith in its integrity. Just as synagogue worship is a "watch and wait" operation undertaken in anticipation of the hoped-for reestablishment of Judah and the Temple, so preserving the forms of Judaism anticipates the time when the substance—the establishment of the true community—can come into being.

To repeat the question, then, we ask: are Christians today in a similar position? Yes they are, and no they are not. On the side of "yes," we may note that all people in our country, Christians included, are under pressure to raise love of country and patriotism above its functional level. The over-the-top tendency we see today is to make "America" itself into an ultimate value in which the country is thought to be incapable of doing anything wrong. In this way of thinking, the idea of God being one who calls the country to account is therefore rendered impossible. God and country, in effect, merge; they become the same thing. We cannot imagine God as above the country, as its Guide, its Judge, and its Redeemer. Also, on the side of "yes" there is a tendency to view the capitalist system as itself biblical and sacred and, for this reason, immune from criticism.

On the side of "no," Christians today are *not* in the same position as the Jews in the Babylonian and Persian Empires or back in their homeland under the Greek kingdoms. We are in a society in which we have vital roles to play in maintaining and changing social systems and social structures. The divisions between economically defined social classes, between racial and ethnic groups, and between other powerful and powerless groups are not "off in the distance" the way they were in those earlier civilizations. They have an "up-for-grabs" nature that brings them closer to us and makes us more responsible for either keeping them as they are or for changing them in the direction of greater justice, greater integrity, and greater morality.

What MacArthur is urging, then, is an effort to preserve the Christian faith in what he determines is its point of purity and integrity in the midst of a world that is now and always will be full of evil. His program for doing so calls for maintaining the biblical faith in what he thinks is its purity. This means, among other things, insisting that the book of Daniel was written in the 500s B.C. as it presents itself as being. This clearly involves a rejection of modern biblical scholarship in its entirety, along with all other features of mainline Christianity that seem overly accommodated to modern civilization. In this, he is like the Jew remaining a Jew in Babylonia-Persia or under the pressures of Greek overlords. He maintains a near-total indifference to the mammoth cruelties, injustices, and waves of violence that are taking place in our world today. He ignores the realities of our time and seeks to blind his readers to them.

But is this way of being faithful actually faithful? We might note here that thinkers like Reinhold Niebuhr, along with MacArthur, share a profoundly pessimistic assessment of the possibilities for establishing peace and justice in the world. The expression, "the Good and the Evil ripen together into the Day of Judgment," has had widespread currency in mainline Protestant religion. Indeed, Reinhold Niebuhr himself was famous for that kind of statement a half-century ago. But for him, and with him most of mainline Protestantism, this does *not* mean that the faithful should hunker down and hibernate in their churches. It means, rather, that "alleviating some poverty here and setting to rights an injustice there" are matters of ultimate concern. And they are so even if bits and pieces of justice and peace are all we can hope for in a world of sinful men and women and of violent ebbs and flows of power. Even though those bits and pieces are only bits and pieces, they are still occasions for encounters with the holiness of God.

THE MEGA-CHURCH AND
THE EVANGELICAL MOVEMENT

So it seems that for much of the *Evangelical* movement, the wish is to remain "faithful" as a *religious* movement while maintaining a calm indifference to the massive cruelties, injustices, and widespread fits of violence in the world. Indeed, where celebrity-leaders of the movement do involve themselves in politics, it is commonly on the side of the oppressors, not the oppressed. When it comes to nonpolitical humanitarian efforts, however, many church organizations acquit themselves far better. In the wake of Hurricane Katrina in August 2005, it was often church organizations that came to the rescue of evacuees. While both FEMA and the Red Cross vacillated between doing nothing and doing the wrong thing (no, this is not unfair), the Texas Baptist Cooks quietly went about the task of feeding thousands of people cooped up in large buildings. Numerous other churches across the United States sent teams of volunteers as well. Whether these churches fit the *type* of mega-church is not clear. However, there did not seem to be a regal minister involved, just "good church folk." However, they clearly had to be organized to do what they did. And they were able to mobilize a humanitarian project on rather short notice.

But what of the mega-church? Does its only interest in the world lie in the world's being a field for evangelism and conversion of a maximum number of people to their brand of Christianity? Could it, and would it, mobilize a humanitarian project in times of emergency? These are good questions, perhaps best understood by the motivation that could drive the mega-church to humanitarianism: growing the mega-church membership.

Apart from emergency humanitarian action, it would not be "in character" for the mega-church to betake itself to an intense opposition to the ways of the world. Its bland, noncommittal attitude toward issues would not fit with well-articulated opinion about anything. It is not likely to "take sides" in the realm of doctrine or in the sphere of social, economic, and political opinion. Nor is it likely to have much to say about the role of Christian churches in the political-economic issues of the day. But neither would its style go readily with an opposition to the strident opinions of the evangelical faithful. Opposition, we may note, is a firm attitude. And firm attitudes do not appear in the mega-church. Actually, it is not likely to betake itself to a camp in favor of or opposed to any stand on any *social* issue. If its leaders had to address matters about the anti-Christ and the coming end of the world, they would probably echo what the end-time Evangelicals say, but they would do so without conviction. Their seeming to agree would be more like someone saying what he is supposed to *say* rather than expressing something that he actually *thinks*. Even the obvious irresponsibility of such writers as John MacArthur would be unable to awake him from his ideological indifference and lethargy.

What these mega-church preachers would do, rather, is similar to what singers do when they sing songs with little concern about the words of the musical compositions they sing. In Protestant churches, people commonly struggle to sing hymns in such a way as to make them sound pious and godly. In doing so, they reproduce tunes as best they can, but they do not appear to concern themselves with the words they are repeating. It does not occur to them to consider the meanings of the words that they utter as they sing and to wonder "do I really want to say that?" Similarly, a mega-church leader or spokesman could look at words like those of MacArthur, and he could repeat them as part of the "song" of his mega-church operation. They would be no more serious to him than would the words of many songs and hymns to the people who sing them. It is just part of the music or just part of the game. To the mega-church leader, the important thing is the music, not the words. It is the enthusiasm generated within his worship service and his church program that concerns him. *This* is what matters. If there are some words that we could not agree with if we considered them, we solve the problem by not considering them.

Throughout the career of the mega-church and in all of its programs, there seems to be a strange blend of the fierce partisanship of the wing of Protestant Christianity, which is called Evangelical by its proponents and a bland, noncommittal and undefined enthusiasm. Neither the partisan-ship nor the noncommittal attitude can be an option that a proponent of civilization in the best sense of that term could favor, for neither sees a need for the *moment of uncertainty* that all civilized thinking, properly so called, requires. But it is not only the civilized man or woman who has this problem. So also, and perhaps even more, does the Christian. For the Christian, the term *truth* has to do with Jesus Christ. It has to do with Him, and with Him always and supremely. When we say that the Bible is true, therefore we mean that it points to Jesus Christ who himself *is* the Truth. It means this, and it means only this. To say that it means something else, such as that a Prophet Isaiah, speaking in 720 B.C., could foretell the *name* of a Persian emperor who was to rule 200 years later is to have a source of truth *other* than Jesus Christ. It is, in this sense, to "empty the Cross of its Power" (1 Cor. 1:17).

This does not mean that the Bible is unimportant. On the contrary, we know Jesus Christ in and through the testimony that the Scriptures bear to him. Without the witnessing of the whole Bible from Genesis through Revelation, the name "Jesus" is just a name. But through the Bible's testi-mony, the man bearing the name Jesus becomes "the way, the truth, and the life." Yet we must not allow this importance of the Bible to become a thing *sui generis,* that is, a thing in itself.

If such bibliolatry is wrong, what about the noncommittal attitude of the mega-church? If it does not promote a strong attachment to certain beliefs, it also does not promote wrong belief, at least not with conviction. Its tendency in society is to put aside what divides and to find what unites. It will bring people together by making what divides them unimportant. In the end, the mega-church favors bland indifference to fierce partisan-ship. That indifference to truth is, we may say, better for business, includ-ing the business of religion. But there may come a point where Truth does matter. In these points, Truth is a pillar that holds up a community. If bland indifference is better (or less bad) than fanaticism and even than fierce partisanship, it is *not* better than truth and humane values.

Returning here to the program of the mega-church, note again this church's bombastic style of worship. And note again the function of the compass groups where the imperative of church growth is somewhat re-laxed. In these small compass groups, discussions are to a degree unsuper-vised. Therefore the possibility exists that a genuine Christian critique of modern civilization could take place and that a serious probing of the souls of modern Americans could develop. But these fortunate occurrences are inhibited by the environment in which the groups form and meet. The heavy weight of pious enthusiasm in combination with moral and ethical indifference makes it difficult (or impossible) for people in the groups to follow the leads of their best judgments and their incipient moral sensitivities. Whatever paths they pursue in their discussions, they find themselves quickly immersed in the pretentious triteness of the music and preaching that goes on in the auditorium.

6

THE MEGA-CHURCH AND
THE NECESSARY MOMENT
OF UNCERTAINTY

Every Christian group, every Christian tradition, and every Christian worshiping community is one-sided in one way or another. In no location on the Christian map will we find the Gospel in its fullness, nor will there be any site in which the presentation of the Gospel is pure. People's perspectives are limited. They see everything from one angle rather than another. In looking at anything, certainly anything of importance, they always "highlight" certain features of a complex reality while giving less than due attention to others. People are finite. They are creatures. They may be made in the image of God, but they are creatures nonetheless. And just as they are always located in one spot of ground rather than another, so they see any object—a tree, a mountain, a building, in one way when many other ways of seeing it are also possible. It is part of wisdom to acknowledge this limited or partial character of our perceptions of all things. It is part of Christian wisdom to confess that we see the wonders of the Christian Gospel from one of a multitude of possible angles.

Alongside the limited character of our perspectives are the factors of egotism and pride. In our condition of separation from God, we are always "on duty" for ourselves. We seek to create inlets of security and mountains of glory that are intended to take the place of those that we lose when we stray from our Divine Source. Whenever we look at the Gospel in all its richness, this impulse to do for ourselves what only God can do forces its way into our perceptions. It pushes us to highlight those features of the Gospel that will make us look good, either as individuals or as members of certain groups, for example, of nations, races, social classes, or sects.

If a person is wealthy and powerful, he will think that wealth and power are, by their nature, from God and for God. He will see it as God's will that he have a large estate. If he is poor and powerless, he will rejoice in believing that the "meek will inherit the earth." In neither case is he innocent. His wish to be exalted or to be part of something (a nation or other group) that can be exalted influences his perception of the Gospel.

Distortions of the Gospel arising from limited perception and from bias are, of course, not the whole story. On the contrary, each of the many Christian traditions and groups also holds up special features of the Gospel that we do well to welcome and study. A Baptist, steeped as she is in a freely flowing Spirit of God would do well to look into a well-done Catholic Mass and to perceive there the mystery of God's presence as it appears in the structured liturgy that has been celebrated through the ages. The Catholic, comfortable and "at home" in the Mass in which the holiness of God reverberates with such force, would be well advised to accompany her Baptist neighbor to her church one weekend and to feel there the spirit that flows freely when not hemmed in by forms and patterns. Both would do well to consider the special discipline of the Quaker who has learned to "wait in silence for the Lord." If there is a "down" in every Christian tradition, there is also an "up." There is both distortion of the Gospel and special vision of it.

In the mega-church, however, there is a certain "down" for which there is no compensating "up." There is a blurring of the Gospel by the mega-church that is brought about by its very nature as a mega-church. Unlike other churches, even other large churches, the mega-church arose from the work of leaders who set out to build very large churches. They defined "success" as having a large population of "constituents" (attendees, members) and undertook to achieve exactly that kind of success. Their fatal error was in making growth to a large size a project and giving it priority. Certainly a Christian leader who speaks with conviction, with integrity, and a love of the Truth may see his congregation swell as numerous people respond in faith. But to such an honest and truthful preacher of the Gospel, that is something that happens, if it does. It is not his ambition or his project to make it happen. His ambition and his project are to proclaim the Truth of the Gospel. Just what else will happen is then, as he sees it, the decision and the business of the Holy Spirit, not his.

Because the mega-church has made this one fatal error, the error of emphasizing growth over Gospel, it will inevitably travel down many wrong roads. These mistaken turns and directions derive from the ill-advised project of bringing about a very large church. Other traditions may make similar mistakes. Indeed, it is certain that they will make them. But they do not close off the way back by defining "success" as growing to a very large size. They are open to being challenged by the features of the Gospel that they ignore or shortchange. Baptists and Catholics show openness at various points in their church life. But because all churches do take wrong turns from time to time, the following discussion will apply to all churches, as well as to the mega-church. What we say here, however, has special relevance to the overgrown religious projects of the mega-church.

Central in this discussion is the essential concept of *the moment of uncertainty*. All responsible thinking about what is true and what is good, we assert, requires that a searcher go through a process of inquiry. This process inevitably involves a moment when she is not sure what she will learn when the process is complete. The procedure can be thinking; it can be observation; it can be allowing aesthetic intuition to arise in consciousness; it can be "waiting for the Lord." But whatever it is, there must be a moment when inquiry has begun but has not yet reached a conclusion. This "not yet" must be accepted and endured. *Without it, there is no possibility of reaching truth.* Nor is there any hope of correctly distinguishing what is good from what is evil. Without it, there is no chance of being right, nor any possibility of being moral. Most notably, as per this discussion, there is no chance of being Christian.

Certainly, insisting that they know "right now" and have no need to endure the moment of uncertainty is something Christians have done throughout their history. Followers of all traditions have done so. But there is always a possibility that a better and more sober moment will occur in the life of believers, and that they will accept that moment. In the case of the mega-church, however, the project of growing ever larger rules out that moment as a matter of principle. A church leader cannot aspire to see his church grow continually and to a maximum degree and, at the same time, cultivate the essential moment of uncertainty. On the contrary, certainty and being correct "right now" are essential items in his toolkit. He cannot get on without them. For this reason, he cannot be truly Christian, cannot have arrived again and again at his Christianity through rounds of thought, and cannot have encouraged others to do the same. (Nor, for that matter, can he be responsible or civilized, for the same reason.)

In this chapter, we develop this point. In doing so, we criticize all Christians who insist on the "right now" nature of what they feel is their knowledge of the true and the good. But we do so in anticipation of applying our analysis to the mega-church.

THE DILEMMA OF OBJECTIVITY

When we speak of the proper relation of human beings to God, we use a number of words and expressions. We say that a person is to "have faith in" or "believe in" God. We assert that a human being should "trust" or "have confidence" in the Lord. We proclaim that what is proper for people is to "worship" God. We decree that what is "meet and right" for men and women to do is to "serve" God or to "do his will." In the mainline Protestant tradition (among others), these are not acts of the mind or the will that people can decide on their own to perform. Rather, they are responses to God's initial actions toward people. As the writer of Psalm 40 put it, "the Lord has put a new song into my mouth, a song of praise to our God."

Common to all of these expressions is that God is an *objective reality.* He is the ground and source of all objects. As such, he is "out there" and distinct from the people who believe in, worship, or serve him. The worshiper is "here," and God is "there." To worship him is to be a subject or a self that addresses an object outside of, or other than, the self. To say this may seem to state the obvious. Yet there is reason to take pains and to dwell on the matter, for although a worshiper may seem to be praising the Lord, she may in reality be more interested in the *subject* of the praise, herself, than in the *object,* which is God.

People are constantly struggling to win approval of others. In an effort to do this, they effect a self-presentation or a self-image. They appear, like actors on the stage, in front of an audience consisting of everyone around them. And they see themselves as they imagine the audiences around them see them. They therefore become, in imagination, their own audience. A man may assume an air of the "tough guy." In presenting himself in this way, he thinks that others see him as being such a "tough guy." And seeing others as seeing him this way, he sees himself as the honored "tough guy," which, he thinks, exists in others' image of him.

Because people are presenting themselves in this way in everything they do, the *self* that they present can become equally important, or more important than the object of their perceptions. *That is, the person who believes in God can become more important to himself than the God in whom he believes.* He, as the one who trusts in God and serves him, can assume a greater grandeur for himself than the God whom he trusts and serves. Instead of encountering a God who is supremely *Other* than himself, he exalts himself precisely *as* the one who serves God. In this way, he exalts himself in his pretense of being one who exalts God. In effect, when he praises God, he is really praising himself. Yet he is unaware of the muddling and lack of distinction accompanying his praise process.

SELF-PRAISE AND IMMEDIATE JUDGMENT

The nature of this praise takes on a distinct form when a person is praising herself rather than God. Again, the difference is that everything has to be *immediate, in the now, where the self is located.* When she asserts that something is good or evil, others must accept what she says, and they must accept it *right now*, without delay, thought, or question. There can be no hesitation, for to delay the judgment is to destroy it. It has to be accepted "on the spot" if it is to be accepted at all. She asserts, for example, that homosexual activity is seriously offensive to God. In making that statement, she expects a listener to concur. And in her expectation that others in fact make the same judgment, she sees herself as a basically fair-haired "good" person who is on God's side. She basks in the warm glow of people's agreement, which she assumes to be forthcoming. She thinks that they think that homosexuality is offensive to the Lord, so it must be true. Or, more to the point, they will believe that she is one who believes the right thing. She is a "right believer." She sees herself as good because others believe that she is good.

The belief about the good or evil of anything exists, then, in the space in which a person and the others around him believe they should be and are "of one mind." And the truth or validity of the assertion resides in the fact that everyone affirms the same opinion. It is a "shared" or "agreed upon" attitude. The sharing of the attitude is the essence of the matter. It is not an opinion that has a distinct content. That is, the person holding the view and the others around him are not sharing an opinion about a subject that is external to their opinion-holding; instead, their opinion is simply about themselves. There is no objective reality "out there." If there were such an objective reality, their opinion could be right or wrong. The facts could be what the people say they are, or they could be contrary to what the people say. But this is about attitude, not objective reality. Because the sharing of an attitude is what it is "all about," there is no possibility of being refuted by messages from an external, objective reality. When the person says "homosexuality is offensive to God," he means that those are the words to a song that he and the others around him are singing. That is what it is, and that is all that it is.

The moment of uncertainty has no place in such a warm and cozy social circle. To say that we need to think about the morality of various forms of sexuality, or that we should carry out some form of real inquiry on any topic, is to flee from the social circle. It is to leave this circle behind, to part from it, in the quest for an objective truth or goodness that exists separately outside the circle. Formerly, the validity of the assertion was simply that it was being shared with the circle. In this way, the terms *true* and *agreed upon* come to mean the same thing. By even speaking of thinking or testing, we refer to something outside the group of people who share the attitude. Even if someone were to say that she had given the matter careful thought and had inquired and had concluded that the people were right about homosexuality, she would be disloyal to the group. As the people in the group see it, the truth of the assertion about what is right and wrong comes from the fact that *they,* that is, they *together,* say it. It does not come from some other basis that one might reach through thought or inquiry. In saying that she had concluded that they were right, she implies that there was a possibility that they *might not* have been right. Even allowing that as a possibility is a sign of disloyalty to the group.

Each person in a compass group wants to be thought of as "good." So let's say the group says that a "good" person is one who thinks that homosexuality is evil. If any one person were to disagree, she would lose her "good person" badge and would even be seen as an "outsider" to the group. If she were to say that there was even a possibility of entertaining another opinion, she would be an outsider. And no one wants to be an outsider.

The view that homosexuality is evil exists, we may say, in the interaction between someone who asserts it and someone who assents to it. It is in this way a *social fact.* The two people involved form a small social group. The two people together enjoy a warm glow of camaraderie with each other.

The topic of their conversation, the evil of homosexuality, is grist for the mill of their fellow feeling for each other. That fellowship is then the underlying support for the assertion. The statement about what is evil floats, so to say, on the camaraderie between the two people. To question the statement is to throw cold water on the warm glow of fellow-feeling. And since the two involved *like* that feeling, they affirm the statement.

Otherwise stated, the assertion is that knowledge of what is good and evil has to be immediate and without hesitancy or even a hint of the tentative because only in this way can it retain its persuasive power. To hesitate is to doubt. To doubt is to destroy the belief and a person's ability to praise herself as one who holds that belief. The circle tightens, even closes, around the so-called truth as the group holds it. Exclusion is a natural consequence of questioning, or even thinking over, this immediate thing being treated as truth.

THE SOVEREIGNTY OF TRUTH

And where then is truth? Let's come at this in another way: All authentic righteousness is object-oriented. A person affirms what is good or does what is right because it *is* good and right. The goodness of an act resides in the act and not just in how we may feel about it. The Samaritan does what he can to help the robbed and beaten traveler. He performs that act because the traveler needs him to do so. The beaten man's need takes over and assumes sovereignty in the situation. This may be the entire focus of the Samaritan's attention. Or, if the unfortunate traveler's plight does not by itself evoke the desire to come to the man's aid, a perception of the Good may do so. The Samaritan may perceive that it is *good* to come to the victim's rescue. The image of the Good then assumes a sovereignty and controls the Samaritan's conduct. True, the purity of the Samaritan's action may persist for only a moment. Once he has performed the act, or determined to do so, he may then congratulate himself for being such a fine fellow. But we believe that there was at least a *moment* when all the Samaritan cared about was the traveler's plight or about the Good itself.

We can also speak about *Truth* this way. Say a person asserts that trees do not grow in areas of little rainfall. We then become curious about what moved the person to make such an assertion. We want to explain her "speech behavior." Perhaps, we think, the act of saying what she said about trees makes her appear knowledgeable or "on the right side." Or it may influence what the rest of us do; perhaps we will avoid traveling through an area that has little rainfall and therefore presumably few trees, and she has reasons of her own to want to thus influence our travel plans. Actually, there could be all sorts of reasons for her making such a statement. But among them, certainly a prominent one would be that trees do not, in fact, grow where rainfall is slight. That is, this person may make this statement because the statement is *true*.

Truth, like goodness, is objective. It is "out there." Truth is not necessarily convenient to assert. Truth is not always what will "work" in persuading people to do what one wants them to do. And truth is not always what a person finds most pleasant or agreeable to believe. The separation of *Truth* from the biases or wishes of an observer is central to its meaning. If a person declares that he is concerned to communicate Truth, but then insists that the content of Truth is something that is approved or desired, he is not, indeed, speaking of *Truth*. To be itself, Truth has to be independent of what people want to believe or consider it good and virtuous to believe. Once a person has determined that he will seek the Truth, he must reject all feeling that it is more pious or noble or worthy to believe one thing rather than another. It is never simply "good" to believe a particular statement; nor is it ever what a person does in order to present himself as good.

To pursue Truth is always and necessarily to concern oneself with the indicators of truth that are proper to the object being considered. If that object is one that people can *see* (or perceive with the five senses), looking and seeing are the only way of arriving at truth. If it is a conclusion of a process of thinking (as in a mathematical statement), then thinking or calculating are the proper means. If it is an intuition based on one's perception of the contrast of being and nonbeing (life and death), then disciplined intuiting is the method. In every case, the person who pursues Truth "waits" for that which is "out there" to reach her or come into view. It does not matter whether people, or the whole world, think that it is good and godly to believe a certain thing. One is concerned with, and only with, the question whether an assertion is *true*.

It is noteworthy that there are many references to the *True* and to *Truth* in the Bible. "Send out your Light and your *Truth*; let them lead me," says Psalm 43. These references assume that *Truth* has this objective character and so is indifferent to what is approved or regarded as pious. Someone may say, of course, that he is much concerned with Truth and then go on to explain that by "true" he refers to a set of assertions that have been included in a sacred canon or collection of pious beliefs. But if he does so, he has emptied the term *truth* of its meaning. He has asserted, in effect, that the concept of the *true* can be swallowed up by that of the *pious,* thereby indicating that truth is unnecessary or even unemployed—that we could skip what is *true* and go straight to *pious.* Alas, if the concept of Truth is going to have work to do—to have a *function*—it must be cut loose from piety and human ideas about godliness and allowed to stand alone and by itself.

Both the Good and the True, then, stand tall and in a spot that is exclusively theirs. They are unconcerned and indifferent to what is in *our* minds and hearts. In their majesty, they care nothing about what we want or what we approve of or what we think is religious and "godly." They insist on being what they are and on telling us what they are without regard to our sentiments or prejudices. And just as they do not care what we think, they are indifferent as well with what "people" think. They do not ask to be elected by popular ballot or to be vindicated by a volume of sales (or attendance at a worship service). And they do not wish to assure us that people will think well of us if we take due note of them. To affirm the True and the Good is precisely *and only* to affirm the True and the Good. And that what we say is *true* is our only reward for saying it.

LOVE OF THE GOOD AND THE MOMENT OF UNCERTAINTY

The wish to serve the Lord rather than to merely be viewed by people as one who serves the Lord is tricky. It is rather like trying to rise out of one's self. The reason why we may reject the project of being merely thought to be a servant of the Lord is that people do not approve of that project. What they approve of is actually serving the Lord. Or at least they approve of wishing to be the Lord's servant. But how can a person reject the project of being well thought of if the reason for rejecting it is, itself, to be well thought of? It seems we are trying to jump out of ourselves—of our own skins. For now, however, we are going to take this observation about ourselves and park it by the side of the road somewhere. We will assume that, yes indeed, we wish to pursue Truth and Goodness for their own sakes. There will be at least a moment when all we care about is the True as such and the Good as such.

Basic to this pursuit is the *moment of uncertainty* of which I have spoken earlier in this chapter. The existence of this moment says that there must be a bit of time—we cannot say just how long—when we are unsure or in limbo. We have left one safe harbor and we have not yet arrived at another. We are, instead, in a space that is uncertain and undefined, sitting between a beginning point and an ending point in a "no-man's land" where we do not have our feet on the ground. In this space, we do not know what is true or good, and we cannot be identified or recognized as people who have that knowledge. We are agnostic; we do not know, in this moment, what is noble and right. The acclaim of people will not be forthcoming here; we will not be seen either as espousing right views or as approving right actions. Yet despite this poverty of seeming nobility, wisdom, and virtue, we *must* go through this "no-man's land." We have to think and inquire. There is no way out of doing so if we wish to be devotees of Truth.

This devotion to Truth with a capital "T"—as the Truth—is a matter about which each member of a faith, and herein the Christian, must make up her mind. That is, she must choose to not serve the Lord or to indeed serve the Lord. She must choose to be or not to be a devotee of that Truth which is the Truth of God. And we note that the true road to being a servant of the Lord leads right into this wilderness of uncertainty in which there is no nobility or virtue, but only doubt and uncertainty. Knowledge of the True and the Good may lie over the next hill, but in the valley of this moment of uncertainty, there is no such knowledge. There is only uncertainty and doubt. There is only a hope of arriving later at Truth. There is a question mark where we would prefer a badge of honor, for the honor is within the walk through uncertainty and eventual arrival at some degree of certainty. But a person arrives there only after having truly tested herself and her beliefs. Truth is not fed to us; it is discovered.

The person who wishes to be praised by others as one who knows the Truth and knows the Good will never tolerate this moment. The praises of people that he craves will be forthcoming (he thinks) if, and only if, he has immediate perception of what is true and what is good. To allow a moment of doubt is, for him, to abandon the certainty that he thinks is essential. More, it is a relinquishing of the esteem and prestige that are his heart's desire. To move away from this goal and to allow the moment of doubt is difficult and inglorious. But if we wish to embrace an authentic godliness, this is a move we must make.

UNCERTAINTY, LOGIC, AND EVIDENCE

This most necessary moment of doubt occurs in all logical thinking. And, all real *thinking* is logical thinking, with its most basic form being the *syllogism*. In this construct, there are two premises and a conclusion. We may, for example, say "all loving actions are good." We then add, "spanking a child to keep her from running into the street is a loving action." The first statement is a major premise. The second is a minor premise. From the two premises we then derive a conclusion. We say, "spanking a child to keep her from running into the street is good." If, then, we accept the first statement and the second statement, we *must* of necessity, embrace the third. Agreement with the two premises compels acceptance of the conclusion.

The moment of uncertainty occurs in this process. It is true that the conclusion is contained in the two premises, as a baby is in the womb of his mother. But the whole point of talking about logic is that we do not see this immediately. If we did, there would be no need for logic as a subject of study or learning. What happens is that we make the first statement or premise. We then make the second statement or premise. There then follows the moment of uncertainty. We are, even if briefly, in an intellectual "no-man's land" or zone of agnosticism or not-knowing. Then, as the moment passes, we *see* that the conclusion follows. We did not *see* it immediately, but in due course we do. We have jumped from one building to another. We were sure-footed on the first and sure-footed on the second. But for a moment, we were suspended in the air between the two.

We go through this process if, and only if, our interest is in the objective truth. If we were concerned, instead, to establish our own standing as being people who are good or right according to some external standard, our focus would be on the reactions of the men and women around us, not on premises and conclusions. The matter of vital concern to us would be what others assert and agree is true, not what is, indeed, true. And this agreement of others is quite slippery. We have to grab it, or it will slip away from us, grab it without skipping a step, without hesitating to think, without reference to statements that are logically implied. Therefore it is only by abandoning hope of being popular among these "others" and widely acclaimed by them that we can be devotees of the Truth as the Truth.

Of course, we might think that these others may be inclined to engage in logical reasoning. And if this is so, then we could appeal to these others through logic. But if we say this, we do not correctly assess what is taking place. For example, here comes someone who wants the agreement of another person. Truth to this other person is what others will assent to. And this other person also craves being "right." There is, therefore, a reciprocal assertion and assent. And it is here that there is no room, or time, for hesitancy or doubt.

Let's put it another way. If one person goes through the process of thinking and then appeals to another to see, or at least seriously contemplate, the correctness of her thoughts, she expects the other person to go through the same thought process, including the trip through the moment of uncertainty. Can she be sure that the other will do so? Can she *trust* the other to tolerate the season of uncertainty? She is not at all sure of this. It will take a certain moral courage or "guts" to wait for the other to go through that process. If appearing to be "right" and seeming to be on God's side is terribly important, she will instead blow a trumpet for what is immediate and does not require thought. She will say things that "have a ring to them," as it is said.

We have then two giants engaged in a stand-off with each other. On the one side we have the demand for immediate consent to a statement about right and wrong. On the other, we have the plea for patience as we go through a process of thinking or inquiry. The two giants are made out of different materials that have different textures. The one is concerned with praising ourselves. The other is devoted to the True and the Good as objective realities. If a Christian is serious about being a Christian, he must choose the process of thinking *and* its moment of uncertainty. If he fails to do so, he is seeking to be "seen by men" and he "has his reward" (Matt. 6). The Truth of God is not involved.

Along with the need for thinking, there is also the requirement of seeking *evidence* as a basis for making statements. We stand where we are and we look. As we look, we see what is there to be seen. The sights in front of us are present in a place before we see them. They have an existence independent of our act of looking at them, or not looking at them. We are here; they are there, and they present themselves to us. What they are has nothing to do with what we want them to be. Nor are they concerned with what we think they should be, what we would approve of. It is simply a matter of what *is* there. The "is there" abides in noble and majestic indifference to what we desire or approve or, for that matter, consider to be pious and godly.

Here, too, there is the moment of uncertainty. A person looks at something. She looks in order to see what is there. There is, of necessity, a moment between the determination to look and the act of seeing what is, in fact, there. Perhaps she wants to know the color of the car parked in front of her neighbor's house. To that end, she turns away from the house and looks. She then sees the car, and she sees that it is blue. There had to be an instant of time, perhaps a brief one, between the looking and the seeing. To be correct in her assertion about the car, therefore, she has to tolerate that moment between the time when she has started to inquire and the subsequent moment when she has perceived the color of the car. Although simple, this example provides a model or paradigm of the appeal to objective truth.

In addition to the moment between the beginning and the conclusion of an observation, there is also the possibility that an observation may not be possible or may be troublesome or expensive. A person feels called on to make a judgment, but the data—the evidence *given*—are not sufficient for determining whether one thing or another is true. Either it is not there at all, or it is too little or too vague to justify drawing a conclusion. Where this is the case, judgments should be tentative. A person says it appears that something is true, but he stands ready to change that judgment as more sights and sounds present themselves. Or he should be agnostic. A person says, "I do not know." If a person is knowledgeable, these words will proceed from his lips frequently. If a person respects the Truth, these words will be an everyday occurrence.

Although all of this may seem obvious, it nevertheless states a rule that is violated constantly. If we listen to the conversations around us, or those in which we are involved, we will see instances every day of people making assertions when they have not waited for the evidence necessary for making them. Nor will we be hearing them express the appropriate tentativeness. In politics, religion, and social affairs, people are constantly saying that the car is blue when they have not yet seen the car. They just agree that people who are "nice" and "godly" affirm that the car is blue.

There are motives for claiming certainty. Let us say that a person forgoes the moment of uncertainty because being immediately sure is essential for her self-image. She seeks to maintain an image of herself as being "on God's side." But she does so because this image maintenance serves as a badge that is a cover for motives that would not otherwise seem acceptable. Among these is the quest for *power*. Like many other people, she has frequent occasion to either seek power or to have it thrust upon her. Frequently, power is thrust upon people like her because giving her that power serves the interests of the larger community. By endowing her with the ability to determine what others will do, the community is able to maintain order within itself. Government officials and police officers serve a clear public purpose and enable citizens in general to live in peace and to pursue their individual goals without conflict with others who are doing the same. Maintenance of "law and order" is clearly to the benefit of people in general. (In the Bible, Paul is clear on this, Rom. 13:1–7). So she may have power for this reason.

Or, to push "good power" further, conceding it to certain persons or groups, or forcing it on them, –serves to equip the community to pursue collective goals. The community's defense of itself against human enemies and natural disasters is clearly a case in point. So also are projects that serve people but that must be undertaken by the community *as such.* Among many ancient peoples, as well as among modern communities, provision for irrigation of farmlands has, by its nature, to be the community's and not just an individual's task. There are many other examples.

But it seems to be characteristic of human beings that once individuals and small groups become powerful, they wish to preserve and enhance that power for its own sake. They no longer view it as just a means to the end of serving community interests. Rather, the means becomes the end; people with power treasure that power itself. That others must do as these people command is inherently rewarding and that is why they seek to establish power of command. Throughout history and throughout the world kings and emperors have elaborated their royal courts far beyond what is necessary for doing their "job." Communist leaders fell victim to this wish and so ushered in the era of totalitarian rule in the 1930s. They billed that reign of terror as a defense of the "working class." In capitalist societies, the wealthy captains of industry similarly identify their project as that of becoming ever wealthier and more powerful. They then justify their enjoyment of wealth and power by speaking of the marvels of the "free market." In this way, they can, in effect, enslave workers under the banner of "freedom." Along with the wish to be "God's pet," then, the desire to preserve and enhance ownership of estates, personal prestige, and personal power proves a serious obstacle to living through the moment of uncertainty.

In addition to being something demanded of individuals as they make judgments, the moment of uncertainty is also built into institutional *structures* and *procedures.* Within structures such as police departments, prosecutor's offices, and courts, rules are made and followed. In the prosecution of crimes, these rules require a "stop, look, and listen" approach to the matters at hand. The rules do so as an explicit antidote for the rash judgments human beings are prone to make. Instead of moving forward with a "get him" procedure, the people involved in criminal trials are required to go through a process of thinking and noting of evidence from a beginning point to an end and, in so doing, to live through the moment of uncertainty. An elaborate structure of rules has been established to ensure that the hasty judgments people are commonly prone to make are held "at bay" for a time. Mandated procedures accomplish this goal, at least some of the time and to some degree.

In these procedures, the people involved are required to go through certain steps. The accusation has to be made in a formal way. Witnesses have to testify in the presence of a person accused of a crime ("face your accuser"). Once a witness has given her testimony, she has to submit to cross examination by an attorney who represents the person who is accused. Under oath, the witness must address challenges to her testimony by that attorney. Might there be question whether the crime actually took place? Is the witness quite certain that the person accused is in fact the one who committed the crime? These questions are posed and then answered by the witness. The witness could, of course, answer as she wishes rather than correctly. But she is "under oath." She is committing a crime if she knowingly gives false answers. The jury is then required to sit and listen to all the testimony, both pro and con.

Along with *procedure,* there is also a frame of mind or *mood* involved in these processes. The processes do battle with what "normally" takes place. As events usually unfold, an attitude of "get the crook–or the murderer or rapist"–comes over the people who are involved. They are gripped by a certain crowd enthusiasm. As people interact with one another, they get each other "fired up" to proceed with the action against an assumed criminal. In their "fired up" condition, they then feel that what they do is *right.* They abandon all doubt and assume a posture of moral certainty. In doing, so, they are mainly impressed with themselves as being people who are right. The reflection on themselves is the major reality, rather than the *right itself.*

The procedures that mandate a "stop, look and listen" approach are in this way more than devices for getting at the truth. They are also ceremonial affirmations of the *importance* of the Truth. The human desire to be seen as good people who are on God's side has to recede. Its place is then taken by the attention being directed to the Truth itself. This redirection of attention from "I am good" to "the Good is good" does not come naturally to human beings. It requires people to cultivate an indifference to the enthusiasm of crowds and to the implicit praise of themselves that is resident in that enthusiasm. So great is the moral difficulty of cultivating this indifference and directing attention to the Good that people commonly need the *procedures* of which I have spoken to help them do it. Rather than loving the Good for its own sake, people are simply following the rules. But in so doing, they are acting as they would if they were motivated by a love of the Good itself. This is consistent with Old Testament references to the *law*. The law helps us to do what is right when our hearts are not fully "in it."

UNCERTAINTY AND WORD FROM GOD

The term *word* carries at least three different meanings. The first is that a word is the basic unit of speech. It is a sound or other sign that stands for or means something. Its referent can be a thing, an action, or a quality of a thing or of an action. It conveys an image of persons or things and actions involving those persons or things. Or it conveys a feeling about such an image as when we say "wow, look at that!" and then describe an arrangement of things of an event.

The second meaning of *word* is a content or message that is communicated from one person, one group, or one agency to another. Thus I might say, "I received *word* from my uncle John that he would arrive tomorrow." Or, "our congregation received *word* from its sister congregation in Cuba" Or, once more, the Office of Personnel received *word* from corporate headquarters" In every case, a piece of information or a directive is sent and received.

Third, there are messages in which the content of the communication is the *sender himself*. It conveys a personal presence. If I say that I received *word* from my uncle, I may mean that I received a message or communication from him that made me feel that he was with me. In this case, the other contents of his communication are secondary. If I had thought that my uncle had been angry with me, the communication could have had any apparent content, and yet the important message would be that he is no longer angry with me. In the case of the message from corporate headquarters, the content could be foremost. The people at headquarters are no longer silent; we now know what they want us to do. But in the communication of my uncle, it is a personal presence—that of my uncle himself—which is communicated.

When we speak of the Word *of* God, or a word *from* God, all of the meanings of *word* are involved. The personal presence meaning of "word" is often paramount. Here the Word of God is God himself insofar as he is present to a person or to a community. It is God as present *to* someone, distinct from God as he is present to *himself*. But the Word of God can also be a content that can be understood in itself, usually as a directive. I may feel that God calls me to abandon one occupation and to take up another. If I am a teacher or lawyer, I may feel that God calls me to become a minister, or vice versa. Or, God may bid me vote one way rather than another, and so on. Such a content was conveyed by the Hebrew prophets when they cried out "thus says the Lord!"

Distinctive about word from God is that the personal presence aspect of the word and its other contents cannot be separated from each other. God may declare himself to be God to me, with me, and for me, to be, in effect, *my* God. He may also call me to speak and to act in certain ways. There is no neat and tidy separation of one of these from the other, as there is with communications from people. We see this in Deuteronomy 5:5. Moses was preparing to announce the Ten Commandments (a repetition of Ex. 20). He said "at that time I was standing between the LORD and you to declare to you the words of the LORD; for you were afraid because of the fire." Psalm 96:3 speaks of declaring his glory.

Here is where we can see the moment of uncertainty. There may be an instant of time when a person hears, or feels that he hears, –God speaking to him. If so, it was certain that there would be a moment before that communication from the Lord took place. There was a period of time, either long or short, when a person was about to hear God speaking to him, but had not heard Him yet. In this period of time he did not know what the Word from God was going to be. Or he did not, as we may put it, "know the Lord." As a person who wants to be faithful to the Lord, he had to live through this time when the Word of God was a "not yet" and a "maybe soon."

And just as a person who would "ascend the hill of the Lord" (Ps. 15, 24) is one who will greet word from God with a "yes Lord," a "send me," or an "I go," she is also one who will live with patience through the moment of uncertainty. In 2 Kings, Elisha had to live through such a moment when a woman came to him about her child who had died in her arms. He said, "she is in great distress; and the Lord has hidden it from me, and has not told me." (4:27). Similarly, with us there are times when the Lord *hides* something and does not tell us. Faithfulness in such moments consists of accepting the *absence* of word from God. In consists in being ready to hear a word that we have not yet heard. The book of Psalms is full of references to a word from God or an action of God that is hoped for or expected rather than possessed.

Of special importance here is that we do not imagine our way into an idea of what the Word of God is. We must wait, although waiting is not pleasant and certainly not glorious. All sorts of ideas about what is good and godly are floating around, all seeking to claim our allegiance. It is all too easy to grab hold of whatever would please us or would please "people" (or those in authority) and then claim that this is, indeed, a word from God himself. In doing so, we will have help from many quarters. Innumerable writers and speakers would be glad to tell us what they think the Word and the Will of God are. But when we have not yet heard that Word, we do well to view such human council as only possible or tentative and to live through the season of not knowing.

This does not mean that there is nothing we can do. When the Word of God comes to us, it comes amid our thoughts, our study, our wishing, our fearing, and, in general, all of the contents and decisions that are rummaging around in our minds and hearts. Whatever we do as daily devotions and weekly worship is much to the point. But the moment in which God speaks his word to us is a moment that is chosen by God himself.

Until then, we wait, sitting in that moment or phase of uncertainty. Among the things we can do there is serious study of the realities of the world as revealed in the social sciences, in the best of journalism, and in our own observations of the world. All of this is part of the process of waiting. It may be a busy process, as waiting goes, but it is a process of waiting nevertheless.

What is called for here is similar to the demand of logical thought and scientific inquiry. We are called to live through the moment of uncertainty. It is demanded of us that we repeat the expression, "I do not know," frequently and faithfully. And just as the thinker and the scientist must live through the time that comes between premise and conclusion, or between beginning and completing an observation, so the Christian must live through the time that comes between the prayer to the Lord for guidance and the receiving of that guidance. For that guidance, we may notice, takes place on God's schedule, not on ours.

To capture the mood here, we may quote the last two verses of Psalm 27: "I believe that I *shall* see the goodness of the Lord in the land of the living! *Wait* for the Lord; be strong, and let your heart take courage; yea, wait for the Lord!" (emphasis added). The writer of this psalm anticipates that he will see the goodness of the Lord, and he commends waiting for an action from God. Neither the vision of the Lord nor the Lord's action to vindicate the faithful is a present possession. Both are in the future. When courage and strength are recommended, it is on the basis of what *will be,* not what *is.* Similarly, the writer of Psalm 62 says, "in silence, my soul *waits* for the Lord (verses 1 and 5).

Clearly, then, the mood is one of patience in expectation of a word from God, a word that is not a present possession rather than one to come in the future. We *wait* to hear what God *will* speak to us. There will, of course, come a time when we have heard that word and are not just waiting for it. But that time comes after waiting, not before waiting, *nor as a substitute for it.* A conclusion that follows logical reasoning or observation of evidence is different in mood and texture from a hastily made judgment. And a person who has waited for word from God and then feels that she has finally received it behaves differently from one who has believed she had that word to begin with or that the word was something she could take for granted.

And even after waiting and receiving, or feeling that one has received, word from God, matters are never settled once and for all. The next day, or week or year, a person may receive yet another word from God. God's Word, we may assert, is new—always new. The circumstances in which we feel that God addresses his Word to us are always a bit more complicated than we realize. And the corrupting power of our own self-interest and pride never disappear completely from our perception of God's Will. For example, a person who feels that God wants him to take a strong stand on an issue may perceive the next day that the impulse to take a strong stand was not altogether and "for sure" from the Lord. A wish or a bit of pride may have pushed the perception of God's will in a certain direction. And it is possible that a new word received the next day would have him compromise with his opponents in the interest of peace or because to do so is right. Or the opposite may occur. The man given to compromise may hear God telling him that the time has come to take a firm and uncompromising stand.

To see the contrast, we imagine someone saying in shocked tones, "you call yourself a Christian and yet you" We could put any opinion on any issue after the "yet you" Or, a variant is, "Of course I oppose or support one or another stand on an issue. I am a Christian!" What we need to see here is that these ways of supporting (or opposing) any position on any issue are precisely *anti*-Christian. They assume that we can know the Will of God without going through the examining moment of uncertainty. It is a case of people telling God what his Will is supposed to be. Perhaps the Lord needs our help in making his decisions! Perhaps in response, we should post sentries to guard the gates of opinion. These sentries will not be concerned with what is True or Good, for that is what we must wait for. Rather, they will be concerned with *how we claim to know* what is Good. They will give a "pass" only to those who have lived through the moment of uncertainty.

If the term *anti-Christian* here seems extreme, there is something we could note. We could observe that in the history of Christianity and of other religions, the worst instances of violence, mass murder, expropriation of people's lands, and oppression of helpless populations have been justified in the name of religion and "God." The oppressors and murderers thought that they were good, noble, and "on God's side." We see here reason for the bit of wisdom in politics that says, "if you have to choose between a fanatic and a crook, choose the crook. The crook will want to 'feather his own nest,' but if you let him do that, he will then be reasonable. He might even do a good job for you!" In this sense, fanatical religion is worse than no religion. Or, "religion is not the solution to the human problem. Religion *is* the human problem." But we are speaking here of religion in which there is no moment of uncertainty. There is no moment in which we do not yet know and in which we are ready to learn.

So what about the mega-church? We certainly cannot accuse it of moral or political fanaticism. Indeed, the *absence* of strong moral convictions is one of its basic characteristics. If it is "fanatical" about anything, it is about its own growth. And this is a concern that, by its very nature, resists a preoccupation with anything else. This moral lethargy, however, cannot be regarded as an escape from the fanatic's clutches that threaten our civilization and all civilizations, for if the promoters of the mega-church do not have a fanatic's agenda, neither do they have any way of opposing it.

The proper opposition to ideas about morality that are themselves immoral does not come from moral indifference. It arises, rather, from a moral passion that sets itself in staunch opposition to the twisted moral conceptions of the fanatic, whatever they may be. Or, even better, it arises from a moral passion that opposes violence and oppression committed by anyone against anyone. Only with such a contrary moral passion can there be an antidote to wrongdoing that thinks it is right-doing. But it must be a special kind of moral passion. It must be a passion that comes after the moment of uncertainty. Only the person who has lived through that moment can be said to have earned the right to be passionate about what she favors and what she opposes. We cannot expect any help for this from the mega-church, for it cannot be passionate about anything other than itself.

7

THE MEGA-CHURCH: FUNDAMENTALISM AND CERTAINTY

In the branch of Protestant Christianity called Fundamentalism, the moment of uncertainty is ruled out in principle. The Fundamentalist's basic idea is that the Faith itself needs to be defended against the corrosive effects of a host of rationalist tendencies in modern civilization. These tendencies, perceived "enemies of the faith," are known by many different names. They are the Enlightenment, rationalism, deism, liberalism, modernism, secular humanism, and others. We must speak of these further.

These various presumed adversaries of the Faith have in common the belief that there is a correspondence between the rational structure of the mind and the intelligible structure of the world "out there." Accordingly, truth about that world is to be discovered either by thinking, that is, reasoning; or observing, that is, seeing, things and events in the world. Together, reasoning and observing make the world around us calculable and knowable. And together, they help human beings understand their world and manipulate the things in that world to their advantage. This belief is what undergirds the entire modern enterprise of science and technology, an enterprise that has had extremely impressive results.

Carried this far, there is no necessary battle with faith, including Fundamentalist faith. Indeed, church leaders in the Fundamentalist camp, like those of other persuasions, have made abundant use of advanced technology in carrying on their work. Their preachers and their churches avail themselves of voice amplification, screen projections, television programming, and other fruits of modern technological development. These devices have been in use so much and so long that no one would think that there is an issue about them, and, indeed, there is none. Even more, fundamentalists have often used scientific understandings of nature to justify specific beliefs. Among these is the idea that the Hebrews could cross the Red Sea because of a certain tide phenomenon that had been previously unknown. Also included here is the belief that the three young men who survived the "fiery furnace" in the Book of Daniel did so because of a "cool zone" within the furnace. Even more important in the Fundamentalist program has been the effort to set up creationism as a viable *scientific* alternative to the belief in the evolution of species.

FUNDAMENTALISM VERSUS MODERNITY: RATIONALISM-EMPIRICISM AS METAPHYSICS

People of rationalist persuasion go further than observing, calculating, and manipulating the objects of the world. They go on to develop a *metaphysical* commitment. They say that the truth about the world and about life is to be found through these resources and is, in effect, exhausted by them. The truth that they uncover is the fundamental and basic truth about reality as such and at its core. Where this elaboration into metaphysics or ontology occurs, all truths—truths about God, the world, and human beings—are those that are brought to light by calculation and observation. And just as this is the case with knowledge of the world, it also applies to knowledge of right and wrong. What is morally right and morally wrong is that which "makes sense" within a scientific understanding of the world and of human beings.

In the eighteenth century, these understandings were thought to arise from the thinking process itself. The mind was seen as a microcosm of reality as such and was therefore a model of the world "out there." This view was called deism for its emphasis on "rational" belief in God. By contrast, in the last century or two, the emphasis has been more on the world as studied through *observation* (with the five sense), which emphasizes "empirical" belief in God. This view is called by various names, but we will settle for *empiricism*. Both of these views sought to ground morality in human capacities for inquiry.

With deism, the emphasis was on thinking. It was assumed that there was a correspondence between the rational structure of mind and the intelligible structure of reality "out there." The thinking mind, then, could uncover and elaborate all truth, including moral truth. The rational mind would discern what is good and what is evil. All wrongdoing would consist of actions that are not reasonable. Actions are not reasonable when they lead to imbalanced or excessive inequalities in power and prestige within a community or to hostilities between communities. A discerning mind, applying itself to the "stuff" of individual and social life, would pronounce a "no" to these actions. That same mind would then approve of actions that promote balance or harmony among individuals and between groups.

In empiricism the emphasis shifts to observation. Empiricism says that we may learn everything about the world by looking at it in a disciplined way. Even morality, the contrast between right and wrong, will yield its secrets to careful observation. In an extreme form of this empiricist view, morality was reduced to *emotional preference*. Instead of an act offending the conscience, it merely seems or feels unpleasant. In this case, there is here no morality properly so-called. Because we cannot *see* the "rightness" or "wrongness" of an act, we cannot attribute these qualities to it. There is, for this reason, only the fact that we like or do not like the things that people do. In this view, if I say that racial segregation is wrong, I mean that I do not like it. That is what I mean, and that is all that I mean. If someone else says racial segregation is alright or good, he means that he does like it. He and I differ, to be sure, but only in a matter of taste, for this is no morality properly so called. There is no "ought" or "'should," nor can there be approving or disapproving of human actions. There can be only liking or disliking of the things people do. Talk about good and evil would in reality be talk about what is subjectively tasteful or distasteful.

Missing in both the rational-calculation view (as in deism and in rationalism in several other forms) and in the seeming counterpart, empiricism, is the contrast of right and wrong as a matter of what Paul Tillich called our *ultimate concern*. Ultimate concern expands beyond the "conflicting" ways of knowing reality offered by rationalism and empiricism. It pushes us to a lonely desert wasteland where night falls and, with it, the total silence becomes a voice that speaks to us of a stark and total contrast of good and evil. We will find, in that contrast, the divide where we either affirm our humanity by saying "yes" to the Right or lose our humanity by following the siren call of the Wrong. We will find ourselves in that place where the decision is absolutely ours, for no one can make it for us. Neither the laws of a nation nor the ever-powerful "public opinion" can relieve us of having to decide. There the prefabricated rules that pertain to each situation in which we find ourselves cannot serve as substitutes for our own decision making. Instead, we must make decisions amid complex twists and turns of events that afford no neat distinctions between actions that are "good" and actions that are "bad," yet which leave us with the serious task of making the "best possible" decisions.

Of course, advocates of both rationalism and empiricism may have a "feel" for this stark contrast of good and evil. Some have acted on it when they find themselves in situations where it costs them to choose what they see as right. Suddenly it matters to them in an unconditional way that they choose what is right in situations where it costs them to do so. When they come up against totalitarian rulers, or a totalitarian "public opinion," they see that something of unconditional importance is at stake in choosing what is right over what is convenient or popular. But to actually make sense of their own choices in these circumstances, they would need to rethink their worldview. They would need either an ontological commitment, an understanding of the "really real," or they would have to have a theology in which knowledge of fundamental matters derives from a movement of God toward us rather than an elaboration of the resources of reason and goodwill that we can conger up from within ourselves.

In biblical terms, what is missing is the Truth that human beings do not reach through their own resources, but that comes to them from outside of those resources. Abraham did not reason his way to God, nor did he discover God by observation. Rather, God came to him. God called him to leave the land of his ancestors and to go to a new and strange land where his descendants would be multiplied and would be a special covenant people. The movement was from God to human beings, not from human beings to God. That is, God *revealed* himself. His revelation of himself to human beings is from outside of the human sphere. It is supremely Other. Yet this revelation does not contradict human reason. It is not antihuman in that sense. Rather, God's revealing of himself to us fulfills reason even while infinitely transcending it.

An examination of history tells us that rationalism and empiricism had seemed adequate in a world that was bursting with promise of peace and justice. These bright and cheerful outcomes were to be brought about by enlightened human beings who had been freed from the superstitions and narrow nationalisms of the past. But this pretwentieth-century optimism has since been dealt harsh hammer blows by the two world wars and subsequent fits of violence that gave the twentieth century its basic contours. It has also fared poorly under the widespread greed and opportunism that seem to infect all sectors of social life. Something of *ultimate concern,* higher, greater, more far-reaching, calls us now, as it has in times gone by. But now we arrive having examined the supposed continuum of knowing our world, and have specified (for now) the parameters of our realities, and even institutionalized these.

THE "WHY" OF FUNDAMENTALISM: ATROPHY OF MORALITY AND OF COSMOPOLITAN HAUTEUR

We cannot assume that we are able to entirely explain what has motivated the Fundamentalist rejection of the rational-empirical worldviews held by "the modern mind." Still, we can surmise that the feeling, whether vague or clear, of the loss of "ultimate concern" may have moved the Fundamentalist to look with horror at the modernist project and to even declare war on it. Fundamentalists could tell that something was amiss. Something precious was threatened. The call to righteousness implicit in all Christian proclamation was in jeopardy. It appeared likely that the "you shall not" of the Ten Commandments would give way to—even be collapsed into—a notion of certain things just being or not being "nice" or, at best, "ideal." Modernism seemed (and may still seem) to be an acid solution that could (and still can) dissolve the demands for righteousness that make Christianity what it is.

Fundamentalists saw then (and see now) that all was not (and is not) well on the theological front, even, or especially, when that front presents itself as religious or "Christian." It was and is necessary, therefore, to sound the alarm and rush to the battle stations. Something has to be done lest the Christian Faith lose its substance and its soul. Rationalist-empiricist trends in the churches have to be opposed. Liberalism or modernism has to be identified as the enemy so that the struggle can be given focus and direction. The real Christian Faith must be either defended or recovered.

True, what propels the Fundamentalist movement may not be specifically Christian or devoted to righteousness as such. An alternate possibility is that there is a collection of people who sit in the middle of a society, in its culture and in its complex of values and patterns for living. This culture and this complex of values form a single, unified system. For the people who live within it, the system gives pattern and structure to life that makes the world intelligible and, to some degree, dependable. People feel that they understand the pattern and that they can count on it. Life is, for this reason, secure and meaningful. A person lives to continue and perpetuate her family; she seeks to build a sense of "self" in her career; she projects an image of herself, her family, and her business that people in general can see and respect. This structure affords opportunity for her to appear as honest, hard-working, and, in general, to be admired and respected. In the interest of winning respect for herself and her family, a person clings to a collection of fundamental values, including norms of conduct, understandings of what is "true," and definitions of the "good life."

Emerging and now standing against this hard kernel of time-tested fundamental values and patterns for living is that which may be defined generally as *cosmopolitanism*. This is a set of images that emphasize and exalt diversity. The new cosmopolitan norm says there is not just one, but there are several, definitions of value and patterns for living. The meshing of these diverse patterns in one community is considered to be "good." That is, the *meshing itself* becomes a value. It is considered good for people of varying cultural backgrounds to live together in a single community. This high valuation of diversity necessarily brings about some attenuation of the specific nuclei of value and social patterns. To wit, it is asked: How can it be of great importance that people live by a traditional code if those people live amid others who live by different codes? How can it be of great importance if this living side-by-side is itself what is valued and cherished? The whole point of any item in the code is a "for sure." For example, we may take the view that man–woman couples should begin their sexual relationship only after they are married. Then we ask, does this not need to be something that is required of everyone, always and everywhere? Must not the view be that this is how all people are *supposed* to live their lives? If there is a belief that the rule holds only within one group while not applying within another, would it not appear that it is not really a fundamental rule or moral principle at all?

Not only does the emerging cosmopolitan norm, this mesh of diverse codes, erode reliance on, and respect for, traditional moral conceptions; but it also subjects people of traditional lifestyles to a state of *status deprivation*.

The sophisticated folk who present a cosmopolitan image of themselves appear to think of themselves as superior. They appear, whether intentionally or not, to flaunt a "better than thou" manner while disdaining the more traditional people as old-fashioned, even "provincial" or "unenlightened." By contrast, those ordinary folk who claim no cosmopolitan credentials develop *resentment*. It seems to them that the sophisticated and worldly-wise cosmopolitan norm is "a put down" and an encroachment, even an invasion. These fundamentalists, traditionalists, experience the "sting" of this cosmopolitan hauteur and so they quite understandably want to mobilize forces against it. It's a case of "you think you are better than I am, but you're not!" And it is virtually a call to arms, at least moral arms, as it is perceived as a threat.

The values, beliefs, and practices that seem vulnerable to this presumed attack of cosmopolitan disdain are those of a particular society at a particular time. The codes by which people of "middle America" live at the time of the ending of the twentieth century and the beginning of the twenty-first century is taken to be the law of God. The items that go to make up the code are often then "read into" the Bible. Sometimes this is easy, for the Bible says something that is similar. Sometimes it is difficult or impossible, for the Bible is silent or ambiguous on a particular matter. The opposition to homosexuality is a case in point. Although it is often asserted that the Bible is "clear" about homosexuality, there are in fact only six references that are even thought to pertain to the subject. They are in Genesis 19, Leviticus 18 and 20, Romans 1, I Corinthians 6, and I Timothy 1. Of these, only the Leviticus references are at all clear, and they are part of a Levitical Code that no one, least of all the Fundamentalists, propose to follow.

We may put the two things together. First, the Fundamentalist is alarmed by the dissolving of the traditional moral imperative, a dissolving that appears to him to be implicit in the various forms of modernism. Second, the Fundamentalist identifies with a core of traditional cultural values and is resentful of the liberal or intellectual cosmopolitan who seems to him to disdain him for that core of values. Whether or not the cosmopolitan is actually eroding the Fundamentalist's values (one), and whether or not the Fundamentalist is correct in assuming the cosmopolitan is on the attack (two), either of these assumptions, let alone the two combined, trigger profound alarm, blinking red lights. Modern ethics is not only threatening but must be halted, the Fundamentalists say.

THE "WHY" OF FUNDAMENTALISM

Pinning Down the Fundamentals

Feeling this alarm and seeing those blinking red stoplights, Fundamentalists do what people commonly do when facing cultural acids threatening to dissolve the values they hold dear. They naturally try to pin down some *fundamentals.* These are points that they hold to be true and good, points that they think their adversaries are likely to deny. They are drawing points or "lines in the sand" that will set "us" apart from "them." It is ironic that these points may or may not be essential, or even real, components of their value scheme. But whether or not these points are at the center of what truly concerns them, they are the matters that are in (perceived or actual) dispute. These points become pieces of ground on which they can place themselves and then say "here I stand!"

These points are the gauntlet that gets thrown down. For the Fundamentalist, there is the classic list that was set forth early in the twentieth century, the absence-of-error read into the Bible: the verbal "inerrancy" of the Bible, the Virgin Birth of Jesus, the Atoning Death of Jesus, the physical Resurrection of Jesus, and the Second Coming. Although there is some variation in this list, these items may serve our purposes. What these items accomplish for their exponents is to pin down what they espouse in such a way as to make clear how they differ from their adversaries. These are points that they *have to* accept while, at the same time, being points that their opponents *have to* reject. The points therefore serve to distinguish the "in-group" of faithful Christians from the "out-group" of disdained modernists or liberals. Everyone can for this reason know "who is who."

Is there some value in this almost arbitrary Fundamentalist critique of modern worldviews? Is there a truly dangerous moral atrophy in the cosmopolitan indifference to specific value schemes? Do some people rightly resist the disdain of others just because they cling to these value schemes? Certainly, different people will have different answers to these questions. It seems clear, however, that Fundamentalism surrenders much of its Christian substance in its battle with modernism by allowing its opponents to define the terms of the debate. The belief in the creation of the world in six days 6,000 years ago is an answer to the scientific question about the origin of the world. It is not an exposition of what the writers of the biblical documents were intending to say. Those writers did not ask *our* questions, and for this reason they did not answer *our* questions.

When the Fundamentalists speak of the Bible as "true," they are assuming a peculiarly modern idea of what truth is. To a great degree, the Fundamentalists have mimicked the very modernists whom they wish to oppose. Their treatment of the Scriptures and expositions of Christian faith are photographic negatives of the liberalism with which they wish to do battle rather than a true opposition to it. They proclaim, "we are of *this* opinion rather than *that*." But the "this" that they identify with is actually formed and shaped by the "that" from which they wish to distinguish themselves. In being shaped this way, their "this" loses much of its positive substance. What they affirm is really modern rationalism-empiricism turned inside out. Indeed, opposing it is becoming it.

Fundamentalism may also occasion a loss of authenticity in the moral life. Common to all moral decision making, properly so called, is that an *individual* must *herself* accept full responsibility for the decisions that she makes. She must take note of what is at stake in any situation in which she finds herself and then decide what is the best, or the least worst, thing to do in that situation. Although there is no way to avoid the imperative to make such a decision, people commonly do try to avoid it. They fall back on rules and regulations. They feel that in "going by the book" they escape the demand that they decide for themselves, that is, hold themselves accountable for their own decisions. Indeed, they fall back on "the book" to ease the stress of, and release themselves of responsibility for, making decisions amid many complexities and uncertainties. This effort to let the rules decide what to do is what the existentialist philosophers of a half-century ago called *in-authenticity*. A person tries to flee from the call of her own humanity by making rules decide what, in fact, she must decide if she is to be a real human being.

The Darker Face of Fundamentalism

If we spell *fundamentalism* with a small "f" and use it to refer to phenomena found in many religions, we can see that it may have a yet more troubled face. Movements found not only in Christianity but also in Judaism and Islam identify the divine with what are, in fact, their own particular projects and or provincial claims. A group struggles to get something for itself but asserts that it is acting on orders from God. It asserts that its claims are holy and good. The claims can be land, buildings, or exclusive rights to exercise governance in an area. And where a group that is not in the grip of a fundamentalist faith might see a need to negotiate and be willing to negotiate with other groups who also have claims, the fundamentalists may not see this need. They have a feeling of entitlement and of being God's servants who are absolutely right, and so they have no need to negotiate or compromise. Therefore they proceed to carry out violence against other groups and assume that they are fully justified in doing so. The aggression of Israel against the Palestinians together with the reciprocating violence of the Palestinians against Israel is, of course, a prime case in point, although there are innumerable others in the world today and throughout history. This, of course, is what the word *idolatry* means. Something in the realm of the finite is given a dignity that belongs properly only to the transcendent and the universal. A thing that is not a god is thereby made into a god.

And we do well to remember that what is opposed to in the Bible is idolatry, not atheism. Apart from Psalms 14 and 53, there is very little mention of denial of God in the Bible. Such a denial is neither considered right nor wrong; there is simply no mention of it. What there is, instead, is a condemnation of *false* gods. And any time that something in particular is wrongly given the status of the divine or godlike, we have idolatry. When this occurs, we have the enemy. We can be sympathetic toward fundamentalist views when they set themselves against the atrophy of morality as such or when they chafe under the (presumed) hauteur of the cosmopolitan or intellectual. But when fundamentalists of any religion see the mistreatment or slaughter of their enemies as good and holy, then we have an enemy that must be opposed unequivocally.

At this point, the atheist might merit some sympathy, for when the atheist denies God, he is digging a hole in the world around him. This is a hole from which "god" has been extracted. But this hole itself may well bear a closer resemblance to the God of Abraham, Isaac, and Jacob, as well of Isaiah, Amos, Micah, and Jeremiah, than the "god" of the fundamentalist! We may remember that the voice of God is often one that is heard precisely in the absence of all voices—in the "silence of eternity." (As always, it makes a difference which fundamentalist we are talking about and which atheist we are referring to.)

FUNDAMENTALISM AND THE MOMENT OF UNCERTAINTY

Much to the point of this discussion, the function of the fundamentals is to avoid the essential moment of uncertainty that we are all called on to go through unless fundamentalism relieves us of so doing. If I accept the fundamentals as truth, I steer clear of this necessary uncertainty as though it were a pit I could fall into. I think I already have truth—right here. I declare that there is no need to defend this truth I think I have because this truth is where I begin. And if question is raised as to why I begin here, I answer that I just do. I could say that it feels right or that I "have faith," but that is all that I can say. Most notably, I do not go where the Christian needs to go, to the foot of the Cross where I meet a Lord who insists that he *is* the Truth in himself and as himself, and not in the doctrines *about* him.

But why does it *feel right* to insist on the fundamentals, the Virgin Birth and the others? It feels right because doing so is a standard item of the surrounding culture. The person who says he accepts the view that the Bible is the "Word of God" in the specific sense of its being true word for word expects others to see the inherent nobility and godliness of such a point of view. To him, this has an aura of the self-evident, just as do all items of a particular society's moral codebook. Even those who disagree, he thinks, must see the validity of the assertion that the Bible is the "Word of God." If they reject it, they do so only as an expression of their pride and as an indication of their unfaithfulness. This helps to explain why a fundamentalist can intone that he "follows the Bible" without going into detail about what such a "following" entails. But if some of the details were given, such as the genocide at Jericho, he would reject them.

Such fundamentalism, then, can be viewed as a form of Christianity that rejects the moment of uncertainty as a matter of principle. Fundamentalism is different from its close cousin, evangelicalism, in minor but significant ways. The fundamentalist wishes to wall herself off on an island of faithfulness to her basic creed. The evangelical has a similar creed, but wants to reach out into the larger society. In doing so, she inevitably compromises, or at least hedges, on some of her doctrinal commitments. She does this so that she will be successful in the act of reaching out. Acting in this way has not been fruitless for this evangelist. She has enjoyed considerable success in America, as has been described in a rich literature on the subject, although with some disagreements about the reasons for the success.

All social groups divide into subgroups, with disagreements between them. The Fundamentalist and Evangelical groups are no exception. There are certain to be pockets within these groups in which the moment of uncertainty takes place and some attention to a voice from outside of the common culture is heard. Even the dilution of Fundamentalist purity that occurs in the Evangelical acts of reaching out could be salutary. It may be stimulus for an inquiry about the Word of God that opens a door for actual inquiry. And, of course, the Word of God has a way of appearing and being heard even when it is least expected. We may think we know who is on God's side and who is not, and we may think we know what the content of God's will is—and is not. But God has his own schedule and his own agenda. His Word will upset our best theories and practices. Part of being Christian is to always expect what we do not expect.

THE MEGA-CHURCH AND CERTAINTY

American Protestantism is commonly divided into two groups, the liberal or mainline sector and the Fundamentalist or Evangelical wing. Within this divided body, the mega-church is definitely on the Evangelical side. It arose and has its roots in that tradition and continues to be within that tradition in a number of ways.

But the mega-church is actually quite different from standard Evangelicalism. The differences have to do with doctrine, not, however, with the *content* of doctrine, but with the *attitude* toward or the treatment of it. Characteristic of the mega-church is a pronounced *indifference* to doctrine. It does not matter to mega-church preachers whether a classic doctrine is affirmed or denied, whether any particular doctrine is accepted or rejected. Of course, when pressed, mega-church leaders will support the classic Fundamentalist opinions. They will favor the Virgin Birth, the view that the Bible is true word-for-word, and so on. But they do not do so because these opinions are important. They do so precisely because these opinions and all opinions are *not* important. And this is what separates them from both the liberals and the partisans who oppose each other, but not out of the rampant indifference we see in the mega-church.

On the one hand we have the liberal, the person who denies the Virgin Birth because opinions are—and therefore *this* opinion is—important to her. She is serious about her opinion. Because there is no credible evidence that Jesus was conceived in His mother's womb without male agency, she says and she believes that respect for Truth requires that we abandon such a belief. This respect for Truth is a moral matter and not just a bit of intellectual game-playing. This contrast of right and wrong *requires* that we submit to the discipline of evidence and logic. Failing to do so would be a sign of disrespect for Truth and, as such, would be immoral.

On the other hand we have the partisan. The partisans of the belief in Virgin Birth argue their case with conviction. To them, the entire edifice of the Faith rests on this and the other "fundamentals." If the Virgin Birth were allowed to fall away, Jesus would no longer be the presence of God with us. We would be left helpless before the crushing currents of modern rationalism and empiricism. All that would be left of him would be a man—a good man, perhaps—but a man nonetheless. And with that vulnerability would come a submission to the entire "modern" world with all of its faithlessness, its lack of respect for church, family, and its continual indulgence in the sins of the flesh.

In contrast to both of these perspectives that share a high evaluation of beliefs and opinions, the mega-church has a very relaxed attitude toward all ideas of what is true—toward doctrine as such. And with this "at-ease" attitude regarding thoughts and ideas, there is no reason for the mega-church to venture forth from a Fundamentalist "home base" into a strange world of differing ideas and beliefs. Therefore the "line of least resistance" is to stand where one is. Whatever has been believed by Evangelical "revival" preachers, mega-church leaders will also believe. They will not argue; they will simply take a certain body of beliefs for granted.

Although both the non-mega–church Fundamentalist and the mega-church "constituent" may share a belief in a certain doctrine and be in agreement on the opposition to a contrary point of view, their reasons for doing so are distinctly different. Where the liberal says that there was no Virgin Birth (or no evidence for it), the non-mega–church Fundamentalist insists that the doctrine be affirmed on the basis of Scriptural truth and as a basis for the affirmation that Jesus is the Son of God. On the other hand, and quite differently, the devotee of the mega-church sees the liberal as in error simply because he is making an issue of what should not be an issue. From this mega-church standpoint, the liberal is affirming the importance of having a *correct* view of the Virgin Birth matter, and it is this affirmation itself that is to be rejected. To wit, the mega-church affirms the Virgin because denying it is bestirring our selves to a preoccupation with beliefs, and it is this preoccupation itself that is wrong. Do not concentrate our attention on questions of doctrine. Doctrine should just "come naturally." Adherence to this stand allows us to wear a badge that says, "true Christian."

This sense of the irrelevance of correctness is something rather new in Christianity. The history of Christianity is actually a saga of *points of view* serving as the banner by which one group is set apart from another. It is replete with accounts of leaders who establish and defend certain views while attacking and declaring as anathema certain others. Rarely do we find indifference to matters of doctrine. Certainly, there are some groups among whom a preoccupation with liturgics or styles of devotion fill up the space that could have been occupied by doctrine. And there are others, such as the Pietists, among whom the cultivation of the "heart" seems to make matters of the "head" not so important. But in no case is there the kind and extent of indifference that we find in the mega-church.

Also true, in responding to divisions along doctrinal lines, it could be argued that the doctrines as such were not always what was important. As H. Richard Niebuhr argued in his 1928 book, *The Social Sources of Denominationalism,* the real fault lines dividing one part of the body of Christ from another were social rather than intellectual or doctrinal. Within a nation, one ethnic group was divided from another. And divisions of upper, middle, and lower classes appear within an otherwise united national community. In the first millennium of Christianity, the division of the Eastern Church from the Western Church reflected a broad sociopolitical divide of the East from the West. And it is likely that the disputes about the Trinity carried on by Arius and the Orthodox (Athanasians) reflected social divisions that are not clear in history books but that would have been clarified had there been a sociologist busy and at work at the time! But even so, matters of doctrine were important, even if more as banners carried by competing groups rather than as the substance of the divisions.

Whether in their substance or as banners or emblems, doctrines were important. They mattered and made a difference. To anyone who proclaimed the Gospel or who served as administrator of a body of Christians and their clergy, there was a point of view that defined what it was, as we say, "all about." The doctrines were the basis for the life of the group. And even if an Evangelist had a wish to gather a goodly number of sheep into his fold, he wanted that abundant company to adhere to the body of doctrine. This is what he would have meant by saying that there were *many.* There were many who accepted, prayed, worshiped, and set their hopes for eternal life within a community defined by its *beliefs.*

In the mega-church we see something quite new and different. In this new kind of religious community, the people involved do not take their stand on something that is thought or believed about an objective reality. The Lord whom they "praise" is not an *other*. He is not *other* than the group; he is not situated outside of it. Nor is he to be sharply distinguished from it. There is little reference to a "beyond" or an "out there" that is the source of the group's life and the object of its loyalty. What is treated as important, rather, is the subjective life of the group, the act of worshiping itself. Just as a man who loves a woman may be more concerned with himself as the one who loves (as the lov*er*) than with the woman who is the presumed object of his love, so the worshiper is preoccupied with himself—or the group with itself. Here, the *activity of worshiping* is what is significant, rather than the God who is worshiped. Here, where liberal opinions are opposed, it is not because they are incorrect. It is, rather, because they proceed from an act of reasoning that would threaten to dampen that enthusiasm. Reasoning hence becomes the opposition.

Whereas a Protestant congregation may see itself as a community that is formed by and lives off of "justification by faith" (Rom. 1:17), matters are quite different in the mega-church. The mega-church is formed by and lives off of itself. It lives off of the enthusiasm that is generated within the events that form its life. It this sense, it is like a "rock" concert. In the rock concert, there are performers. These performers are few in number. And there is an audience consisting of people who are very many in number. The performers elicit enthusiasm within the huge audience before them. The audience *authenticates*, through its enthusiasm, the celebrity status of the performers. The emotional crescendo produced within the concert is self-generated and self-perpetuated. Nothing from outside—no theory or "point of view," no ground or source—is needed to do so. Similarly, the mega-church generates its own verification. It authenticates itself.

Further, the "we–they" divisions among groups that are important elsewhere are not so for the mega-church. In other traditions, doctrines are important. They are important because the followers of the tradition feel that, by adhering to them, they (among other things) identify with an honored "we" that stands in contrast to a deprecated "they." We, the Protestants, adhere to "justification by faith," as against those Catholics who do not (or so we think). We, the Catholics, adhere to the succession of bishops, which Protestants do not. Liberals and Evangelicals similarly claim a state of "belonging" to their respective religious social circles on the basis of opinions that they hold dear. But in the case of the mega-church, there is no such "we" that stands against an alien "they." Rather, the "we" is supposed to be *everyone*. It intends to draw all people into itself, not to set itself off apart from others. Its passion is not so much to be right or correct as it is to be inclusive. To be in the mega-church is not so much to be part of "a religion" that is set over or against other religions, but instead to participate in a religious "Wal-Mart" that just wants to attract ever more customers.

And the "everyone" is quite egalitarian. In traditional societies, people in the "upper crust" take pride in being set apart from the common people beneath them. And to the end of maintaining that distinction, they cultivate fashions and styles. These fashions often change frequently, and by doing so they protect the distinctiveness of upper-class social positions. Even if the members of the "unwashed" mob beneath them imitate some of their styles of clothing and other adornments, they would not be able to claim equality because they could not keep up with the constantly occurring changes. Fashions and their rapid changes preserve a special place for those of high social status. There are, of course, many other symbols of "elite" status. These include houses, entertainments, and even the churches people attend. And, although all this is true, it is also true that this superior position depends on the larger community that includes the lower classes. Only within such a community can there be a location "up above." From this perspective, like the top floor of a house, "upper crusts" must have "lower crusts" to keep them "up!"

But in the mass society in which we live, the "elite" factor, while still present, does not dominate social life as it does elsewhere in the world. The vast television viewing audience takes the place of the elite group as a dominant factor in society. Instead of a noble elite or "upper crust," we have a *mass*. We have people spread out like dots that extend as far as the eye can see. The audience at a rock concert, which consists of thousands of people listening to live performers, is symbolic of what we have become. We Americans want to be part of that audience; indeed, we wish to be immersed in it. We want to participate enthusiastically in its applauding of performers. We want it to define who and what we are. We do not want to be set apart from others as an elite group wants to be distinguished from the common people. Rather, we want to be gathered into and made part of that vast audience.

We see this in the ways in which people address one another. Decades ago, if a person met someone and asked him what his name was, the person asked would have said something like "I am Peter Randall," or "I am Margaret Owens." If you ask the same question of people just like them today, the answer is likely to be "I am Pete" or "I am Maggie." In the earlier era people stood out and were identified as members of families that had a place within the community. Today a similar pair of persons would be any two grabbed from the "everyone" that is *out there* in the world. They would, in effect, be a man and a woman plucked out of the mass, like cups of water taken at random from the ocean. There is little to distinguish any one of them from others. They do not "stand out" as members of a family or lineage, or by the village where they grew up, or by their standing as servants of important people. Rather, each is an individual, and one who is only marginally different from others. A man named "Tom" is different from others bearing that name only by a few details. He is not really different. He and the other fellows named "Tom" are all just small units in a large mass.

What we have in the mega-church is such a mass. It consists of a large number of people. The number *must* be large. The people attending the worship events must be enough in number to be credible as an "everyone." They are like an ocean that has strong currents, with each individual feeling that she is a drop in the ocean and is swept along by the currents. It is the fact that she is a drop in an ocean that makes her a real person. She depends on the ocean for her reality as "one of" the people in the crowd. She may then find herself in an inlet or a bay of the ocean. In that smaller collection, she can be known as "Maggie." Indeed, calling people by their first names is what creates the inlet. In that place there are people who actually know one another, even if it is only by their first names. But the identity she has in that small group is made authentic and real only by the fact that the small group is an inlet of the larger ocean; the small group is not an independent reality. It would not be that group if it were only that group. Its being part of that ocean is its essence as the group it is. The group is not the small town of long ago, and the people in it are not the "folks" in that town. They are, instead, a few who have momentarily pulled aside from the vast multitude to be that small group. In this sense, "Tom" and "Maggie" are simultaneously part of the human ocean and members of a smaller group, with each part or aspect of their belonging being dependent on the other.

We can now see why the *moment of uncertainty* does not take place among the people in the mega-church. There is no need for a person to think through what viewpoints he will accept or believe in because, to him, his thoughts and beliefs are not sufficiently important. If a person reflects on an issue, perhaps the issue about whether it is all right (or mandatory) to have women clergy persons, he will not call up in his mind what his basic principles are and then consider how those principles apply to the gender identity of the clergy. He will not, that is, have to *think*.

Why not? We can see that if he is to engage in thinking, he must first assume that it is *important* that he think the *right* thing. For the person who *thinks*, there has to be a contrast between right thought and wrong thought. And avoiding the one while adhering to, or arriving at, the other must be a matter of importance. It must seem to him that, thinking that women should not be clergy when, in truth and in the eyes of God, they should be, is a disaster. Similarly, thinking that they should be when the Lord thinks that they should not would be to fall into the pit of error and impiety. Further, thinking that they should, when indeed they should, is avoiding disaster and sailing into the calm waters of Truth. The same would be true of thinking that they should not, if that is the truth. In any case, to think the right thing—whatever that right thing is—is serious business indeed. And where actual thinking is actually involved, this is dangerous business. So to avoid the dizzying heights of the serious, the easy way out is to avoid undertaking the enterprise of thinking. It is simpler to just keep from rocking the boat and to take refuge in the mega-church.

By contrast, the rather uncomfortable act of living through the moment of uncertainty is a price we pay because it is important to reach the end point of our thinking. If we are to arrive at that destination, we are required to travel the road that leads to it. Like Dorothy in the *Wizard of Oz*, we go through a jungle with demons, ghosts, and witches to get to the Oz of Truth and Goodness.

In the mega-church, what we think or what we believe is not terribly important. The mega-church itself and the enthusiasm that forms its life are important. Believing one thing rather than another is not important. And because holding to correct points of view or Truth is not important, there is no need to live through the moment of uncertainty to arrive at Truth. The enthusiasm generated by "praise teams" (choirs) and visible in the overhead screen is what is needed. And this enthusiasm does not require a moment of uncertainty. Indeed, it must reject such a moment because suspending judgment is not consistent with the "full speed ahead" imperative or with the enthusiasm or "praise" associated with it. It would be like throwing water on the fires when we wish that the fires would burn brightly.

It is true that, if pressed, mega-church leaders will confirm conventional beliefs. But their doing so is qualitatively different from a similar confirmation voiced by a Fundamentalist or even an Evangelical. The Fundamentalist confirms the belief that the Bible is true word-for-word because that belief is important to her. It matters. Or, if not that belief itself, something that it implies is terribly important. The leader or advocate of the mega-church will confirm that same belief, but she will do so because it does *not* matter. The liberal will, of course, deny that all of the words of the Bible are literally true. She will, instead, insist that scholarly study of the Scriptures go forward without inhibition. But she, like her Fundamentalist adversary, considers the Truth to be important. In the mega-church, however, the assertions that evoke fire in the Fundamentalist and that generate iron resolve in the liberal occasion nothing but a yawn. And this is why she can confirm those beliefs. It is because the Truth, to her, is "no big deal."

We can see this in the issue about women as ministers. In many Fundamentalist churches, denying that women can be clergypersons would come easily. It would require no thought, because it has tradition behind it. The powers of thought may be mobilized to explain it, but if they are, they are called to active duty to account for what is *given,* not to consider options that are "open" until one is chosen and the other is closed off. The view that women should be allowed to command—to "fill" pulpits—by contrast, would have to follow from a process of reasoning. There would be a general principle about the quality of God's people ("neither male nor female", Gal. 3:28), and then a further statement about serving as clergy or as leaders would be *deduced* from it. The moment of uncertainty would occur while the deduction is going forward.

If a woman were to appear as a minister in a mega-church, on the other hand, the process would be different. Instead of being justified by applying a general principle to the specific case, it would just happen. The woman would appear as minister in front of an audience, and the enthusiasm of the moment would be the justification. If any accounting were desired, it would be just that the Holy Spirit had called her to lead as minister or shepherd and had called the brothers and sisters to follow her as flock. This actually happened in Puerto Rico in a large Pentecostal church, seating 5,000 in its auditorium, based, as was stated, on *Mita* as the name of the Holy Spirit.

WHAT IS WRONG?

So is Truth "a big deal?" In the philosophical tradition of Western civilization, the answer is definitely "yes, it is a very big deal." Within all of the controversies between thinkers and the many rivalries between points of view, there is this constant: To think is to inquire about what is *real*. It is to reflect on that which by its nature is "out there." It is something that exists independently of the subjective life of an individual. It is that which is *other than* the individual himself and to which he may relate. And it is in relating to that which is objective that he becomes human. He flees from the perpetual "round and round" of his interior life to that which is not that life and which is other than it. He then becomes a human being in the process of relating to the other-than-he.

Let us try an exercise in imagination. We have a man who dreams of having a beautiful woman as a wife (sweetheart, lover). It turns out, as he sizes things up, that he has two possibilities. He can have a beautiful *dream* wife. She is a "Laura." Laura is superbly beautiful, has a scintillating personality and an alert, wide-awake mind, but she's only a dream. His dreams of her are, however, quite vivid. He has cultivated that life to the point where his "Laura" looks and feels like a real woman. As an alternative, he has the possibility of marrying a woman who is quite ordinary in face and figure. Her personality, although pleasant enough, has no special sparkle. She is ordinary in every way. But she is *real*. He can see her and touch her without mobilizing his imagination, for she is really and truthfully *there*.

Now if he must choose, which will he prefer? Because his imagination of "Laura" is quite vivid, we might think he would prefer the beautiful dream sweetheart. But let us pause and let these two possibilities settle down in our minds. Once they have assumed their proper places in our awareness, would this not seem to be correct: The man would prefer the ordinary, even dowdy woman who is *real*. He would prefer her to the other woman no matter how beautiful "Laura" is and no matter how vivid his image of her may be. When all is said and done, we human beings hunger for *reality*. To be human, we must connect with that which is other than we, which is "out there." To be caught in an imaginary world—to spin in a purely subjective life—no matter how vivid that world may be, is a species of hell. Even if the dream is as vivid as is reality, the fact that we *know* that the dream is a dream while the real is real is ultimately important. And in due course, we will give up the most beautiful and vivid dreams for just a little hunk of reality. "Give me a piece of reality" will be a desperate cry. Thus the subject matter of philosophy is "the really real" and the knowledge of it.

With all of its enthusiasm, the worship life of the mega-church is caught in this subjectivity. They may sing praises to God ("*Adonai*") and to Jesus Christ and his sacrifice of himself on the cross, but no matter how much they do this, they do not escape the whirlpool of their own subjective life, even if it is a subjective life shared by a crowd. To escape the prison of subjectivity to the freedom of the real world "out there," a person or a group needs to go through the moment of uncertainty. There has to be the waiting for that which is *not me* to grasp that which *is me* (for grammar's sake: that which is *not I* grasps that which *is I*). We see this in Plato's *Dialogues* in which a questioner slowly and bit-by-bit brings a person to a point where he sees the *real* for what it is. The really real is something that comes to us. It comes to us even if it does so in the form of a memory of the really real that we contemplated before we were born, as it does in Plato.

The failure of the mega-church is tied up in a decisive way with one of its basic and defining characteristics—its wish to grow to a large size and then to grow ever larger. This imperative is "jealous;" it does not want to share its place in the affections of the mega-church and its people with any other project. Notably, it does not want to share its place with a concern for Truth in our encounter with reality or for justice as we relate to the world. If to grow into having a large and larger number of "constituents" is what we are up to, then everything must be formed and shaped to achieve that goal.

For the Christian, the objective Truth is person. It is Jesus Christ as the Truth-with-us. And he is not an idea we have in our heads. He is real. His coming into the world was an event in human history. It took place; it happened. And as an event, it was supremely *other* than we, and supremely other than our own inner life. Jesus was a "not-us" (a "not-we") who may, at a time and in a way of his own choosing, reveal himself to us. We do not have control over his revelation of himself to us. We cannot make it happen. Neither, however, can we prevent it from happening, as Paul found out on his way to Damascus.

Thus what is proper for the Christian is to strive to be *teachable*. She should be ready to listen and to learn. As the writer of Ecclesiastes said, "guard your steps when you go to the house of God; to draw to listen is better than to offer the sacrifice of fools; . . . Be not rash with your mouth . . . for God is in heaven, and you upon earth; therefore let your words be few"(5:1–2). We should always be ready to wait. God will speak to us in his time and in his way. In the meantime, we abide in that moment of uncertainty.

The mega-church is not alone, of course, in seeking to escape the moment of uncertainty. The history of Christianity, both in its establishment (or church) form and in its sect form, is a continuing saga of efforts to escape or circumvent the moment of uncertainty. People do this by identifying the Word of God with something that is concrete and specific within the created order. It may be made equal to a doctrine or set of doctrines. It may be made the same as a code of conduct or set of moral rules. It can be treated as the same as a structure of church government, perhaps with bishops and popes. It can be equated with forms of worship and liturgy. In these varied ways, people seek to bring the Word of God that they meet in Jesus Christ down to earth. They treat it as being the same as some forms of thought or action that are to be found in the human realm. All of these are devices for fleeing from the moment of uncertainty. They are also devices for fleeing from the Word of God.

In criticizing the mega-church as we have, we do not mean to imply that *only* the mega-church is vulnerable to such a critique. We mean only that it is vulnerable to criticism in its own ways, which are different from those of other groups or traditions. In truth, we all seek ways to escape the moment of uncertainty. What hope there is for us lies in the fact that God will make a shambles of our pretensions to have his Truth under our control and will speak a word to us that is always a new word and which is, indeed, his Word.

Contrary to the dicta of the mega-church, we must pursue the moment of uncertainty, for this is Christianity in process. At every point, we must acknowledge, declare, and insist that the proclamation of Truth as objective is the business that we are about in the Christian Church. And because we are called to be busy in seeking Truth, we cannot—indeed we *dare* not—allow the numbers of people whom we count in our congregations to be a standard by which we measure the rightness, the validity, or the authenticity of what we do.

8

---※◆◆◆◇---

ECUMENICISM AND ITS LIMITS: THE BOUNDARY LOOKS OUTWARD

The rise of the mega-church in recent decades poses a new problem for Protestant churches. A trend toward mutual acceptance of the varying traditions has been underway for a long time, with remarkable results among both Catholics and Protestants. During a long span of history, each of the many religious groups cultivated a sense of uniqueness and superiority, but the vogue more recently has been for people in each tradition to regard those in the other groups as being brothers and sisters in Christ. The differences between them are viewed as matters of emphasis or preference, rather than issues of fidelity or infidelity to the faith. The member of a Methodist church may assure her Baptist neighbor that the neighbor is welcome in her Methodist parish; she will not try to "woo" the neighbor away from her "own" church. Indeed, she will strive mightily to show her neighbor that she recognizes and honors the "church she goes to." This ecumenical spirit even bridges the gap between Protestant and Catholic. It does so frequently and in many ways.

Because of this pervasive spirit of mutual recognition and respect, the churches are ill-equipped to deal with a genuine threat when it appears on the horizon. They have little in their toolkits that would enable them to either recognize or cope with a basic challenge to the Gospel when that challenge presents itself as being "Christian." They have been so busy opening up their hearts and minds and expanding their vision that they do not recognize an occasion where it may be necessary for them to close off those minds and hearts. Yet the mega-church may provide precisely such an occasion. Baptists, Methodists, Presbyterians, and others may pride themselves on being open to each other. But in the mega-church, they have a new kind of adversary, one who bears the others no goodwill. And the appearance on the religious horizon of this mega-church adversary requires the other churches to mobilize their ability to close off and declare opposition. No longer can they cherish only tolerance. They actually must see the need to develop an *intolerance* to that which is opposed in a basic and fundamental way to the Gospel they cherish.

Churches are human communities organized around the Gospel of Jesus Christ. As such, they have always had a concern to declare "here I stand" for the Gospel and to reject that which will dilute or destroy it. To do this, they have had various ways of drawing *boundaries.* They allow variation in belief and practice within these boundaries, but they reject as alien to the faith whatever is outside of the boundaries. In Galatians, for example, Paul insists that the believer must base his entire faith on what God did and does in Jesus Christ, that he therefore cannot and must not supplement that faith by adopting Jewish ceremonial law (dietary rules and circumcision). To allow that addition would be to imply that something other than the Gospel of Jesus Christ is necessary and so to deprive the Gospel of its power. The whole point about the Cross of Christ is that it is the *only* thing needed, as well as the *only* thing that is adequate. Either the Gospel is *sufficient,* Paul said, or it is nothing. Paul drew a line.

Boundaries, however, by their nature face in two directions. They face inward, and they face outward. In the outward face of the boundary, those items of belief or practice that are alien to the faith are to be rejected. Often, they are to be rejected with passion, for the Gospel is at stake. Certainly, the Christian can maintain an attitude of goodwill toward his neighbors of other faiths. He can be open and accepting to people who espouse Moslem, Buddhist, or other religions and can count them as friends. But this acceptance is toward them as neighbors, as fellow human beings, and as people who share moral concerns and humanitarian projects. He can share with them a concern for what is good in individual, family, community, national, and international life. He can also admire the achievements of Greek philosophy, Buddhism in its various branches, Hinduism, Confucianism, and Islam in their mighty efforts to cope with the dilemmas of human existence.

But there is then a line to be drawn. She does not share with them a common cause to the point that implies that faith in Christ is just one of a number of religious options. The Cross of Christ must be and remain, for the Christian, the center of what ultimately concerns her. Therefore, if a church or a group presents itself as "Christian" and uses Christian symbols while it clearly has its faith located elsewhere, the line must be drawn. The group must be considered to be outside the boundaries of Christianity. In many cases, these groups will naturally exclude themselves. Examples of these would include Christian Science, Jehovah's Witnesses, and Mormons. But in other cases they seek to include themselves within Christianity, and for this reason the Christian community itself must draw the boundary lines.

The inward face of the boundary, by contrast, seeks to include all that can be included. It is an underscoring of the very existence of the boundary. This boundary itself warrants some attention. If there are essentials in what is believed or what is practiced in any community that is to be called "Christian," there are also numerous nonessentials that are woven into its life. And just as it is important to develop a firm backbone in the matter of the essentials, lest the faith dissolve into a formless mass of ill-defined "spirituality," so it is also important to be somewhat flexible about whatever is within the boundaries of the Gospel. Of course, a too-great insistence on unnecessary details in religious life can threaten Christianity just as surely as can a surrendering of core essentials. For example, if a Baptist insists that churches must have a congregational polity and therefore views Methodists with their "connection-al" organization as being outside of the zone of faith, there is danger that Christians will dissolve into a collection of warring factions, as, indeed, they have often done. If Christians get "fussy" about matters of doctrine, such as a literal understanding of Virgin Birth or of the Creation, "fussy" is the sum and substance of what they *will* be. Faithful is what they will *not* be. The Cross of Christ will be drained of its power (1 Cor. 1:17). If the cross is essential, it is *all* that is essential. Therefore the boundary says whoever or whatever group stakes all hopes for fullness of life on and declares all loyalty to "Christ and Him crucified," (and who has a "right spirit" that produces "fruits" of the Gospel) is within the boundaries of the Faith.

The basic *logic* of the Gospel—and of the church's boundaries—is the same in both the demand for the exclusive and the demand for the inclusive. Both of these demands are intended to ensure that the faithful put all of their trust in "Christ and Him crucified." The demand for the inclusive is to be expected; it is inevitable that churches will develop features that are not essential. To be an actual church, a congregation must bring about a polity, a ministry, a code of ethics, and forms of worship and of implementing the education of its people. It must also generate systems of ideas including ideas that explain all that it does and how its various beliefs and practices pertain to the Faith in Christ Crucified. But none of these actually defines the essence of Christianity as such. The varying ideas and practices will have only a loose relationship to the central core of the Faith. To insist overmuch on any of them would be to question the *sufficiency* of the revelation of God in Christ. A balance must be found.

We must thus affirm the importance of the boundaries in this twofold way. Boundaries look *out,* and they look *in.* They exclude and they include. And they do both of these to ensure that faith is based on the rock on which it must stand: on the decisive work of God in the Death and Resurrection of Jesus Christ. Our focus in this chapter is on the outward look of the boundaries. In the next chapter we consider the opposite, the inward look.

THE BASIS OF THE BOUNDARIES

Christianity has never been considered by its adherents to be just a case of, or instance of, "religion." Nor is it a program or strategy for achieving "spirituality." It is, instead, a faith in which the believer throws herself entirely—heart, mind, and soul—on the gift of God's grace in Jesus Christ. The life, death, and resurrection of Jesus are where the believer's faith begins, where it continues and where it ends. Although a variety of ideas and songs and liturgies may fly hither and yon around the Christian, her gaze remains fixed on the Cross of Christ, albeit it does so *through* those ideas, songs, and liturgies. Here is where God reaches out and lays hold of human minds and hearts. Here is where there is relief from the burdens that human beings carry with them everywhere. Here is where a heavy load of guilt is lifted and God's forgiveness "poured out." Here is where there is refreshment for souls whom God has made hungry and thirsty for Truth and for Righteousness. Here is where there is a *command* that is at the same time an *invitation* into the wholeness of life. Here, in effect, is everything that matters ultimately.

Behind this point of beginning and ending, there is the view that we human beings are alienated from the ground and source of what we are—that is from God. In our every action, we push ourselves away from God. It is not just in our bad or foolish actions that we do so, but in our every action, or, better stated, in action as such. In the biblical account of the Garden of Eden, Eve and then Adam responded to the serpent's call to eat the forbidden fruit. They performed, in that act, the very first thing that they *did*. Until that point, they were in what Paul Tillich called the state of "dreaming innocence." They were capable of deciding and acting, but had not yet done so. The eating of the fruit was the first occasion in which they made a decision and took an action. In this sense, sinfulness or at least alienation is an ingredient in this particular human action, and thus in every human action. And this sinful alienation is in our noble and wise deeds just as it is in our wicked and foolish actions.

True, human beings can perform right actions. Actually, most people perform right actions most of the time. But because there is this big gap between us and God, there is no assurance that we will continue to do so or that we always will do what is truly right. Like a driver who takes his hand off the wheel of his car, we may continue on the right path for a time. But sooner or later, we will go wrong. We see this in, among other things, the "religious" person who becomes self-righteous and who presents a haughty rather than loving presence, often while insisting on observing rules that are unnecessary or wrong.

There is a reason for this behavior. In pushing herself away from God, a person also puts a gap between herself and her fellow human beings. It is God who holds a person up, and in holding her up, binds her *in* community and *to* community with other human beings. When a person encounters another person, she meets in that person a "wall" that limits her own ability to control all that surrounds her. If she then respects that boundary and honors the other person's reality as a person, she does so because she is supported by God. God holds her, so to say, in full community with the "other," that is, the other person. Where the support of the ground and source is lacking, so also is the community. The alienation of people from God, then, is always an alienation of person from person.

We see this in the fact that we never love our neighbor as ourselves. A man may honor another person, but he always holds back a bit of that honor, as though it is dangerous to let it all go. True, a man may say that another person is "good," but he may feel the other person to be not quite as good as the man himself, or not "good" in ways that are important to the man himself. No matter how much we may love other or honor others, there is always this level of holding back. And because this gap is never fully overcome by even the firmest of human bonds (husband–wife or parent–child), life is filled with jealousies and envies and, in due course, by conflict and tragedy.

We also see this sort of human tragedy in the matter of ranking and power. It is inevitable, of course, that there will be rank orders within human communities. Even if everyone were equally talented and equally industrious, it would be necessary to have "authorities" so that the life of the community could be ordered. But if people were "in God" and so in community with their fellow human beings, this authority would be strictly for a purpose. Those who rule would be those who serve, by ruling or administering. In fact, however, people in their state of separation from God almost always elaborate on a position of authority and elevate the position's power beyond its proper place as a platform from which to serve. They always seek to preserve and to enhance their own power and their prestige. They will do whatever they can to accomplish this. And then, having accomplished it, they will make up a good reason *why* they would be "at the top." Following the work of Reinhold Niebuhr, we may say that this is a definition of *sin*. Men seek maximum power, *and then* they undertake to justify that power.

Important in this analysis is that the problem is in the human *will*. It is not that we lack wisdom or understanding. It is, rather, that in our state of separation from God, we are anxious and afraid. And in that desperate situation, we seek to quiet our anxieties by exalting ourselves in one way or another. We know somewhere in the depths of our beings that this is wrong. But we bury that awareness under layers of religious or ideological justification, saying that our exalted position is the will of God. In principle, we *could* tough it out and decide (will) to do what is right. But it is inevitable that we will not. Yet the fact that we *could* do what is right leaves us guilty for not having done so. This state of guilt is basic to our human situation.

The Gospels address this state of guilt. Jesus is the man who is in full communion with the Heavenly Father and therefore in full communion with us. As the man from God, he evokes anger in people, for he exposes their pretensions to appear "good" precisely *as* pretensions. It is inevitable, therefore, that he will be crucified or otherwise crushed wherever and whenever he appears. But in doing so he is absorbing the hostility of people that is directed against Him, and therefore against

God. By absorbing it, he lifts it and takes it away. To wit, I might say, I strike him in my anger; but, seeing that he simply accepts my anger and suffers it, I find my anger gone. It is not there any more. And being without my anger, I am able to affirm God as my God. And I am able to affirm my basic community with my fellow human beings.

What is critical here is that the Crucifixion of Christ is the decisive event in which God reaches out to human beings. He reaches across the gap that humans have created by their actions and restores the bond between him and these humans. He lifts them up so that they are no longer anxious. And not being anxious, they are able to be back in fellowship with him and therefore with one another. This is a volitional matter, one having to do with the will rather than the intellect.

Further, it is because of this encounter with the Christ whom we crucify that we are able to *know* about the encounter of God with people. It will solve the problem of epistemology. If I, as the great sinner, find myself released from my alienation from God and restored to fellowship with him, this finding myself in that state is how I know that Jesus is the Christ and that he wins and obtains the pardon that I need. It is not a matter of the intellect. I did not, by astute analysis, perceive that God forgives and restores me in Christ. No amount of brilliant philosophizing can accomplish this. Nor could any amount of observation and "research" do so. Rather, it is *as* the one who is forgiven that I perceive that, through Christ, God forgives the sins of the world.

In terms of epistemology, or how we know what we know, we have here a radical departure. We cannot join Descartes by his winter stove and determine to doubt all things and then to take a rock bottom point that we cannot doubt and build up from there. We will not get from "I think" to "I am." What we will do, instead, is to find that we are worse than we thought. We will find ourselves pushed down into the depths of despair about our separation from God, and then, dropping to the bottom of the pit, we will discover ourselves to be sinners, yes, but *forgiven* sinners. And as forgiven, we then perceive that we could know how sinful we were only because we had *already* been forgiven. Without God's pardon, we measure ourselves by the standards of the world. And by those yardsticks, we might do all right, for we are respectable middle-class folk who bathe frequently and have good table manners. But it was because we already knew God through the Cross of Christ that we knew how sinful we were. We might say that we dropped to the pit and then met God there. He then lifted us up.

To put it another way, we find that just as Christ rose from the dead, so in him we are *alive.* Or we find ourselves to be alive. This awareness that we now live when we had been dead is how we know what we know. Here is our epistemology.

This does not in any way lessen the importance of the Old Testament. There, too, men met God as the one who forgives. We see this in Psalm 103, among many other places. And Jesus himself is presented in the Gospels as the fulfilling of what God began in Abraham and continued through Moses, the monarchy of David, the calling of the great prophets, and the Exile and Return. What is distinctive is that in Christ we have a definitive and final encounter of God with human beings in which a full creation of the *new person* takes place.

THE BOUNDARY LOOKS OUTWARD (IT EXCLUDES)

We can see now why the boundary that looks *outward* is necessary. Human beings have developed philosophies of many kinds and have done so at all times and in all places. Some of these are so brilliant that we can only stand in awe of what has been achieved. We need merely to think of what Plato and Aristotle wrote and of the fact that the work of the latter followed closely on that of the former. We may also reflect on what was accomplished in the Roman Empire in the realms of law and administration; in both cases, we have a civilization that was capable of producing creativity of great magnitude. No less awesome would be the creations of Buddhist spirituality and Hindu faith. Moslem civilization, coming after Christ, has also achieved great heights of mind and heart. But at no point in all of these do we find a man who is in full communion with God being crucified and so getting at the very heart of the human separation from the Creator of the world. At no other point do we find the forgiveness of sins that makes us "New Creatures." So without relaxing in the least our admiration for achievements that have been accomplished elsewhere, we insist that the Cross of Christ is where we begin and where we will continue.

Never, that is, may the Christian allow her faith to be seen as just one of many forms of "spirituality" that are more or less equal in elevating human beings above their selfishness, greed, conceit, vanity, or preoccupation with immediate pleasures. Once this allowance of a lifting of ourselves *by* ourselves is made, the Cross of Christ is "emptied." It loses its power. The view that people can, by cultivating a spiritual capacity that has been lying dormant within them, lift themselves out of their human situation is rejected. The Cross has its power for people who—and only for people who—assert that they have *no* capacity for a wisdom that will lift them above their misery. For this reason, they depend entirely on God's gracious action in Jesus Christ. Clearly, there can be no compromise here. Either Jesus Christ is Lord, or he is not. The Christian, therefore, may have goodwill toward his neighbors of other faiths, but she does not relax her insistence on the primacy and uniqueness of the Gospel of Jesus Christ.

The matter was particularly serious in the early centuries of the Christian era because there were other faiths that found it convenient to use the paraphernalia (symbols, ideas, ceremonies) of Christianity while denying its central core in the Crucified and Risen Lord. Under the label of Gnosticism, many of these were *dualistic* in their mode of thinking. Reality, for them, was to be divided into good spirit and bad matter. These may also be referred to as the realms of the infinite and the finite. Bad matter—the finite—was the cause of suffering in human life. The remedy for suffering was therefore to leave the realm of matter behind and to rise to the sphere of spirit. In the Gnostic movements, this was elaborated into a series of steps or stages in which the soul rose from the bad creation to the good reality that is above and aloof from it. It was a matter of learning or knowing; indeed, the word *gnostic* means *knowledge.* It was not just knowledge in our modern technological sense, however. As Paul Tillich said, it was knowing of an existential kind. It was a knowing carried out by the entire self and not just by calculative intelligence. And it was a knowing that had to do with the anxieties people suffer as they face the stark contrast between life and death, between being and nonbeing. It was *existential* knowing. Yet, even though existential, it remained knowledge in the sense of a knowing that can be cultivated *in* human beings *by* the agency of other, more knowledgeable, human beings.

Gnosticism was, in this sense, *religious.* It had to do with what concerns people ultimately, but it was religious in a way that was totally distinct from that of Christianity. For in it, the problem plaguing human beings was a failure to *understand,* even though the understanding that was lacking was of an existential character. And the solution was therefore for a person to move himself through the stages that separated his initial imprisonment in the realm of "stuff," and of heartbreak and tears, to the glorious sphere of pure spirit beyond. This ascent may or may not involve a "rigorous" rejection of the pleasures of the flesh. But it is a human project in any case.

By contrast, the Gospel of Jesus Christ saw the human problem as resident in the *will*. It was in a willpower that had been bent and twisted by separation from God. A person, alienated from the ground of his being, is unable to decide for the good, for obedience to good and love of his neighbor. In principle, he could make such a decision, for he has command of his *will*. But in practice he cannot, or, better stated, does not. This combination of "could" and "does not" leaves him responsible for his departures from the Will of God. It leaves him, that is, *guilty*. He stands accused and convicted because he could have *willed* the good but did not. He had the ability to choose to serve God, but in his anxiety he always chooses a path that veers from the one to which God calls him. And because the defect lies in his *will,* the remedy has to be in an *event* that takes place in history. For only in something that *happens* in the world and among people can a person's *will* be addressed and lifted out of the morass in which it has imbedded itself. There has to be a historical event. Specifically, it must be by the life, death, and resurrection of Jesus Christ.

If, then, Gnostic movements find it convenient or useful for their purposes to use images, symbols, beliefs, and practices of Christianity to promote *their* solution to the human problem, there is a dilemma. Inevitably, they will change the Christian images to fit *their* program. They will certainly wish to deny the physical reality of Jesus and of his suffering and death. Most commonly, they seek to make him into a phantom or a purely "spiritual" being uncorrupted by the flesh. This is, for them, necessary because in order to use him they need to see him as a spiritual being who leads people *away* from the flesh toward a realm of pure spirit. To do this, he must be purely spirit himself. He *cannot* be an actor on the stage of history which is what, in biblical and Christian terms, he *must* be.

Thus was the battle joined. To distinguish Christian faith from Gnosticism, the church fathers needed a point of departure. They needed an assertion that Christians must make and that the Gnostic thinkers must deny. Thus in the Bible the writer of 1 John wrote:

> By this you know the Spirit of God; every spirit that confesses that Jesus Christ has come in the flesh is from God, and every spirit that does not confess Jesus is not from God. And this is the spirit of anti-Christ, of which you have heard that it is coming and it is already in the world (1 John 4:2–3)

The vehemence of this passage indicates the importance of the assertion that God as the Son was present in the world *in the flesh*. He was not just an image or a spirit floating in the air. Nor did he only appear to have a human body. He was present as a body in the world as we know it. Jesus was, to the authentic Christian, the "Word made flesh" (John 1:14). He was in the world as a body that was present in time and space and among people. His earthly life consisted of a series of events that took place in human history. His Crucifixion and Resurrection were events that took place at a certain time and in a certain place.

Here was the *boundary*. Here was a point where Christian faith was on one side and any "other" or alien faith was on the other. At this point, all equivocation and all compromise come to an end. Everything depends on standing firm on this spot. It is a matter of life and death, indeed, of eternal life and death. In Paul Tillich's terms, it is a matter of ultimate or unconditional concern. So here we have a boundary looking outward. Here tolerance was *not* called for. Here there is no room for a "well maybe" or an "and also." There are no "two ways." There is just one, and the Christian will take her stand here and stake everything on it.

MODERN IDEOLOGIES

If Gnosticism was the great adversary of the first centuries, others exist today. In our time, there are religions and ideologies that describe a process that they say is taking place in history. They then assert that there is, in these processes, a movement from what is bad to what is good, or from misery to happiness. Such a change from bad to good, they further assert, in not just an "at the moment" occurrence. Nor is it something that just "happens to happen." It is, rather, a basic process that takes place at the very core of reality. It is a fundamental metaphysical process. The movement within it from one stage to another is therefore something that happens as a matter of necessity. It occurs in reality as such.

Marxism is a prime case in point. Its view of history is modeled on the dialectic of Hegel in which there is tension between opposites that gives rise to a new reality in which the tensions are resolved. In the modern era, the tension is between socioeconomic classes. The capitalist or investing (bourgeois) class makes wealth from wealth. The working class (proletariat) makes wealth from labor. There is tension between the two because the investors make their wealth by exploiting the workers. The tension between the two will then generate a "revolution" in which the working classes will, in effect, take over and usher in a society without exploitation and without classes. Significant here is that this is in actuality a metaphysical process. The tension between investors and workers does not just "happen" to be taking place. Nor is the resolution in the socialist-communist society merely a fortuitous outcome. Rather, it is the nature of reality as such to bring about this process and produce this outcome.

The difference between a Christian view and this Marxist understanding of historical process does not have to do with the supposed Marxist denial of God, as is commonly supposed. Rather, it is that Marxism posits a false god. If Marxism asserted only that a tension between investors and workers *appears* to be taking place and that a *probable* outcome of such a tension is the appearance of a classless society, there would be no quarrel with Christianity. A Christian might observe events and think that those events are unfolding as Marxism suggests. Or she could hold the opinion that a rather different sequence of events is taking place. There would be no *prima facie* reason to prefer one image of history over the other. Neither would be more noble or pious than the other, any more than it is more noble to think that a car we are looking at is blue than it would be to think that the car is yellow. It is a matter of what we *see* and nothing else. And further, the concern for social justice that seethes beneath the surface of all of the work of Karl Marx and of his followers resonates very well indeed with the thundering of the Old Testament prophets. At several different points in their writings, many texts refer to concern for "the stranger, the widow and the orphan." Others refer to "the oppressed" or "the poor." In some references, it is God who "loves" those who are without power (Deut. 10:17–18). In others it is the good king (Ps. 72:4, 12–14). In still others it is the "you" to whom the prophet is speaking (Jer. 7:5–7, Ezek. 18:5–9). The loaning of money "at interest" as a stratagem for despoiling the poor of their property is condemned (Neh. 5:11, Ps. 15:4). At several points in Leviticus, laws regarding respect for the rights of the poor or helpless are stated and then followed by the expression "I am the LORD." To acknowledge God as the Lord, that is, is seen as *requiring* a tender concern for those who are without power or wealth. In this sense, the entire life and work of Karl Marx would seem to be an "echo" of the prophetic tradition of the Old Testament. Regardless of whether it is straight or twisted, it is a real echo.

The problem arises when the dialectic that Marxism describes is viewed as something that is *necessarily* taking place. Rather than a process that just happens to be going on, it is an unfolding that issues from the very core of reality itself—or from reality as such. When this is the belief, the dialectic of class conflict issuing into the classless society takes the place, in effect, of the action of God in history as described in the Old Testament. There we see God choosing a special people. We see God punishing that special and chosen people for their infidelity to his Covenant with them, that is, for their worship of foreign (controllable) gods and for the fact that the wealthy and powerful among them oppress the poor and power- less. Going further, we see God's promising to restore his special people to their former glory and righteousness and to make of them a "beacon to the nations." All of this is viewed as an activity of God, for he is a god who "keeps covenant." He makes promises and keeps them. The certainty of its occurrence rests in God's will and intentions and not on an impersonal metaphysical process. To abandon faith in a willing, intending god and to place confidence in such a metaphysical process is then a case of idolatry.

What the Marxist does is to build his image of reality on the same mold, or with the same structure. There is an original innocence when human societies were not yet rent by divisions of the community into upper and lower classes. Nor was there the exploitation of some people by others that is brought about by class divisions. There is then the "eating of the apple," in which some groups claim to "own" the means of production and there- fore the product that comes from those means. In the final stages of the process, the working-class people rebel and bring about a society that has no classes and in which the original goodness of human nature can at last blossom. Point by point, this analysis parallels the biblical view of history. It is different in that it substitutes a social and economic process for the will and work of God.

If it is true that Marxism makes an idol of a social process, it is no less true of capitalism and the devotion to "free enterprise." Here, too, the question is whether an idea or a process is hardened into a metaphysic. A writer may describe in some detail the workings of the *market*. She may see glory and wonder in what is achieved when people *compete* and, in so doing, provide quality goods and services at low prices. She may also see in this wondrous "market" a process in which effort "flows" from areas of excess production in which prices are low (say shirts) to those in which goods are scarce (say shoes) and in which prices are therefore high. But here, too, the prospect of idolatry lurks in the background. Market processes may properly be seen as occurring sometimes, under certain circumstances, in certain ways, and to certain degrees. But what happens is that people come to see the "market" as having a metaphysical status. They see it as something that takes place at the very core of reality, or *reality as such*. Its processes are not seen as things that happen sometimes and under certain conditions. They are viewed, rather, as matters of necessity. Reality itself is so structured as to ensure that these things will happen. The "market," in this sense, has a godlike character. And belief in it becomes a case of *idolatry*.

In sharp contrast, the Christian faith insists that Jesus is Lord. He is Lord always and everywhere and over all things. Faith in him, for this reason, will not allow acceptance of any such metaphysic. It will take *sacredness* away from the market and insist that markets are what they are and *only* what they are; he asserts that they do what they do and *only* what they do. They may work well at certain times and under certain conditions and in certain ways. But there is no *necessity* that they work well under any particular set of existing conditions. While sometimes wondrous in their effects, market processes are not basic in the structure of *reality as such*. Here, too, the Lord of the Bible reigns supreme. As a "jealous" God, he allows no process in history to be basic or a matter of necessity.

Of all the value-schemes that are outside of the boundary of Christian faith, none is more prominent and pernicious in the modern world than *nationalism*. People are loyal to their countries. This loyalty or "patriotism" is not, in principle, wrong. Human beings are organized in groups of all kinds—families, communities, and nations. These groups, as the focus of *belonging*, are part of the goodness of the created order. And aspects of their organization that are designed to maintain peace and order in human affairs are also good. Paul makes this clear in his comments about the Roman emperor (Rom. 13).

But here, too, the prospect of idolatry hovers in the background. There is a possibility—perhaps we should say a danger—that the country will become, to its people, an ultimate reality (a god) and that loyalty to the country will become an ultimate commitment. Where this happens, the citizens of a nation come to believe that "what their nation does" is by its very nature the same thing as "doing what is right." The "does" and the "is morally right" are the same thing as a matter of necessity. If someone asserted that a nation (its government) did something that was morally wrong, the people of that nation would see such an accusation as absurd on its face, for if their nation did something, that thing could not be wrong. It was right purely and simply because it was their nation that did it. To assert that the nation did "wrong" therefore would be a contradiction in terms and possibly even a case of blasphemy, for the nation has been given a godlike status, and the gods logically cannot do wrong.

All intense loyalty to country involves this risk of idolatry. We can draw boundary between what does and what does not fall into this trap. Let us say that an accusation has been leveled against a nation, perhaps the United States. If someone considers the accusation and tells us that she thinks that the accusation is unjustified or incorrect for reasons she spells out—that what the nation did is right—the person's response is, in Christian terms, an acceptable choice. She takes a position that can be discussed in the give-and-take in which people seek to consider options and to make correct judgments. I, or any one of us, may disagree in a particular case. I may think that the United States did wrong and that the nation is "guilty as charged." A case in point would be the involvement of the United State in the crisis of the Sandinista government of Nicaragua of the 1980s. But here the nation's defender and I (the nation's accuser) can discuss the details and possibly even come to an agreement. But if the defender says that "having done wrong" is a thing that *by its nature* cannot be asserted of the United States, then we have an idolatry of the nation.

We see, then, that Christianity has boundaries that look outward. A Christian may "love his country," but he always does so as one who loves God *first*. This is a point where we must take a stand; for failure to do so is not properly honored as "tolerance" or "inclusiveness." Rather, it is to be disdained as unfaithfulness. Without a "here I stand," we do not have Christianity. We may have a case of being nice, "reasonable," or friendly. But we do not have faith in Jesus Christ.

THE SPIRITS OF THE TIMES

The word *spirit* occurs frequently in the discussion of non-Christian faiths, those that are outside the boundary. For the Gnostic devotees, what was good for human beings was to leave, step-by-step, the realm of matter behind and to rise to the realm of *spirit*. When Max Weber wrote (in *The Protestant Ethic and the Spirit of Capitalism*) about the role of Protestantism in the genesis of capitalism, he spoke of the *spirit* of capitalism. If Marxism did not use that term, it was because Marx preferred the expression *class consciousness,* which is a similar idea. In the case of nationalism, we often hear about the *spirit* of the nation, or people are described as having a patriotic *spirit.* At a less serious level (or so we might like to think), when people talk about high school and university athletic competition, they often speak of *school spirit.* It is to the end of cultivating that *spirit* that bands play and cheerleaders lead, that is, lead the crowds in high-powered cheers.

Even in the matter of romance, we might recall a popular song of some years ago, one about the city of Rome and its "spirit," in which these words appeared:

> Good-Bye, farewell to Rome
> City of a million moonlit places
> City of a million fond embraces.

There is a dialectic in these lines. "Rome" would not have the connotations it has without the moonlit places and the fond embraces. Our history books do not give it that meaning, do they? Did Cicero see it this way? But, today, the "fond embraces" would just be nice hugs if it were not for the fact that they take place in the "moonlit places" that are found in large numbers in "Rome," the places to which the singer bids farewell. So let us note that what we have here is also *spirit.* It is the *spirit* of a city that is made to be what it is by the occurrence of "embraces" in its "places." And, at the same time, the "embraces" have a romantic nature that derives from the aura of the city of "Rome" in which they take place. There are, of course, other cities that have *spirits.* We could think of San Francisco, New Orleans, New York, Paris, Granada (celebrated in a song with that title), among others.

Spirit is something that arises, like a mist from the ground, in human crowds and communities. It is in this sense just as much a human creation as is the realm of spirit that Gnosticism believed in. And it is just as aloof from historical events, notably the events to which the Old and New Testaments bear witness. In this sense, devotion to these spirits is both outside of and alien to the Christian faith.

THE SPIRIT AND THE MEGA-CHURCH

To relate the concept of *spirit* to the mega-church, we need to consider the way in which the term is used in the Christian faith. In biblical and Christian faith, the term *spirit* does not refer to a nonmaterial essence or force that is "out there." Nor is it the spirit of a nation, of a class, or of "the youth of today." Rather, the *Spirit* is always a *spirit* that moves among us. It moves among us through and by something that takes place on the plane of history. There is an event. This event occurs; it happens. It takes place within the world of objects and people, of nations and empires, of the pull and tug of groups with groups and of individuals with individuals. It takes place among people who love and hate, who face life with fear and with courage, and who seek to gain from life things that are wonderful while seeking to avoid things that are terrible. In *this* human existence in *history* these events take place. And the Spirit has to do with these events.

In the case of Israel, the history begins with the call to Abraham and continues with Moses and all the prophets. It then proceeds though the monarchy of David and through the Exile and Return. At every point, the *Spirit* of God is an acting and moving presence. It is a presence through which the actions of God that occurred in the past become effective as actions now, albeit as actions that were always complete in the past. Just as God led the people of Israel out of the land of Egypt, so exactly *as* the God who led the people then, his Spirit leads the people now. The Exodus was a completed action then, but by the *Spirit* it is effective as an action of God in the "here and now." Similarly, for Christians, Jesus was crucified and rose from the dead. His doing so was an action completed 2,000 years ago. But by the Spirit it is effective as an action now.

There is, then, this difference between the *spirits* of Gnosticism, of nations, of groups, and of the "youth of today" on the one hand, and the Holy Spirit of Jesus Christ, on the other. The former is a nonmaterial essence that people appropriate through human wisdom, through group enthusiasm, and through inner self-assertion. The latter, the Christian *Spirit,* is an event in history in which an event accomplished in the past becomes effective *as* event in the present. The God of Abraham, Isaac, and Jacob speaks through the prophets. The Father of our Lord Jesus Christ speaks to people in Jesus's Name now. The event of the past bursts forth, so to say, *as* event in the present. It is the *Spirit* that has a historical grounding.

There is a question before us, then, concerning *spirit* as known in the mega-church. The Church certainly has *spirit,* as that term is normally used. In its music, its preaching, and its groups and programs, it evinces great enthusiasm. There certainly is *spirit* in its midst! But is this *spirit* an effective reverberation in the present of what took place in the historical past? Or is it a nonmaterial "ooze" or "oomph" that unites people in a shared contemporary enthusiasm? This is an important question, for in its answer we have a response to the question whether the mega-church is Christian.

Let us say that someone visits the mega-church. She attends one of its worship services. She is a person who is familiar with how worship is carried out in other churches, including churches of different kinds. She has known the Catholic Mass, the Baptist preaching service, and all sorts of worship events that seem intermediate between those two. At the opening of the event in the mega-church, a leader, armed with guitar, will say something like "is it not a beautiful day in which to worship the Lord?" To this visitor, the words "worship the Lord" seem strange. There is something insubstantial about them. Is "worship of the Lord" indeed what is taking place here? Something is certainly happening, but is *worship* what that thing is? Somehow, the word does not seem quite right. And the person who has this problem may well be one who attends a Baptist Church one Sunday and a Catholic Mass another and has no trouble perceiving that what takes place in both of those settings is *worship.*

So why does she have this problem here at Ocean Tide Church? The answer may be that there is a self-generated enthusiasm in the mega-church that separates the spirit that is present in it from the *historical grounding* of Christianity. Certainly, there are references to the event of the Crucifixion in the prayers and songs of Ocean Tide. A line frequently heard in the songs is "I am so glad you came to save us"! And many other expressions with that same meaning will be heard. Indeed, if anything, the repetitions of it are excessive. They would make a visitor wonder whether what is taking place in that event is a real remembering of the events of the Gospel. That is, is it a remembering in which what took place in the past becomes effective *as* event in the present? And what is there in this total event that makes it an effective act of remembering of the events of the Gospel?

Consider: A man purports to love a woman. To convince her that he loves her, he says "I love you" over and over again. Would not the sheer repetition of that expression raise doubts in her mind about whether it is true? Her thinking might be that if he does indeed love her, his love would be manifest in a variety of ways. He would reveal his love in many things that he says, some not specifically intended to do so. His facial expressions and "body language" would give him away as full of love for her. In innumerable things he does, he would reveal that he has a wish for her to be happy and comfortable. There would be, we might say, many "faces" of his love for her. If all he does is repeat "I love you," he may well be reporting a *lack* of love in his heart and in his will.

Is there not something similar in the worship of the God who acts in history and who is God to us in and through these events? The worshiper would certainly want to speak of the Crucifixion and Resurrection of Jesus Christ. But he would want to talk about many other things as well. Just because this worshiper is devoted to a Lord who is "out there" and not just the product of his imagination, the worship would manifest his devotion in a variety of ways. And in each of these ways he would pause and gather the thoughts that arise from his encounter with the holiness of God and with the righteousness that is manifest in the Gospel. Then when he speaks, his utterances would be testimonies or instances of *witnessing.* The very variety of his forms of words and actions would be a finger pointed with the words uttered, "behold the lamb of God who takes away the sins of the world . . . . behold the lamb of God who takes away *my* sins!" There would be a sense of the *historical grounding* of all that is said and done. In this regard, we may note that traditional Christian hymns display a much greater variety of themes, moods, styles, and musical features than do the songs of the mega-church.

If this historical grounding is missing, what we are left with is *spirit,* pure and simple. It is a spirit that is a product of the life of the group as a group. It would arise from the interaction between people that takes place within the group and that makes it a group. As such, it would be a disembodied spirit. It would *not* be the Holy Spirit of the God of Abraham and Moses who is also the Father of our Lord Jesus Christ. In this way, the mega-church would be outside of the boundary.

The occurrence of enthusiasm is not of necessity such a disembodied spirit. The Bible has innumerable references to a joyful singing of the praises of God. Psalm 98, for example, Versus 4–6 say:

Make a joyful noise to the Lord all the earth.
Break forth into joyous song and sing praises
Sing praises to the Lord with the lyre,
With the lyre and the sound of melody.
With trumpets and the sound of the horn.
Make a joyful noise before the King, the Lord.

It is notable that these verses are an expression of the *faith of Israel.* The writer stands in the midst of the people of Israel—of the Covenant Community—and expresses himself as one of the people. Behind him are the people who fled Egypt and went through the waters. Before him is the expected action of God to vindicate his people and his Righteousness and his Justice. The writer of the Psalm is *not* an entrepreneur. He is *not* building an empire for himself based on the enthusiasm that he is generating. He is *not,* indeed, seeking to call attention to himself at all. Rather, as the writer sees it, there is Israel, and there is what God is doing for Israel. There is what God is doing to vindicate his Justice and his Righteousness. And in these actions of God, we view the history of Israel about which he wishes to "sing praises."

9

ECUMENICISM AND ITS INCLUSIVENESS: THE BOUNDARY LOOKS INWARD

If the boundary of the Christian faith looks outward and excludes philosophies, ideologies, or "spirits" that have another starting point or another ending point, it also looks inward. The Christian faith thus seeks to *include* all, beliefs, practices, and codes of conduct that are, in truth, inside its boundaries. This is just as delicate a task as is the task of looking outward. The Cross of Christ can be deprived of its power by an excessive strictness concerning unessential details (while it is *looking inward*) just as it can be weakened by the lax and limp acceptance of all faiths as being simply different expressions of "religion" (while it is *looking outward* as per the previous chapter).

THE MANY SIDES OF THE GOSPEL

We might take the Gospels as the primary example. Let's start here with the last verse of the Gospel of John (21:25). Speaking of the risen Christ, the writer says, "But there are many other things which Jesus did; were every one of them to be written, I suppose that the world itself could not contain the books that would be written." Here there is permission given for the written word (given what will eventually become the Gospels that we know today) not to include "within" its boundaries every detail. We should keep in mind that the Gospel itself is a living and growing item. It is not only the *document, the Bible,* but it is also testimony that says "look" Jesus Christ. It is the witness that the early Christians made to each other about the teachings, life, death, and resurrection of Jesus Christ and about his continuing presence among them as the people who "gathered" to remember him. And, as such, it opens the way for an evolution in definition and understanding in our own day. There is thus an *expansive character* to the Gospel, once it is out in the world.

One form of this expansion is in the number of "believers." As the writer of Acts said, "And more than ever believers were added to the Lord, multitudes both of men and women" (5:14). This increase in numbers of believers continued and, in due course, made Christianity the dominant faith in the Roman Empire and beyond. This persistent swelling of the ranks had a lot to do with why the history of Christianity came to be almost identical with the history of Western civilization.

But the expansion is in more than just numbers of adherents. It also has to do with *concepts*. As the churches increase in numbers and assume an ever-greater place in the societies in which they are found, there is a need for an *accounting* for what is going on in all aspects of the life of the church. Doctrines and practices, including liturgical traditions and moral codes, have to be made understandable. A person who wishes to explain them or to persuade another person about them has to use *words* to do so, and these words have to be derived from the concepts of the culture in which the speaker and the hearer live. To make sense of the statement that "God was in Christ, reconciling the world to himself" (2 Cor. 5:19), a person has to use words that a listener would understand, and these have to be the specific equipment of a specific culture.

Inevitably, the use of these concepts will bring the faith down from the heights of holiness and will compromise the Gospel's message. The presence of God in Jesus Christ, is, after all, far too great for the human mind to fully grasp. Human minds cannot "wrap themselves around it," that is, around the immense concept of this presence. God, by his very nature, is a mystery. He is outside of the terms or categories by which people think. The very word "God" can speak of the Lord as great, but it can also diminish him. People everywhere in the world have gods. To speak of a "god" is to use a term widely understood in many societies and cultures. The exact meaning of "god" certainly varies. In some societies, the term would refer to an impersonal sacred power, whereas in others a "god" is an entity that thinks and intends. In most societies, a "god" is a core of sacredness tied up with a particular people. Is the God of Abraham, Isaac, and Jacob just another one of these gods? There must be something that he has in common with them; how else could the prophets speak of false *gods* (idols) as compared to the True *God?* The Christian insists on a vast difference between God and the gods, but how do we account for that difference? Actually, it takes the whole Bible to account for it.

There may be reason why the Old Testament speaks of the "day of the Lord" as being a day of "clouds and thick darkness." There may be reason also to see, when we speak of God, a total contradiction between a usual conception of a powerful "lord," on the one hand, and, on the other, the humble Christ who, by an act of his own will, goes down to defeat, "even death on a cross." What is involved in these ways of speaking of God is that we are speaking of *that* which by *its* very nature cannot be spoken of. That is, no set of concepts derived from human cultures is adequate. For this reason, Christians rummage around among the items within the cultural armamentarium—the terms and ideas of a culture—in an effort to say what cannot be said. The hope is that God will reveal himself in the midst of the inadequate, confused, twisted, and bewildering ways in which people try to speak of him, that is, that God will reveal himself as being that which, by its nature, is outside the realm of human thought and human speech.

A complete history of Christian thought, of which there are several in print, would give accounts of the many ways in which Christians have sought to explain their faith. Such a history would take the reader through the uses of the Platonic and neo-Platonic metaphysics of the first 1,200 years of Christianity. It would continue with the architectonic philosophy of Aristotle, which became prominent in the thought of Thomas Aquinas in the thirteenth century. These Platonic and then Aristotelian philosophies provided major ways of organizing Christian thought. The history would then move on to the rejection of philosophy, as an endeavor of the human mind, in Martin Luther and John Calvin. Then it would move to the rich display of metaphysical (or ontological) and antimetaphysical concepts used by thinkers of the last 200 years.

For our purposes, it is enough to note here that Christians have made an effort to "capture" intellectually the act of God in Jesus Christ and hold it in the many forms of speech found in the world. This effort has never proven successful. Try as we might, we are human beings and, as such, are clumsy and stumbling in using the vocabularies we have. The hope is that God, in his mercy, will reveal himself *through* and *in spite of* our bungling efforts. A result of this effort to use the terms or categories of culture to talk about that which, by its nature, *transcends culture* has resulted in the fireworks of varying and often competing theologies. These different forms of thought are sometimes made absolute. For this reason they become mutually hostile.

Also, we may note that there are different *moments* in the gospel narrative. There is the moment in which Jesus teaches; the moment in which Jesus is crucified and the world descends into darkness, and the moment in which he is raised in glory from the dead. And as people and groups seek to run to the Gospel and put their hope in this, they always run to and cling to varying phases or moments in the unfolding of the Gospel. There is the "moment" in which a person stands accused by God of his sinfulness, and the "moment" in which he is united with God through the sacraments. The former is emphasized in the Western Roman Catholic tradition; the latter has its day with Eastern Orthodoxy, a branch of the faith that spreads its wings from Greece through Eastern Europe to Russia. The former features the crucifix, a cross with Jesus on it; the latter has ornate, reshaped crosses in which the moment of suffering and death is overwhelmed by the new union with God.

In Protestantism the Lutheran tradition, with its base in the feudal societies of northern Europe, featured the dark side of the human being. It emphasized the "moment" in which sin reigned supreme and the individual's only hope was to be justified by the grace of God. And, as one who is justified, the believer was to stand firmly and obediently in his place in civil society. He was to submit to the rule of those in authority over him. The believer transcended the law in his faith, but he lived *by* the civil law as long as he was in the temporal order. By contrast, in the Calvinist wing of Protestantism, that same commitment to "justification by faith" led to a "moment" in which all the structures of society and culture were to be constantly reformed in response to the Word of God and the lordship of Jesus Christ. This continual *reforming* was to take place in the more fluid social order of the emerging capitalist societies of central and western Europe and of the British Isles.

Similarly, in America there was a contrast between two broad forms of faith. There were the settled communities of the eastern seacoast, villages transplanted, in effect, from England. In the Congregational and Presbyterian churches of these towns, the believer put on a somber face as she contemplated a Word of God that laid claim to all of life—to government and to business and to community life. The Word of God brought the believer to a "moment" in which she, as a forgiven sinner, took the responsibility for the whole structure of community life. That whole of life was on her shoulders. As God's servant, she had serious business to attend to.

In another and a quite distinctive form of the faith, the preachers of the Gospel wandered out into the frontier where people had fled from the settled life of the East and were building farms and communities. They ventured into a zone in which life was "wild and wooly." Out there the people wanted a faith that would lift them out of the disorderly life they were living, or seeing around them, to one in which they would build communities and families. For them, the Gospel "moment" was filled with emotion as they first confronted their sins and then were released from their sins. The increased emphasis on the salvation of the individual plus the decreased concern for structuring community life (in this branch of Christianity) help to explain the rift in American Protestantism in which mainline forms of the faith are distinguished from its evangelical versions.

Out on the frontier, the Baptist lay preacher was part of a company of people who found themselves "saved by the Blood of Christ." Among them, there were a few men who were to become preachers. For these men, the "moment" was one in which they "stood out" within the company of converts to the faith. Compared to the others, these preachers-to-be were especially committed, capable, well versed in the Scriptures (there being little else to read), and gifted as speakers. Each of them was "one of" the brethren, but one who "stood out" for his enthusiasm and ability. This preacher-to-be would take up preaching and, in due course, would be provided with a small income enabling him to devote himself to the work of pastor on a full-time basis.

For the Methodist, on the other hand, the "moment" was one in which a lone individual went through the experience of "Justification by Faith." It was her journey, and hers alone. She would join with others, but the joining was secondary to the justification of the individual sinner. For this reason, church organization had an *instrumental* character. The polity or government of the church was designed to get the job done, to get the Gospel to individuals. Here, the preachers were young men who intended to make their careers via circuit riding. They went on horseback from one frontier village to another. They established churches and then traveled among these small congregations, preaching within each in its turn. In due course, some congregations became large enough to have their own pastor or to share him with only one other congregation.

In both England and America, a group that appeared around the edges of the religious scene, but did so persistently, was the Society of Friends. These folk were also known as Quakers. That latter name was applied to them because they "quaked" at the presence of God who spoke to them in the *inner light*. The presence of this group in the history of Christianity should be instructive for us. Nowhere has there been a group that appears to have veered more sharply from the doctrines that other Christians cherish. And nowhere has a company of people deviated more drastically in their ideas of how to worship (the "quiet" meeting) and of how people should relate to each other. It is also true that there are few places in the entire history of the faith where the wind that blows across the pages of the Gospels, and especially through the Sermon on the Mount, shows itself with *greater clarity and force*. Nor are there many locations in which Jesus's commands to "resist not evil," to "love your enemies," and, in general, to love all people of all kinds and in all places, have been more conspicuous. Perhaps here especially, we should think about the "moments" of the Gospels. If there was a "moment" when Jesus was crucified and raised from the dead, there was also one in which he preached the Sermon on the Mount and uttered those *rigorous* commands that call the Christian to rise above the "give-and-take" ethics of ordinary morality.

We could go on and on. The history of Christianity is a fireworks display in which the varying "moments" of the Gospels produce different forms. Each of them is, in its own way, authentically Christian. But none is the whole of the Gospel.

REVERBERATIONS IN THE LARGER CULTURE

There is another way in which the boundaries of the Christian faith look inward. This is the way the Gospel sends shockwaves through all realms of society and culture and is, for this reason, evident in its effects in zones of life that are neither religious nor Christian.

In the beginning of the Gospel of John, we read: "the Word became flesh and dwelt among us, full of grace and truth." The word flesh does not mean just a man, but men; the Word is present among human beings, men and women. By being in *a* person, the Word is in *people*. And this does not mean simply in the body, but also in everything about human beings that makes them human, their minds, hearts and spirits, their anxieties and high-voltage hopes, their hates and their loves. In *all of this* the Word of God was present. But there is more. The "flesh" here refers also to every-thing about human beings that makes them social and binds them into communities. There is the way their life together is organized in families, in neighborhoods, in nations, and kingdoms. There is also their shared or common consciousness. There are their religions and their ideologies. There is their aesthetic life complete as it is with music, art, sculpture, and poetry. There is, therefore, *culture* in its most broad and inclusive sense: social consciousness as community. Some music is religious in theme and style (such as in hymns). Other music has themes that celebrate life in other ways (such as in victory from conflict, in love with romance). So much of culture is nonreligious.

If we could think of all of this social organization and culture as being like an atmosphere (or an ocean), we could say that the Gospel sends not just ripples but huge waves of shock throughout it. What God did in Jesus Christ reverberates through the entire layer cake of ideas, sentiments, and collective images that make up a human society and its way of life. God's action has effects throughout a society and in all aspects of its culture; it permeates the cultural atmosphere. Many of these reverberations of the Gospel do not have an ostensibly Christian character; nor do they appear to be "religious." Yet they are shockwaves of the Gospel nonetheless.

An example of such a reverberation is the classic story or stories of the Lone Ranger. Or perhaps we should say of the Lone Ranger and his faith-ful Indian companion, Tonto. This is a story set in the Wild West of the United States. Although many of the people in the West were part of the overflow of population in the East and were seeking to establish in zones from Nebraska to California the same life they knew in the East, others were more the "desperado" type. These were lone men who lived a purely "adventure-seeking" lifestyle. Some were men who just had no taste for the settled life of family and community; they therefore sought to go out in search of all sorts of adventures. Some were the leftovers of the Civil War who found themselves without family or neighborhood. For them, there really was no life except one of the "kicks" of the moment. Some quite consciously sought to "live fast and die young."

In the lore of the West, there was indeed an account of someone called the "Lone Ranger," also known as the "masked rider of the plains." He was, as the expression suggests, "masked." *That is, he had no identity.* His was the pure case of the unattached man who could live as he chose. But while thousands like him sought a life of "wine, women and song," or even of "cigarettes, whiskey and wild, wild, women," he saw a different way of living, or we could say of living *out* what days he had left. He chose to devote himself to *helping* the settled people and families who were constantly running into trouble with bandits. To help them was all he wanted; it was his end goal. When he had finished a task and was talking with the people whom he had delivered from the "bad guys," he would leave immediately. The people would turn to say "thank you" to him, but when they did, he was no longer there. All they saw was the back of his horse with little puffs of dust off the horse's back feet as he rode on to his next helping assignment. He did not want anything for himself, not even to be thanked!

We can see in this fictional character an "echo" of Jesus Christ. And we see it in a zone of life in which religion is not explicitly present. The Lone Ranger did not preach, and his career did not lead to crucifixion. (Unless of course, the mere loss of identity was a death-crucifixion in itself.) But he found fullness of life by coming to the aid of his fellow human beings. He supported the establishment of family and community life, although he did so as one who lived outside of those forms of life (as do, we may note, Catholic priests and nuns). He did what he did as one who would not participate in regular life but who would help those who did. He was anonymous, just as Jesus abandoned his specific identity as the Son of Joseph and as a Jew in his Crucifixion. And the Lone Ranger wanted nothing for himself. To *help others* was the whole of life for him.

At a far more general level, the historical occurrence known as the "Enlightenment" can also be seen as a reverberation of the Christian faith. There are, of course, debates about this. Some see the Enlightenment only as a cultural action in which human beings sought to exalt their own powers of reason to the point of putting God out of the picture entirely. And the Enlightenment certainly did honor and exalt the powers of reason. And it certainly did pull away from the Evangelical view of God as active in human affairs. It abandoned that view in favor of either having no God or of having the "watchmaker" God of deism, which offered the rational belief in God to those who required this pathway. But these negatives are not the whole story. The Enlightenment thinkers were emulating, in a way, the Greek philosophers. But they did so with a difference. In fact, it has been argued that they changed one basic feature of Greek thinking. To the Greeks, *history* was unimportant, for what was important was *above* history. They saw history as cyclical. By contrast, history moved forward in a straight line according to the Enlightenment thinkers of the 1600s and 1700s. They believed in *progress*. Their thinking was, in this way, less Greek and more Hebraic. It took its clue from the biblical view of history as moving from the call to Abraham to the establishment of the Kingdom of God. Here history does not go around and around; rather, it moves forward, toward a Good Society yet to come.

This "echo" is evident in America in various ways. The statement (in the Declaration of Independence) that "all men are created equal" could be viewed as coming from the biblical faith in a God who counts each individual as infinitely precious. It could also be seen as deriving from the detached impassivity of Greek stoicism. But there is a seriousness about it that reflects the biblical encounter with a Holy God more than with the "reasonable" ontological views of the Greeks. Further, the system of "checks and balances" in the three branches of the American government derives from an understanding of human sinfulness. These checks and balances combine a concern to make government effective with a wish to keep any one person or group from claiming excessive power. The belief that such a prophylaxis is necessary derives from the biblical view of human beings as unreasonable and prone to seek excessive power or glory for themselves whenever they can. Here again, the Gospel reverberates in the layers of culture and society outside the narrow sphere of religion.

A sharp cry for justice for the poorer sections of society has been heard frequently in the last few centuries of Christian history. This began with many of the sects that made up the leftwing movements of the Reformation era (1500s, 1600s). Some of these movements were religious and others were secular. But both made a sharp trumpet-call for justice. In varying ways, they demanded a change in society in the direction of greater justice for the poor. Some seek to do this by establishing little islands of justice in the midst of an oppressive society. Others have sought to bring pressure on the larger community to change its own structure in the direction of greater social and economic equality, or, at the very least, greater justice and a better life for the poor. Opposition to slavery, for example, coupled with a concern for freed African Americans, was a feature of Protestant church life, that is, of *some* Protestant church life. It was often in the predominantly middle class groups that this appeared with the greatest force. The social gospel that began in the late 1800s and continues to this day represents this thinking. In much of neo-Orthodoxy (or neo-Reformation) thought, the theological basis changed. But the passion for justice continued. The liberation theology of Latin America (and elsewhere) that began in the 1960s reveals this passion as well. These are based on abundant biblical texts that make the same cry. Among these are Psalms 15, 72, and 82; Jeremiah 7:5–7; Ezekiel 18:5–9; and Nehemiah 5.

In these texts, justice for the poor is demanded as an *implication* of loyalty to God. Yet nowhere are "the poor" made heroes (as in Marxism), nor is concern for them made into the whole of faith in God. The focus is always on the godly community as such—as a community. Justice for the more humble within it is there as an important implication.

We see this implication again and again. In the *Jeremiah* text, the prophet says that God will be favorable to the Hebrews if they will "amend their ways." This amending consists of not worshiping foreign gods and of not oppressing the stranger, the widow, or the orphan. The writer of Ezekiel speaks of the man who "does right" as one who "does not oppress anyone, but restores to the debtor his pledge." He also "gives his bread to the hungry and covers the naked with a garment and does not take accrued interest." In *Isaiah* 58, the writer, called the "Third Isaiah," says that a "true fast" that God chooses is to let the oppressed go free and to share bread with the hungry, to bring the homeless poor into your house, and to cover the naked." Then, he says, "your light shall break forth like the dawn." In Nehemiah, the writer is a Hebrew who is in the service of the Persian King Artaxerxes. This king sends Nehemiah to be an administrator over the Hebrew exiles who have returned to Israel. In that capacity, Nehemiah notes that well-to-do Hebrews are oppressing their poorer countrymen. They do this by loaning money to the poor to pay "the king's tax." Then when the borrowers cannot repay, the lender takes their property and makes slaves of their children. As administrator, Nehemiah then compels these wealthy people to restore the poor people's property to them and to cease collecting interest on the debts. In Psalms 72:4, 12–13, the good king is seen as one who "defends the poor and needy and crushes the oppressor." Although many of the texts pertain to individual acts of charity, others enjoin political and structural measures designed to achieve justice for the powerless.

Although much of this concern for justice is an "in-house" religious or Christian occurrence, we can see reverberations of this concern in movements taking place outside the house of Christian faith. Marxism is, of course, the largest and most prominent of these. In addition, many socialist and more moderately liberal trends are examples of the same thing.

Among these are the struggles of labor unions, women's or feminist organizations, environmental organizations and movements, antiwar mobilizations, and so on. There is, of course, a question as to whether these are reverberations of the Gospel or events that would have occurred in capitalist or industrial societies without the Gospel. This is a question for which there is no definite answer, for we cannot repeat our history with Christianity withdrawn. But if we compare Western Christian-dominant culture to the great cultures of the East in which religious passion of the Christian sort has no connection whatsoever with concern for economic or "worldly" justice, we will be inclined to think that the Gospel of Jesus Christ is much involved. Note that what dominated Eastern religions was more of an acceptance of, even a detachment from, the material world.

What we see in all of these "reverberations" is that the Gospel does not just stand by itself as a "religious" event, or as a matter of "theology" or of "the Church." Rather, the action of God in Jesus Christ was something that happened in human history. And it finds expression in many and diverse parts of the social relations and cultural creations of human beings. In many cases, these expressions that are outside of the narrow realm of religion may even have a prophetic assignment and task directed *to* the religious realm, as narrowly conceived. That is, it may be a call from God to testify to *the churches* about the churches' proper calling where the churches have proved unfaithful to the command of God, as, of course, they do with some regularity.

Not everything, then, that seems inconsistent with the Gospel of Jesus Christ is fully and clearly outside of the boundary of the Church. The boundary, instead, embraces much (but not all) of the inconsistency and then looks *in* at it. There are, of course, those things, those various occurrences, not fully embraced throughout history—even recent history, For example, there is Nazism, which seems to be a more definitely pagan movement. And while these echoes of biblical faith cannot be described or honored as fully Christian, neither can they be totally dismissed as outside of the broad reach of the faith. Echoes, we may note, are not the "real thing." They are not the actual sound, but neither are they altogether alien to the sound. They are of the particular nature characteristic only of echoes. Note that the echo reflects back at—is formed in response to— the source sound. The echo is thus, by its nature, both *a derivative of* and *an oppositional counterpart to* the source sound. Some echoes are more pure than others, with nothing impeding a perfect reflection of the source sound, whereas other echoes are reflective of all sorts of interferences and even corruptions.

True, many echoes of Christianity have been lifted up and made into far more than Christianity. The *concern for justice* for the poor is cut loose from its biblical and prophetic grounding and made to be the sum and substance of the struggle. And the Christian, while sharing the interest in justice, may want to reestablish that grounding. She does so because she believes that faith in God as revealed in Jesus Christ is the only sure grounding for the passion for justice and fears that this passion may wither if it seeks to become its own basis (Cf. John 15:6). If it does not wither, it may become fanatical. That is, it may so emphasize one concern for justice as to shortchange other justice issues or other very human concerns. The Christian also wants to stay close to the biblical–Christian base because she wants to keep things in perspective. She wants to keep the concern for social and economic justice in dialectical tension with other concerns of the Gospel. The same Gospel that demands better pay and working conditions for coal miners, for example, must also "speak to" the well-to-do parents whose child has died of leukemia. It must also address people who struggle to establish order in family life. *Any* one-sided value system needs correction from other sides.

Still, Christianity has faced features that balance off other features. In much of frontier Evangelicalism, the pressure on people to stop drinking, smoking, and dancing became so great that there was little to say to sinners who did not practice those vices. Nor was there a way of looking beyond them to other issues of community concern. It also occurred, not infrequently, that pressure for the conversion of the sinner pushed the churches into a preoccupation with their own life as churches. As a result, they had little vision of how a Christian goes about living her faith in business and other nonchurch activities. And, conversely, liberal churches have often been so wrapped up in seeking to be "inclusive" of people with diverse racial, ethnic, economic, and sexual identities that they leave some of the "people in the pews" without comfort or help. These are the people who suffer from tense personal relationships or a general emptiness of life. These are also the people whose world has been changed from colorful to a drab black and white because of personal tragedies such as the death of a child. These, like all people in all Christian circumstances, look to the Gospel to see if it has something to say to them that will make a difference. To them, a presentation of Christianity that seems entirely preoccupied with tolerance (or better than just tolerance) for races, ethnic groups, genders, and sexual orientations is not wrong but certainly is, in the moment of other personal need, irrelevant. It leaves many of the people for whom Christ died "high and dry."

One-sidedness is *always* a problem. It is a problem both inside and outside of the household of faith. To be passionately concerned about a certain implication of the Gospel, as the Christian is indeed called to be, is to put the follower of Jesus Christ in a place where he needs to pause, look around, and address a different implication. This is what the advocates of liberation theology did when they coined the expression, "preferential option for the poor." Awkward as it may be, this expression was designed to hold in tension the passion for justice with a wish to include all people, *even* the rich, in the "circle of love." Such interest in the "yes but" together with the "and also" is part of our calling as Christians.

THE MEGA-CHURCH AND THE BOUNDARIES

The theme here is that the mega-church is outside two boundaries; it is neither Christian nor a church. In saying this, we may seem to violate the open and accepting spirit of modern church life. Denying the title "Christian" might seem to be, at best, pretentious and, at worst, bigoted. It certainly "goes against the grain" to utter such negative commentary about any organization, movement, or person that presents itself as "Christian." Today's culture encourages us to disapprove of polemics and to insist on tolerance for varying points of view.

Today, we do indeed live in a country where "freedom of religion" is a matter both of the spirit of the times and of the Constitution and the laws that stem from it; however, we have never before been confronted with an adversary so vigorous and so dangerous as is the mega-church. Certainly, there has been competition among varying Protestant groups. Each presents itself as having ideas about how church life should be carried out and of how "Christian living" should be promoted. And each group thinks that its ideas are, in important ways, "better" than those of others. And some think that they, and they alone, are truly Christian. And, this being the case, each would like to attract more people and especially more people who consider themselves to be Christians.

Yet there is a definite difference between (a) this competition among churches that are all Christian, and (b) the struggle to keep at bay movements that are outside the boundaries of Christianity. Some of these other-than-Christian movements exclude themselves and are, in this sense, not a problem. Groups that are exclusionary, such as Jehovah's Witnesses and Mormons, have been perceived as threats, as is evidenced by the sometimes vigorous persecution to which they have been subjected. But even here the issues are often outside the realm of religion as such. The Jehovah's Witness's refusal to participate in the nation's wars could account for some jaundiced attitude of the majority toward them. The Mormon tolerance of polygyny (or polygamy) was (and may continue to be) a far greater cause of trouble. This is true even though the main Mormon body abandoned plural marriage a century ago. It explains in part the Mormon flight from Illinois to Utah. The Masonic groups also suffered a great deal of bad repute in certain periods, although without losing appeal to many men.

In none of these cases, however, do we have a movement or trend that poses the threat to the Christian faith of the sort that occurs in case of the mega-church. Each of these alternative forms of faith appealed to groups of people who were on the margins of American cultural and social life. By contrast, the mega-church is a movement that plants itself in the very center of American cultural and social life by imitating forms of cultural expression that are the most popular and most dominating in American life. Thus it appears in the middle of American life rather than on the edge. For a model to emulate, it looks to the structures that dominate American life. It wishes to imitate whatever is *big*. It could be big business, big government, or, most suitably of all, big entertainment.

To a great degree, the mega-church models itself on the "rock concert" in which but a few performers display their talents before a massive ocean of listeners—usually young people who are adoring and enthusiastic. The mega-church aspires to duplicate the intense emotional expression and experience that arises within such oceanic gatherings. Also like the rock concert, the mega-church avails itself of music and song—of lyrics and tunes—that are simple and simplistic and that convey an overwhelming triteness. Nothing is too banal or too bereft of content to serve as the vehicle for its expressions.

The same is true of the prayers (always brief) and the sermons (always long). A great deal of ingenuity is exercised in finding clever ways of delivering a message that is supremely trite. It is not considered important to actually say something. Listeners are not asked to think or follow a sequence of ideas. Indeed, to have discernible *content* might seem to detract from the desired bombast of the moment. We may see that the audiences (the proper term) have been prepared for these mega-church performances by American television. The viewers of that medium are accustomed to advertisements in which clever ways of being silly make up an approved form of communication. They have also learned to expect news to have a "sound bite" character that demands no discernment of the listener and does not expect her to have questions or to want things to be explained step-by-step.

The mega-church is thus an archetypical American enterprise. It is supremely *modern*. It appeals to what Americans are accustomed to in business and entertainment. It is for this reason that people in such large numbers are drawn to it. And once they appear en masse, the very abundance of participants makes the enterprise appealing to still more. Bigness begets bigness.

WHY THE MEGA-CHURCH IS OUTSIDE
THE BOUNDARY

To explain why the mega-church is outside the boundary of the faith is not an easy task. In the history of Christianity, contrasts between forms of faith, those within the boundary, as well as distinctions between what is Christian and what is non-Christian, have usually been presented as matters of *doctrine*. Where battle lines are drawn, they usually divide people who hold one set of opinions from those who adhere to a different set. Points of view about God, the world, the nature of human beings, the source of evil and suffering, and the nature of salvation seem to be the prime matters of concern.

This may be, in part, a matter of how history is written. If we were well acquainted with the Gnostic movements of the second and third centuries, we might well find that they had a liturgical or cult life and an educational program that formed the real center of their activity, with their metaphysics being secondary as something designed to explain all the rest. But because historians have greater access to written documents than to cult practices and are, for that matter, inclined to think in terms of philosophies, they write history in such a way as to emphasize thought rather than liturgics.

In the case of the mega-church, the primacy of doctrine or "thought" must fade away because the life of the mega-church, by its nature, retires doctrine to a place at the bottom of the list of concerns. Its leaders and followers can espouse rather traditional or conservative views. But they do so, not because they care passionately about the views they affirm, but precisely because they do *not* care with passion, or at all. Just as a person who loves music will often sing a song without being concerned with the words, since it is, to him, just music, so the preachers and the listeners in the mega-church can sing "saved by the Cross," without being concerned with the meaning. They do not care about "justification by faith" in such a way as to stand on it, defend it, elaborate on it, or even to preach on it. In this way, the mega-church is either entirely nondoctrinal, or, at most, it espouses only a doctrine "lite"—a minimal real doctrine.

Actually, this lack of or minimal attention to doctrine is a big part of the mega-church's appeal. To take a stand on anything, whether doctrinal or moral, is to gather a set of people who are like-minded. But it is also to repel another set, those who are otherwise minded. The genius, if this is the right term, of the mega-church is to settle into a place where there is no strong stand on anything and therefore no stand that will alienate some of the potential "constituents." The music and other features of the church then provide the church's appeal to very large numbers of people.

This being the case, we must look elsewhere for specific features of the mega-church that identify it as either within the boundaries or outside the boundaries of Christianity. We could begin by noticing the abundant ways in which the mega-church chooses to distinguish itself from others. Bill Hybels announced this intention when he said early in his career that a traditional church service would be a "turn off" for people not accustomed to it, and for this reason something very different was needed. Accordingly, he fashioned his "seeker" services to be of a quite different sort. These events would, by intention, be more familiar and understandable to a person who had not been to church in many years—or ever. Everything about these services would be different from the "usual" and would supposedly be more attractive.

The mega-church rejects all of the usual paraphernalia of churches. The building itself would not look like a church. Rather, it would bear a close resemblance to a corporate headquarters. Inside, there would be no pulpit that would look like a pulpit, nor would there be crosses or other of the usual symbols or objects seen in Christian churches. Neither would there be an organ; instead the music would be provided by guitars, drums, and, in general, the instruments found at rock concerts. The place where the events take place is called an "auditorium" rather than a "sanctuary." These features, along with the totally unfamiliar music, would distinguish the operation so sharply from the usual church that a visitor would see no resemblance.

This is evident especially in Ocean Tide Church (note again, this is not its real name) of which we have spoken in other chapters. Years ago, it was a standard Baptist church and had a building that a passer-by would easily recognize as being a church. With long, sloping walls on the outside, it seemed rather like a tent—a traditional symbol of the belief that Christians are people who are "just passing through" this world. In its setting it was really quite beautiful and expressive, probably one of the better architectural presentations of Christianity in a modern, urban setting. Some years ago, however, that building was torn down. It may have been too small for the burgeoning congregation, although by most standards, it was rather large. It was then replaced by a building that is altogether nondescript. It is without special personality of any kind. It could indeed, be a corporate headquarters.

Do these efforts to leave behind a whole host of objects and practices that are reminiscent of Christian churches put the mega-church outside the boundary of Christianity? Although tempting, this question cannot be answered in the affirmative. There is no guarantee that every expression of faith in Christ crucified and the reverberations of that faith in worship and in ethics will always look like churches as we usually think of them. Many Protestant churchgoers will be dismayed at the events that take place in the most "mega" of mega-churches. But they might have similar trouble with a Catholic High Mass and with a noisy Pentecostal service. They might be quite bewildered, and even bored, in a quiet Quaker meeting. Discussions of whether the mega-church worship is good and right are certainly legitimate. But we do not perceive the presence of Jesus Christ in our world with enough clarity to say that the "bombast" of the mega-church is outside the boundary of Christianity. If we do not like that bombast, we may recall that in the Old Testament, one of King David's wives (Saul's daughter), Michal, was disdainful of David's participation in ecstatic dance. She regarded it as being undignified for a king (2 Sam. 6:20–23)! Bombast was not unknown in Israel. Indeed, it was the special role of groups of "prophets" to display ecstatic outbursts. In this, they played a role different from that of the priests who were to devote themselves to formal ceremonies.

There remains one feature of the mega-church that will provide the basis for putting it outside of the boundary of Christianity. A Christian attending a mega-church may have sensed that something was badly amiss. But if this Christian is open to diversity in expressions of this faith, she will not be able to "put her finger on it." Nor can she even be sure that her intuitions are correct. This remaining feature is *the mega-church's project of becoming very large.* We say *project* quite seriously, for we do not assert that simply being large puts a church outside the boundaries of Christianity. We may be skeptical or even critical of churches that seem to be overgrown, so that they lose the character of being congregations. But we cannot say that they desert the faith in being so bloated. Rather, what does bring about the real rupture is the *intention,* conceived early on, to become very large. Large size *as an objective* is the problem. Some might think that there is little difference between the fact that an enlargement occurs and its being intended, but we assert here that this intention is the very crux of the matter.

We can see why. The objectives of ministers of the Gospels and Evangelists are many and varied. A Methodist wants personal piety, while the Baptist wishes for people to form independent "gatherings" in which the Holy Spirit is present. The Quaker and other sectarians want "simplicity" of life, while the Catholic has in mind a people who stand in awe of a majestic Church and its impressive array of bishops, popes, and traditions. Innumerable other examples of this variety could be given. But nowhere among these objectives will we find that growing to a large size is one of them. It is simply not a Christian objective, nor is it one that an authentic Christian pastor would ever set for herself.

There are cases where church workers set "goals" in terms of membership of churches, of church attendance or of financial contributions to be received. This setting up of goals is common, especially in the Methodist tradition. Such striving is dubious, but it is not by its nature wrong. Church leaders could just be saying that if a minister and congregation are sufficiently energetic and full of Christian warmth and love, they will probably bring in a certain number of people. Or if the Gospel is so proclaimed that the thunder of God's presence lifts people out of their mundane lives into something that is much better, a goodly company of folk is likely to gather. It is another matter entirely, however, when *unrestrained and indefinite growth* is itself *an objective.* This is *never,* in itself, Christian.

Once becoming very big is set as a *goal,* a minister or other leader is constrained by the exigencies of achieving that goal. The goal controls *him.* What he will do and will he will not do, what he will emphasize and what he will not emphasize, is determined by that which will "work" in maximizing attendance or membership. The goal has sovereignty; it commands "do this" and "do not do that." It does not allow other objectives to come on the scene and speak. It pushes them into silence. It allows no concerns about Truth or Justice to be heard. The minister himself, confident as he may seem to be, is in fact beholden entirely to the floods of people who may or may not swell his constituency.

Missing here is the sovereignty of the Gospel of the revelation of God in Jesus Christ. An authentically Christian evangelist or minister is always under the constraint of the Gospel. She is never free to pursue other objectives with hefty commitment. Whatever she does, she must put her activities under the rule of the Gospel. The Gospel must always come into view as sovereign and, indeed, as *all* that matters. Of course a minister, being human and beset by anxiety, may fail to do so. She may swerve from the "straight and narrow" in an effort to achieve prosperity or prestige. Leaders of a congregation may similarly be alert to the "place" of their church in the status ranking system of the community. But in principle she and they remain beholden to the Gospel. Thus Paul said that he is under "constraint" to preach the Gospel. He therefore gets no personal credit for doing so and cannot brag about doing it. And because he would like to brag a bit, but *just* a bit, although to do so is foolish, he supports himself by his craft (tent-making) and seeks none from the churches (1 Cor. 9:16). The constraint then, is to "preach the Gospel," not to build a large church.

To put it another way: The people in a congregation should be aware of each other and of the minister as holding and pursing Gospel values—*other than and distinct from* being a numerically "successful" congregation—or *enterprise.* They should be aware that their calling as a congregation is to point away from themselves as a congregation to him who is their Lord. It is to be, above all else, *faithful.*

Also notable about a mega-church's *project* of becoming very large is that it puts a barrier between it and other Christian churches that is far greater than the walls that divide the churches from one another. The minister will no longer think of himself as "one of" the ministers of the community, nor will his church be "a" church in the city that it calls home. Both minister and church will see themselves as unique and set apart from all others. This distinctiveness might be attributed to the *imperialism* of the mega-church. It seeks to grow and, in fact, does grow so vigorously that it cannot avoid being viewed as competing with surrounding normal-size congregations. It will see itself that way; certainly other congregations and their ministers will see it that way. This will inevitably hold up a barrier of a sort and of a power of a kind that does not divide other churches.

But there is more to it than just this. There is the fact that the mega-church defines itself as qualitatively different from other churches. It is not just a church with more members or larger attendance than others. Rather, it is a different *kind* of operation. A boundary has been set. On one side are the Christian churches. There is among them a great variety in worship and personal piety, in doctrine, in forms of organization, and in relations to the larger community. There is also among them a great display of varying motives and great mixtures of faithfulness to the Gospel with all kinds and degrees of failure to be faithful. But in all, the Gospel is present, and, with it, a Lord who continually reasserts his sovereignty in the midst of confusing human motives and intentions. In the mega-church, however, the project of growing ever larger has been put on the throne, which rightfully belongs to the Church's Lord. The project of growth has established itself as Lord of the mega-church.

Jokes have been told about the people of one church going to heaven and thinking that they are the only ones there. The fierce and often destructive attitudes of Protestants and Catholics toward each other—to mention only one division—are quite serious. Yet there has always been a way back. The bridges between the groups have never been completely burned. With all of their mutual hostility, Catholics and Protestants have always been *interested* in each other. Each has seen a real, even if alienated, form of Christianity in the other.

It is this *way back* that is missing in the case of the mega-church. When its leaders determined that they must grow indefinitely, they burned the bridges that led back to authentic Christianity. They are now "mega" *rather than* Christian churches. Indeed, they are "mega" rather than Christian, and they are "mega" rather than churches. What they are, rather, is entertainment businesses masquerading as churches. And because they, unlike the usual entertainments, put on a facade of church, they exist in opposition to, as an enemy of, the worldwide Christian church.

10

———

A THEOLOGICAL BASELINE

If the mega-church is not Christian, as we have said, we must have a clear idea of just what we think the label *Christian* involves and implies. Only if we have an idea of what the contours of the faith truly are can we see clearly enough to deny that title to any person, organization, or set of ideas. To make such a denial is a serious matter. If a church says it is Christian, and we say that it is not, we must have a firm basis for our negative attitude. Without such a firm basis, our denial could be the worst form of presumption. If it takes some daring to say "I am a Christian," it must take even more to assert that "the other person is not a Christian." We must have a good idea of what is involved in *being Christian* in order to be bold enough to say that something else—or someone else—*is not Christian*. And we need to establish and maintain a place to begin, a way of knowing this, a *theological baseline* for any such endeavor.

DIFFERENTIATING WHAT IS CHRISTIAN

Of special urgency in this undertaking is to make the assertion and establish the point that *knowledge* of what is involved in the Gospel is important. If we wish to be faithful to God and to the Gospel, there are things that we need to *know*. The Christian faith is not just an instance of "religion," and being Christian is not just one case among many ways of being "religious." Nor is being Christian merely a matter of being enthusiastic. Nor can we simply put on a pious facial expression and utter religious-sounding words and phrases. We need, in addition to all of our expressions of zeal, to *understand* and to *describe* how that which is Christian may be set apart or distinguished from that which is not Christian. This ability to understand and describe is especially important here because knowledge is devalued within the mega-church movement. Here, in this inquiry, we come to the heart of the distinction between God and mega-church activities in the name of God.

Author Lyle Schaller, who discusses church growth in his book, *From Cooperation to Competition,* distinguishes "losers" and "winners" in the coming "competition." The seminary-trained person, even the highly dedicated seminary-trained person, will be among the "losers" in the competition about to take place. People whose expertise is in business and not in theology will, on the other hand, make up the company of "winners." David Wells begins his book entitled *No Place for Truth* with a discussion of students in a theological seminary who doubt that a course in theology has enough value for fledgling ministers to justify the expense to the seminary of providing the course. Common to both of these statements, that of Schaller and those of Wells's students, is a belief that the nature and content of the Christian faith are purely and simply obvious. There is no need for scholars or thinkers to spell out what is involved in it, nor is it required that the Christian faithful learn and master a body of content pertaining to it. It is simply "there."

In the face of this anti-intellectual approach to the substance of Christianity, the case must be made that there is such a thing as understanding—or failing to understand—the Christian faith. And if understanding is preferable to its absence, it is also necessary that there be thought and scholarship pertaining to the subject. We must value being able to differentiate between that which is Christian and that which bears a superficial resemblance to Christianity but is not Christian. Otherwise, we throw ourselves, expecting to swim, into a murky sea of misrepresentations and spiritual (if that) ambiguities.

THE "WHY" OF THEOLOGY

Behind this insistence on knowledge of the faith is the observation that human beings and human groups are always generating *spirits* of one kind or another. It is by so doing that they emerge as groups rather than just as collections of individuals. If we say that there is "school spirit" at "Primrose U," we mean that the "U" is a *reality* and is one to which the students *belong*. There is the thing, and then certain people are "part" of that thing. The "U" is not just a collection of academic customers at a scholarly retail outlet. And it is the "spirit" of a nation that makes it a nation rather than just a place where a bunch of people live and in which they set up a government for their common benefit. Wherever there are such spirits, there is a feeling of belonging. And there is also a feeling of goodness and even of holiness. To have the *spirit* and to be moved by it is considered good and worthy of honor *in itself.* The sensation of righteousness is spawned.

Those who are moved by the spirit of a group (nation, community, family) fall in line with three features of group life. First, they think of the *group as a "thing"* that has a "welfare," and they are motivated to work for or "serve" the group and what is considered to be its "good." Quite often an individual who sacrifices something for the group is given special honor, as illustrated by the praise of soldiers who risk their lives in war. Second, they live by a *code of conduct* that has arisen within the group. This code consists of an elaborate set of ideas about what a person is supposed to do under certain circumstances such as when and whom he should marry. Much of this code consists of taken-for-granted ideas about good and bad, although some of it is codified as *law.* And, third, there is a *hierarchy.* Some people are "up" in honor, prestige, and authority, whereas others are "down" and still others are in between "up" and "down." And the high rank of those at the top is itself sanctified by the spirit while those at the bottom view their humble or despised place in the community as sacred or as the will of God or of the gods.

Such a *spirit* of a group or community serves a purpose. It enables people to live together in relative harmony. And it fortifies them to resist outside forces, whether natural or human, that would destroy the group *as* a group. In this sense, the spirit embodies the "good" and the "right." If some have more prestige and power, it is for the "sake of the group" that they are endowed with these attributes and privileges, for they supply administrative services that maintain order and pattern within the life of the group.

But then something goes wrong. The hierarchy, in effect, takes over. The people within a community who enjoy high rank in the ladders of prestige and power appropriate the *spirit* for their own purposes. Although the hierarchy exists for the benefit of the group as a whole, the elite groups come to see their superior rank within the community as their due. It is a superiority to which they feel that they are entitled. As they see it, they have a *right* to be "up" while others are obligated by the gods to be "down." For this reason, they elaborate royal courts, build elaborate structures with which to glorify themselves, and elaborately project their positions as rulers as being all important.

And then, having lifted themselves to positions of power and glory, they, in effect, pick up a lasso and throw it around the head of the *spirit*. They get control of the *spirit* and of all that pertains to it—ceremonies, physical objects that serve as symbols, and ideas or explanations. Although originally, *spirit* had to do with maintaining the group as a group, it is now "domesticated" and recruited to the service of the ruling elites, whatever they are. The spirit is no longer free, and it is no longer a force binding the community into true community. It now sanctifies and preserves the order by which the top echelon in the community—society—"lords it over" the remainder of the community. The state of affairs in which the king with his royal court is on top and all others are arranged under him in the hierarchical order is defined as the sacred order. In effect, *God* or the gods and that *hierarchical order* are coextensive. The spirit is the spirit of that community and of its hierarchical structure. However, where God is said by those "at the top" to extend down into human hierarchies, for reasons of exalting themselves into presumed holiness, we have worship of something other than God. In the language of the Bible, the word for this is *idolatry,* the sin of worshipping something other than the monotheistic God.

But this is not the model of the Spirit spoken of in the Bible; that Spirit (with a capital "s") is *free.* God, through his Spirit, calls the people of Israel to be his special people. He declares that they will be his people and he will be their God. But he is not tied to their social hierarchy or their codes of conduct. He is not even tied to their existence as a people, as is indicated by several references to the possibility that he may destroy them and raise up another and more faithful people. He remains always sovereign, all-powerful, and righteous. No human hierarchy, no religious or political hierarchy, takes on any part of his rule, his will, his role.

The people who follow him are free. His will—what he commands his people to do and to be—is of a certain sort. It is his will that they live *as* community. The very idea of the Good or the Right, in effect, *means* community. Actions are right to the extent that they provide for and promote this binding together. They are bad to the extent that they disrupt or destroy community. In this framework, hierarchies can exist. Codes of conduct certainly have a place. But both the hierarchy and the codes exist for the sake of, and *only* for the sake of, the community. They have no value of their own apart from the community. Kings do not have any inherent right to rule. They rule only for the sake of the people over whom they rule. Kingship is a means to an end, not an end in itself (Cf. 1 Kings 12:6–7). And codes of conduct are not established as a set of arbitrary decrees of God. The rules facilitate relationships within the community and, in this sense, are servants of the community just as are the rulers.

If this is true of kings and kingship, it is also true of community as community. Properly, the community is not a thing—a reality in itself. It is, rather, a collection of people, or perhaps we should say, of persons. It is made of individuals and in the final analysis, it is the individuals who matter. How any factor of common life affects individuals is therefore the final test by which the factor is evaluated. True, we often speak of the community as such. We even treasure the community itself. But we do so because we speak of many individuals and not just of one or of a few. A person may, at some point, risk or give her life for the community (family, nation). But we mean by that remark that she sacrifices herself as one person for the sake of a large number of individual people. It is a case of "one" compared to "many." The soldier who holds the enemy at bay with her weapons while her buddies escape and does so at the sacrifice of her own life is, in effect, counting many "ones" to be more important than one "one." In this sense, to do something for America is of necessity to do something for Americans, for *persons,* lots of them perhaps, but nonetheless for individual persons. This sacrifice is not for a thing, but for many human lives.

If, then, we separate the concept of Right or the Righteous from particular hierarchies or codes of conduct, we necessarily mean that it has to do with individual human beings. It may have to do with large numbers of them, but even so the concern is for individual human beings. And if we say that we also treasure the bonds of family and friendship by which individuals are bound together, the same principle remains. We treasure the individuals who are thus bound, and we treasure them *as* bound to others in relationship. But these relationships are *of* individuals to each other and only *of* individuals. There is no "relationship" that exists independently of the individuals who are related. Similarly, there is no "America" that exists independently of *Americans.* When a king and his royal establishment claim that their positions are sacred and holy, they, in effect, bring the *Spirit* (the sacred, the gods) down and make that Spirit captive to their established relations. A leash is put on the Spirit—as on a puppy or a dog—to keep it under control. But when the *Spirit* is free, it is not bound to such structures. A society ruled by a Spirit that is independent of that society *as* a society is going to be more egalitarian. Not being tied to existing structures of "up" and "down," it values all individuals in the same way. In this sense, it values them equally. If there are hierarchies, with kings or other officials, those hierarchies exist only for the benefit of the community. *The human-designated rank-orders have no value or dignity in themselves.* People who are "up" in authority are so because it is of benefit to the community for them to be so.

Similarly, codes of conduct exist for the sake of, and only for the sake of, the community. These codes exist for the sake of the individuals who make up the community. These codes exist for the benefit of individuals in that each of them is joined with all the others in a structured or patterned way of living. But that structure or pattern has no value in itself. It is good only to the extent that it enables individuals to live together both as individual decision makers and as persons bonded with others in ties of affection and loyalty.

When the concept of the *Right* or of the *Righteous* is freed from its binding to particular social structures and cultural patterns, it tends, by its nature, to take on a certain content. It tends to favor equal justice with regard to the *goods* that are distributed unequally in virtually all human societies. It favors a comparative equality in the distribution of food, clothing, shelter, and the other things that people need to live comfortably. It also favors allowing men and women a maximum ability to make important (and unimportant) decisions for themselves, consistent with the good of the larger number. And it favors a generous allocation of respect and dignity to all in the community, including, or perhaps especially, to those who may not appear to have a claim on the dignity.

We speak, then, of a Spirit that is *free* relative to social structures and cultural patterns. And we speak of Righteousness and doing Right that are similarly *unbound* to forms of social relations and to the codes by which people live.

THE GOD OF THE BIBLE AND THE SPIRIT

We could distinguish the True God from the "gods of the peoples" in these terms. We could say that the True God is alone and aloof from human communities and from all that they contain. The True God, that is, is aloof from the social hierarchies by which some people are thought to be "above" others while those others are believed to be "beneath" them. As far as God is concerned, these hierarchies are some business—and busy-ness—of human beings and of no concern to him. There is no reason to have a king unless the existence of the king is of benefit to the people over whom he rules. The True God is also alone and aloof relative to the detailed codes of conduct by which people live. He is not opposed to the ordering of social relationships. Indeed, he favors the peace among people that is made possible by a dependable set of prescriptions pertaining to relationships among people. But these patterns of social relations, for example, marriage, are valued for their ability to facilitate peaceful relations among people. They do not have any value in themselves.

But how did we come to this idea about what the True God, the Creator of Heaven and of Earth, is like? Did we see that such a god is necessary for the peace of the world and therefore set up the aloofness of God as a standard by which to measure the gods people worship? If so, we have here a bit of human wisdom. We think that by wisdom of mind and tenderness of spirit we have managed to set up this standard for judging the gods people worship.

This, however, is *not* how we do things. We do *not* have a standard that we have devised and that can then be used to distinguish the True God from the "gods of the nations," for actually, we do not have in our minds an image or idea of such a god. Our minds will never, in a million years, concoct such an image of a god. For us, the very idea of "god" is too tied up with social structures and cultural patterns. We cannot, by our own powers of mind and heart, rise above the provincial gods to which we give our loyalty. We see evidence of this in the tenacity with which peoples who are at war cling to the belief that the groups to which they belong are "superior" and completely right and justified in what they do.

In biblical and Christian faith, we do not seek God and find him. Nor do we, by wisdom of mind and by nobility of spirit, seek and find righteousness. Rather, *God* seeks and finds *us*. *His* actions in looking for us precede anything that we can do, and it precedes everything that we, in fact, do. In the Bible, it is always *God* who does something. *God* speaks to Abraham. *God* commands Moses. *God* raises up David and his descendants. *God* appoints prophets to speak his Word. *God* sends his Son Jesus Christ. In all of these sentences, the subject is God; an action of God is the predicate, and a human person or group is the object. By God's action, and only by God's action, the True God becomes a category of thought and an idea that human beings can form and hold in their minds.

The idea of a God who is "free" and aloof from the structures of human community life is then a gift from God. It is not a "conclusion" of our incisive reasoning or the fruit of our morally sensitive insights and thoughts. We do not arrive at God by human design. Anything we do arrive at is at best a human *description*—not God but merely a description. Anything that projects itself as being God itself—when all it is turns out to be a way of speaking about God—is not God.

Of course, we must use words to speak of the God who stands aloof from human communities and their patterns for living. Consider three basic Christian ideas or doctrines: the Incarnation, the Trinity, and the Two Natures of Christ.

The Concept of Incarnation

In the doctrine of *Incarnation,* we have the belief that God is present in the whole life and being of Jesus of Nazareth. God, or God as the Son, who *is* God, is identical to the existence of Jesus of Nazareth. The idea "God-as-Son" and "Jesus of Nazareth" correspond exactly. The classic term by which this is expressed is *Incarnation.* That term may have a somewhat static connotation. It may suggest something that simply *is.* In this sense it has something of a Greek aura about it. It may give us an image of one thing, God, being impressed on another, a particular man named Jesus. But in biblical terms, *Incarnation* has a more dynamic meaning. It suggests an event rather than a state of being. God, or God as the Son, is present and active in Jesus of Nazareth. We may think here of the golfer who hits the ball with his club while the ball sits on the ground. The hitting end of the golf club swings in an arc. For a split second, the path of the hitting end is parallel with the ground. That is the point at which it hits the ball. God, similarly, is above human history. But he moves parallel with the world at the point of contact with the world through Jesus of Nazareth. The Incarnation is, in this sense, a movement and not a state of being.

It is to the end of establishing this point that two of the four Gospels, Matthew and Luke, give birth narratives of Jesus. These accounts of Jesus as a baby appear only in those two Gospels and are not referred to anywhere else in the New Testament. Moreover, the two accounts have very little in common. They both give genealogies of Jesus, but the two lists of Jesus's ancestors are not consistent. Matthew speaks of Joseph taking the baby Jesus to Egypt. Luke makes no mention of that journey. And in neither case is any hint given as to how the writers *knew* what the birth of Jesus was like.

But the two accounts do have one thing in common. In both cases, the intent is to establish that Jesus is the Son of God (the Incarnation) from the moment of his birth and through his entire life. His existence as a human being is, in and of itself, Immanuel—the presence of God with us—that is, within human beings. There is no possibility of separating the Holy Spirit (the Spirit of which Jesus was "full") from Jesus himself. To speak of "God" and to speak of "Jesus" is to talk about the same thing. There is no separation between them.

But let's look more closely at this nonseparation. What is denied by this nonseparation is that there is a "spirit" or "Spirit of God" that we can think of by itself and in separation from the events of the Bible (and supremely from the life of Jesus of Nazareth). If there were such a "Spirit," we could speak of that Spirit itself. We could pay attention to it for its own sake. And then, having focused on the Spirit itself, we could suggest that Jesus embodied the Spirit in certain ways and to certain degrees, or that he taught about it, or that he exemplified it in his behavior and in his words. We would, in all of these cases, be thinking of Spirit in one corner, so to say, and Jesus in another. We do so with the idea of combining them in some way.

And if this were the case, we could think, talk, and write about the Spirit as a distinct entity or being. It would have characteristics and qualities of its own. We could talk about the Spirit by itself. And we could then consider ways in which Jesus may have helped, and may now help, us to understand the Spirit. Or Jesus could help us "see" what the Spirit is like or how to make contact with the Spirit. We have, let us say, the Spirit, and we have Jesus and Jesus may help us to understand the Spirit.

In this case, the Spirit is, in principle, under our control. We have an idea of this Spirit in our minds, and we can talk about it as an idea that we have in our minds. And as it is an object of our thought, we can mold and shape it to fit our purposes. As members of a community, it can become, for us, the spirit of our community. It could come to rest on our social hierarchies, giving them a sanctity that helps to preserve them in times of upheaval. It could merge with our codes of conduct, making these codes and the items in them sacred and holy in themselves. The Spirit could come to rest on or merge with the community that we make up. God, that is, the Spirit, could be identified with the country or nation. "America" and "under God" could become synonyms, two expressions that mean the same thing. The result of this is that people feel that they are fighting for the Spirit, indeed, for God, when they wage war against other nations.

To separate the Spirit from Jesus, then, is to bring the Spirit under our control. It is to *tame* the Spirit of God. But when we treat the Spirit as being identical with the life and actions of Jesus, we view the Spirit as having pulled away from us. We no longer have it under our control. It is now independent of us and of everything about us. It cares nothing about our social hierarchies, or views them only as arrangements that may be useful to promote peace and order within a community. The Spirit is not attached to our codes of conduct. It views them as it views the hierarchy, as useful for ordering human life and making that life peaceful. It affirms the nation as an object of loyalty only insofar as doing so pulls people out of their selfishness and enables them to work for the benefit of many people—the community. It takes an especially jaundiced view of "fighting for" the nation, because this occasions a callous indifference toward people who are not of the nation and encourages violence arising from differences of opinion between nations. It puts a question mark beside all sentences in which people in nations explain why their nations are "right" in their conflicts with other nations.

When John the Baptist cried out "behold the Lamb of God" (John 1:29), he pointed us to a reality that can stand aloof from and therefore can challenge our ethnocentrism and our nationalism. We are reminded that we have a Lord who is Lord. And he, just as he is, is a person who is the very presence of God with us. And as such, he is, in his very nature, a challenge to our personal pride and our nationalistic chauvinism.

The Trinity

The concept of the Trinity, like that of the Incarnation, arises from the restless mixing of Hebraic and Greek civilizations. The Greek thought in terms of "down" and "up." The "down" was the world as we know it, full of flux and change and of trouble and pain. The "up" was a realm of infinitely dense, pure being. In this realm, there is no flux or change, nor is their trouble and pain. In a variety of philosophies, Platonic, Aristotelian and stoic, the task of human beings is to *rise* above the lower sphere of trouble to the higher realm of pure being and of bliss.

By contrast, the Hebrew always thought in terms of a God who was active in history. Indeed, the Hebrew could not think of "God" at all except *as* One who was active in named and dated historical events. God is the God *who* made the call to Abraham. He is the God *who* called Moses to the lead the people out of Egypt. He is the God *who* appointed the prophets to warn the people, *who* punished the people and *who* promised that one day he would restore them and vindicate them "in the sight of the nations." This horizontal view of God is constant throughout the Bible. Nowhere in those documents do we find a discussion of God as God (except James 1:17). God is always cited as the one who does things in the sequence of events that we call *history*.

So what happens when this "up" and "down" view of the divine meets and mixes with the "before" and "after" view of God? What can happen and what does happen is the construction of the concept of the *Trinity*. God is one and God is three. God is three and God is one. There are not three gods, for this is just one God. But this one God does not abide in static unity, for he is God *as* the Father, God *as* the Son, and God *as* the Holy Spirit. And just as the Father is God, so the Son is God, and the Holy Spirit is God. We have here a way of thinking of the Hebrew God who is active in historical events and of the Greek "vertical" God at the same time.

As a way of thinking of the Trinity, we might imagine that we have a friend named Maggie. Our friend Maggie is, in her entire being, Maggie. She knows herself with all of her thoughts and feelings, all of her fears and anxieties, all of her wishes and longings. And she knows herself, with all of this, to be *Maggie*. She has a Maggie nature in her entire being. But there is something else that she is. She is also our friend. She is "friend" to me or to you (or both). She is "Maggie" for us and to us and with us. And while this "for-to-with us" feature of Maggie can be distinguished from Maggie in herself, the "for-to-with" is still Maggie. It has a definite Maggie-nature. So Maggie is Maggie *in herself,* and she is Maggie *to us.* There are, in this sense, two versions of "Maggie."

God, similarly, is plural. God is God in himself. He is the Lord of Heaven and Earth. As such, he dwells in aloof majesty. He is complete in himself. He is infinite in being, in power, in glory, and in majesty. He is, as tradition puts it, God the Father. But he is also God to us, for us, and with us. He is God in the specific and special sense of being *our* God. He is also God in the sense of being the *world's* God. He is that about God by which God created the world—the heavens and the earth. He is the Word who was with God in the beginning, and it is by him that God created all that is (John 1:1–5).

The Bible uses a number of terms to refer to this "with us" and "with the world" aspect of God. It—or he—is the *Son* of God. He is the *Word* of God. In many references, he is the *Name* of God (Ps. 20:1). He, or better, she is the WISDOM of God (Prov. 8–9 in which God's Wisdom is female). He is the *Presence* of God. He is the *Spirit* of God. And he is even the *Law* of God, as we see in Psalm 119. In all of these, he is God in the sense of being *our* God. He is the God who creates us. He is the God who expects us to have faith in him. He is the God who commands us and expects us to obey. He is the God who makes promises to us and is always faithful to his promises.

For the Christian, Jesus is the Word of God. As a person and as the Person who he is, he is Immanuel—God with us. He is "Word of God now in flesh appearing." And, as we have seen, he is the Word of God in his entire existence and being as a man, as a human being. And since all human beings are bound together by their common humanity and their relatedness, in being "in" Jesus, He is also the Word of God "with" human flesh as such, that is, with all human beings. By being *in* Jesus, God is *with* us.

Central to this thesis that God is *our* God in Jesus Christ is the statement that the God who is thus with us is altogether and completely *God*. He is full God. He is not an emissary of God, as with someone sent by a king to negotiate with a foreign government for him. He is not a representative, as when a defending attorney represents a person accused of a crime. He is not a substitute or stand-in, as when an important woman has a member of her staff *stand in* for her at a meeting or a ceremonial occasion. He is altogether and fully *God*. He is God as the Son. But *as* the Son, he is God.

The alternative to this would be to see the Son of God as a high and exalted being, but even so as a being who is subordinate to God the Father. He is a highest being *under* God. This view that the Son is a next-in-line under God the Father is associated with the name of Arius, who was active in the fourth century of Christianity. It would seem to have a logic that would commend it to us. But Christians were adamant in the 300s, and are now adamant, that the Son of God is fully God and not an underling, even one who is highly exalted.

Although this subtle point may now seem abstruse, it was a life-and-death matter for early Christians. If Jesus as the Son of God can be a "son" in the specific sense of one who is subordinate to the Father, the sovereignty of God-in-Jesus Christ is fatally compromised. If the Son of God is under God the Father, then other exalted beings can have a parallel position under God on High. Jesus could be God's emissary in charge of religion, which is to say of ceremonies and rituals. The emperor, then, could be a parallel emissary in charge of governmental administration. A third person might be God to the army, and a fourth might be in charge of arts and music. In all of this, it would appear that God the Father is over all of the "sons" and is in charge of all. In fact, however, the "higher" authority over the "sons" would be something on earth. It would be the empire, for it is the empire that has these diverse functions—ceremony, administration, the military, and the arts.

Once, again, we are back to a *spirit* of the world. If the Jesus as the Son is "under" the Father, the *spirit* that governs all things is distinguishable from Jesus. Even if Jesus "gets in on the action," as we say, he is still just vice president in charge of ceremonies, He is subordinate to the *spirit* by which the empire is formed and shaped as an empire. It is the spirit that gives unity to ceremonies, administration, the military, and the expressive arts.

We recognize Jesus as Lord, then, when we insist that the Son of God is altogether *God.* For Christians, he is either fully God or he is not God at all. There can be no compromise. And as God the Son, He is God in a dialectical tension with God the Father. Yet in this tension, he is God. And by insisting that Jesus as the Son of God is fully *God,* we make sense of a Hebraic faith in a God who is active in history when speaking with Greek people who think in terms of a god who is "up" as compared to a world that is "down."

But what about the Holy Spirit, the Third Person of the Trinity? In the Christian tradition, there are two basic meanings of this term. The first has to do with the Gospel as being a gospel for people, for each of us. In the Gospel, we speak of God as active in events in history, culminating in the career of Jesus Christ. But we may imagine that all of the Gospel has been written on a paper. The paper has been folded and put into an envelope. An address is written on the envelope. The address is blurred, but as it becomes clear, each of us sees that the address is hers individually. The Gospel appears as a message that is addressed specifically, especially and above all to each individual. God appears in the specific guise of being *my–your–her* God. Each of us is lifted up as though she were the whole of humanity. Each becomes, that is, of infinite or unconditional importance.

This importance, which reaches up to the heavens and down into the depths, is an event in a person's inner life. It is not something external to him, as when a person who is accused of a crime has "counts against him," written pieces of paper that are recorded and "on file" in an office somewhere. Nor is it like an accused person's exoneration, which is similarly written and recorded. Rather it is entirely subjective; it is "in here," written on the person's consciousness of himself. We could say that it is "psychological." But that term is not accurate. For the awareness we speak of is deeper than a person's inner economy of thoughts and feelings. It is, rather, *ontological;* it is his contact with reality, as such.

The second meaning of Holy Spirit is that it (she) brings about the birth of the Church. This is made clear at the beginning of Acts in the New Testament. The same Spirit that grasps the individual and binds her to the Gospel also unites that individual with a company of others who are similarly bound. A collection of people who might have been just that—a collection of people or, at most, a club—becomes a congregation. They are united by the Gospel, which is *other* than any spirit that they could have generated among themselves. Simply stated, they are *the Church.*

With the Trinity as with the Incarnation, our concern is to establish that the *Spirit* that moves us and our churches is a Spirit that stands aloof from energizing forces found in human groups and in the individuals who make up these groups. It stands aloof from the spirit of the United States of America, of the "free enterprise" system, of community life, of every human project and tradition. It is first, last, and always the Spirit of Jesus Christ as the One to whom the Gospels bear witness.

The Two Natures of Christ

According to the Council of Chalcedon of 451, Jesus was one person, but he had two "natures," one human and the other divine. He had each "nature" in its fullness and its integrity. He was not partly or half human and partly or half divine. We may say that he was not a demi-God. He was altogether human, and he was altogether divine. Nothing was taken from one of the "natures" to give the other its due. He was human, and he was God.

This way of stating matters did not arise from a love of playing games with words. It was, rather, perceived as being essential for the faith. It was essential to establish and to maintain a view of God in which God and the Spirit of God are independent of human social structures and cultural patterns.

To see the special place of "Two Natures" in this, we may consider what is involved in a person's being redeemed in Jesus Christ. The state of redemption or "knowing the Lord," we will note, is not something "objective" or outside of a person. It is, rather, within and has to do with a person's motives and decisions.

In civil society, a person's status as "guilty" or "innocent" of wrongdoing is commonly *objective.* It is outside of the person and has no necessary relation to his inner feelings or decisions. A person may be found "guilty" by a court. His presumed guilt is then recorded in documents that are "on file" in a government office. It is in this way a *fact* that is totally apart from the person's inner life. Within his own mind (and heart), the person may know that he is innocent. Or he may believe himself to be guilty, with or without remorse. But the "fact" of his guilt exists independently of anything he believes about himself.

Some Christians have thought of their prospects for eternal salvation in these terms. In simplest (and "Pelagian") terms, they have a "score" in God's reckoning system. Each deed they perform that is good adds points toward their admission to heaven. Each bad deed takes away points for that purpose. When the moment of decision (death) comes, the person will then rise to the one destiny or fall to the other depending on the points that she has accumulated. In principle, the person could not know what her destiny is until she gets there.

In the concept of the Two Natures, this *objective character* of a person's status before God is stoutly denied. A person who is "redeemed by the Blood of the Lamb" undergoes a drastic change in his inner life. Indeed, his status as "saved" or as "redeemed" *is* his having this transformation in motives and decisions. There is not, and there cannot be, any separation of the two. There is no scoreboard that is external to the individual in which a tally of his progress toward his admission to heaven is kept. As the writer of Psalm 32 said:

Happy are those whose transgression is forgiven,
whose sin is covered.
Happy are those to whom the Lord imputes no iniquity,
and in whose spirit there is no deceit. (Verses 1–2)

We see here that being forgiven is coextensive with having a spirit in which there is "no deceit." The person who is forgiven *is* a person who inwardly loves truth. A person who loves truth *is* a person whose sin is covered.

If, then, the redemption that is in Jesus Christ is not an objective status but a condition of the inner life, how are we to understand the salvation that is in Jesus Christ? Christians have always said that Jesus's sacrifice atones for our sin. By it, our sin is canceled. But this is not to be understood as an event that is aloof from our inner lives. It is objective in the sense that Jesus's Crucifixion and Resurrection were events that took place in history and not just in our imaginations. But that event was saving for us in and through our inner and subjective participation in it. Although the Cross took place "out there," it always does so "in here," in a person's inner life. And its "out there" and its "in here" natures cannot be separated.

If anxiety is an essential feature of being human, so also is the wish to subdue and overcome that anxiety. In the world as the world, human beings try to accomplish this through power, possessions, and glory. In the case of *power,* a person strives to arrive at a state in which he determines what the people around him will do and what events will take place. He wants *dominion* over the world. He can seek power at a local level, as when he wants to control what the people in his family will do. He can seek it at a higher level, as when he wants to take charge of kingdoms and empires. But in all cases, he wants power to quiet his inner anxieties. If people act on his order, then surely the "bogeyman" will be kept at bay!

Closely related to power is *possession.* A person is able to make good within a certain community that certain items are *hers.* These include, above all, land, but also buildings, granaries, silver, gold, and jewels. These properties are then extensions of herself. Through them, she becomes, "larger than life." The properties to which she can point serve as a bulwark against death and the "sting of death." And the same is true of *prestige* or *glory.* If she is honored for any one of many things, that honor will quiet her anxieties. She may be considered "big and important" because of military exploits, of success as a trader, of inherited or acquired position in government, rank in a religious (ceremonial) establishment, or reputation as a fighter, trader, magician, or religious ecstatic. Many of these (and some others) will induce people to look at her with admiration and awe (and envy), and this is a kind of eternity that overwhelms the "jitters" to which a person's creature nature subjects her.

In the doctrine of the Two Natures, then, the same Jesus Christ who is fully God-with-us is also like us in the attributes that distinguish us as human beings. He shares our humanness. He has the same high-voltage wishes, the same intense anxieties that we have. There is nothing that makes us the human creatures that we are that is unknown to him. In this sense, he stands beside us in all of our humanness. He was in every respect tempted as we are, yet without sinning (Hebrews 4:15). And as he joined himself to us in our human dilemma, so he joins us to him in the faithfulness to God that resolves that dilemma. There is reason, then, why Christians have insisted that Jesus was divine and human and that he was human and divine.

DOCTRINE AND THE FAITH

In Western civilization in general, and especially within its more cosmopolitan sectors, the idea of *doctrine* is not in good repute. It has had a lot of "bad press." When people think of doctrine, they often have visions of an intellectual rigidity that inhibits discussion and allows no scope for efforts to ask and answer questions about life. Just to say "doctrine" is to conger up pictures of a self-righteous Puritan and of a closed-minded, arrogant, small-town preacher. In the face of this situation, it is small wonder that many want to run from doctrine as they would flee from a burning car that seems ready to explode. And running, they would betake themselves to a university campus where questions can be asked and answered freely.

This jaundiced view of doctrine is not without reason in our civilization and within the Christian Church, for a thought or a practice that is a response to the proclamation of the Gospel is commonly taken to be identical with the Gospel. We may note that wherever the Word of God is proclaimed with authenticity and force, either because of or in spite of the person who does the proclaiming, there are responses among those who hear. People take note and take heed. They confess their sins; they accept the gift of forgiveness; they believe in the Gospel; they pray and worship; they "amend" their lives by ceasing to do certain things while beginning to do others. In all of this, they hear a Word from God and respond to it. The Word they hear is from outside of the world of finite entities and of sin, greed, and selfishness. But, of necessity, the response to the call of the Gospel is from within that world. People respond by thinking certain thoughts with the use of certain concepts. They respond by praying and worshiping in accordance with certain formulae, certain liturgies, with certain musical traditions, and by means of certain homiletic (speech) practices. The call is from *above* the world, but the responses are those *of* the world.

And among these responses are the embracing, the holding, and the proclaiming of certain *doctrines*. The responses also include *liturgies* or ways of worshiping and moral-ethical *codes* by which people live. In all of these, a call that comes from the infinite and the eternal leaves a residue, so to say, in the realm of the temporal and the finite.

This residue—the doctrines, liturgies and moral codes—is then treated as being identical with the call of God to which it is a response. Something in the finite realm is equated with the call that comes from outside that realm. Certain thoughts acquire a dignity that belongs properly only to the call from outside of all human thoughts. And certain liturgies take on a dignity equal to that of the God who is worshiped through them. Specific patterns of living are viewed as being the Will of God for all people everywhere and always.

This does not mean that we can reject *doctrine* as such. If a response to the call of God is a response within the finite realm, it is, nevertheless, essential. We are in the sphere of the creature, and if we would heed the call of God, we must do so as creatures who live among creatures. And we must use the apparatus of the world as we know it. So the creaturely will, of necessity, be involved. But even as we espouse doctrines, we must do so with an "at ease" attitude. We must see that the thoughts we think are responses to a call that is from outside of all that we think or can think. And for this reason those thoughts are never identical with that *of which* they are thoughts, that is, with the Call from God. Our thoughts are always necessary, but they are never adequate or final. We cannot forgo them, but neither can we depend on them. We always hold them in a "today," but it is a "today" that will yield its place to a "tomorrow" in which we may need to think a bit differently.

This would be especially clear if we surveyed the history of Christian thought, a task that has been taken up admirably by many writers.

We would see Christians using the conceptual armamentarium of Platonic philosophy for several hundred years. We would see that set of ideas giving way to Aristotelian idea-structures in the high Middle Ages and Thomas Aquinas. We would note the rejection, or ignoring, of philosophy as such with Martin Luther and John Calvin and then survey a fireworks of philosophies and rejections of philosophy in such thinkers as Karl Barth and Paul Tillich.

We saw at the beginning of this chapter what is involved. The point is that we need a view of God and of God's revelation of himself in Jesus Christ that is independent of—not tied to—human social structures and cultural patterns. This is what is needed, but it cannot *itself* be a doctrine or a goal. It cannot be the platform on which we stand because it does not have enough of a determinate nature. It is more a standard by which we judge concepts, doctrines, or beliefs than it is itself a concept, a doctrine, or a belief. We can think "independent Spirit," but we do so only to have in mind a standard by which to measure and assess the thoughts, or systems of thought, that we can actually hold in our minds.

This, then, is how we will see the Incarnation, the Trinity, and the Two Natures of Christ. All three are intended to ensure that the Spirit of God is independent of human cultural creations. All three are intended to exalt a concept of Right or of Righteousness that is above and independent of the codes of particular societies, for these codes are partial and limited and often designed to justify the privileges of powerful, wealthy, and exalted groups within human communities.

THE MEGA-CHURCH AND THE BOUNDARIES

We return again to the inescapable "boundary" problem of the mega-church as discussed in the previous two chapters. A common boundary-related feature of religions, ideologies, and other centers of enthusiasm, whether in or outside the boundary, is the generation of a certain *spirit*. This spirit can be the upper zone to which the Gnostic wishes to rise. It can be a nation made into an object of ultimate devotion and loyalty. It can be the élan of a city or of any social organization or group. Whatever the identity and nature of this spirit, it stands by itself. It does not depend on events making up a special history. Or, more to the point, it does not *arise* from the events of the Old Testament and the New Testament. It is, therefore, simply itself, and as such exists outside the boundary.

Such spirits arise constantly in the Christian churches. Wherever an implication of the Gospel or something thought to be an implication of the Gospel is lifted up and made important on its own account, we have such a *spirit*. In early and medieval Christianity, there were many instances in which *self-denial* and especially *celibacy* were, in effect, lifted up out of context and made the important things in themselves. The same was true of *doctrinal purity* in Lutheranism and *success in business* in Calvinist territories. When (and if) these are independent of the Crucified Christ as remembered within a community, they are *spirits*. And devotion to them is outside of the boundary of Christianity. Quite commonly, however, the devotees have passed over a bridge, but they have not burned the bridge. The memory of what they have left behind remains with them, and they can return home to the faith in Christ crucified.

This bridge, however, may have been burned, or at least is badly charred, in the mega-church. It has generated a spirit that is independent of the God who is active in history. It is, *as spirit,* the thing that has become important. Major features of the mega-church, such as the abandonment of symbols and of traditional music are, in effect, an announcement that they wish to espouse a *spirit* that is free of the events of the Gospel. This is why their songs that refer to Jesus dying for our sins have such a hollow sound about them. It seems that the song is the important thing, not the Death and Resurrection of Jesus Christ to which the song refers.

In this, the mega-church may not seem to be different in principle from the other traditions that exalt a principle or an élan to a point where it becomes independent of the gospel-as-history. The mega-church may, indeed, be much like the Pentecostal movements that loom large in the United States and even larger in Latin America. But note once more that they have this marked difference: By making it a matter of policy that *they must grow and then grow more,* they burn the bridge. *They have no way back.* Perhaps somewhere, sometime, a mega-church and its leaders will get busy and rebuild the bridge. It is likely that they would lose much of their "constituency" in so doing. But unless they do that, they remain outside of the boundaries of the Christian faith.

11

———◦•❀•◦———

REACHING OUT IN AN ERA
PLAGUED BY THE PROBLEM
OF MEANING

We have noted that the mega-church, as distinct from the merely large church, has a number of characteristics. It has a *regal pastor*. In many instances, this minister-in-charge founded the church. In other cases, he has taken it over from a founding pastor who retires. The architecture of the building that houses the church is not churchlike. Its appearance is more like that of a corporate headquarters or a university administration building. Inside, there is little to suggest that it is a church. The services are held in an "auditorium" with theater-type seats. Pulpits, altars, crosses, and the like are mainly absent. The music is altogether new. Rarely is a traditional hymn heard. Rarely is there a song that even sounds like a traditional hymn. Instruments are mainly percussion, guitars, and a piano. The sermons are mainly of the life adjustment and positive thinking kind, with evangelical Christian themes appearing from time to time. Yet there is little emphasis on doctrine. When issues arise, traditional fundamentalist beliefs are affirmed. But such issues do not arise frequently, and there is little concentration on just what "we believe." Very commonly, the administrators of the church measure its "size" by noting the number of people who attend on a given weekend rather than on the number of members. There is a membership, but its size is as little as one-fourth or one-third of the number who attend. It consists of the people who have been "let in the gate" by the head pastor after going through a class with him. Of all the characteristics, the one that most defines the mega-church is that its founders and pastors make a *project* of becoming big and growing ever bigger. For this reason, they do what it takes to bring about such growth. In that effort, they imitate the *celebrity* preoccupation of Americans. The minister becomes a star performer who gathers an ever-larger audience. A part of the minister's following is then gathered into small groups that meet either in the church building or in the homes of the participants. In this way, there is a balance between the "celebrity-performer" feature of the church and people's wish to belong to a face-to-face small group. This combination of celebrity performance and small group belonging produces a maximum in numerical growth.

Further, I have argued that a mega-church is *not* a Christian Church. The term *Christian* properly spreads a wide net. It embraces both an Eastern Orthodox Mass and a Baptist preaching service. Yet there are limits. The project of growing ever larger crosses a boundary from what is Christian to what is not. As church people concentrate on theological and moral issues, they ask questions about what is True and Good. The project of growing ever larger rules out that concentration in principle. To focus attention on what is True or Good is, by its nature, seen as a digression from the vital business at hand, which is drawing in a maximum number of people. The Christian, with her Bible open, can no more tolerate that than can a scientist who is told that her laboratory findings must take a back seat to government-approved assertions about human beings or about another subject matter. In both cases, a stand favoring a concentration on the True and the Good is entirely appropriate.

In this final chapter, we undertake to place the authentic Christian tradition within the major dilemma of modern civilization, the problem of *meaning*. In doing this, we rely on the work of one of the premier theologians of the twentieth century, Paul Tillich. What follows is derived from his book, *The Courage to Be*.

THE PROBLEM OF MEANING
IN MODERN CIVILIZATION

In earlier historical eras, people were afflicted by the anxiety of fate and death, and by the anxiety of guilt and condemnation. The modern era is the scene of yet another kind of anxiety, the anxiety of emptiness and meaninglessness. Here the major threat that people confront has to do with the question of *meaning*. People of our era are witness to mighty achievements in the realms of politics and government, of science and technology, and, in general, of the ability to manipulate the objects that make up our world. There is question, however, of where these mighty achievements lead or what they *mean*. Are the achievements just themselves—just what they appear to be—or do they prepare the way for something other than themselves? Do they lead to something that is *good* and *worthy* on its own account and then lead to that which is the Good? Once these questions are asked, there is a possibility that a negative answer will be given. Advances in technology may provide certain conveniences and solve certain problems. But that may be all. There may not be anything that they *lead to*. If this turns out to be the case, as is the implicit fear underlying all engineering finesse, we are beset by the plague of meaninglessness. And once this cloud appears on our horizon, we experience the "jitters," fearing that matters may go even further, plunging us into absolute emptiness. A great, black hole of despair yawns before us and threatens to make a mockery of all that we achieve.

If this *problem of meaning* arises in the spheres of civilization and culture, it also infects us at the level of individual life. It infects everything that each of us plans and does. It is present in all of our efforts, our exertions, our cleverness, and our accomplishments. It is in our fun, our pleasures, and our "good times." It is in our celebrations and our acts of doing honor. It is in our victories and conquests. It is in our families, our jobs, and our friendships. It is in our participation in community and national affairs. It is in everything to which we dedicate our intelligence and our energy.

In all of these, we want the items that we achieve, enjoy, or celebrate to refer beyond themselves to some larger value. When a person does well in planning or executing some productive activity, he wants that good performance to *mean* something. He wants it to have a purpose other than just that of being a performance that was good. He wants a larger community to recognize it as having such meaning. If an athlete and his team win in a sporting event, he wants that victory to be an eternal fact recorded in the annals of the history of sports—or of heaven. If a man enjoys his wife's embrace, or a woman her husband's, he or she wants there to be more than the joy of the moment. He wants it to be recorded "out there" in the world that this "love divine" shook the world and the heavens at a certain time. Whatever efforts are intended, carried out, and brought to conclusion, there must be a reference to something beyond these efforts to a sphere of value that seems to be sufficient in itself.

Some of these efforts are by an individual and pertain to her as an individual. The person succeeds in climbing a career ladder or in winning in a sporting event or in having a tumultuous love affair. She hopes that others will know about what she has achieved in these realms and that they will express admiration for what she has done "for herself." The world is supposed to see her as having achieved *Success* or as having arrived at *Happiness.* Others of a person's efforts, however, are for the sake of a collective entity. An employee succeeds in promoting the organization that employs her. An athlete wins a victory for "dear old State University." The soldier gives her all to defend or promote her country or the values that her country "stands for." There is a social organism, and the individual does well because she serves that organism. There is something "out there" that transcends the individual and that gives *meaning* to what the individual does.

THE PROBLEM OF MEANING IN MODERN CIVILIZATION

Throughout most of human history, these meanings are taken for granted. They are so completely assumed that it does not occur to anyone to question them. A person does not see the extended family or clan to which he devotes his efforts as being a "maybe" reality, as something that could or could not exist. He does not see these collective entities as mere possibilities any more than he sees his stomach as being a "maybe" reality. The larger family as a focus of concern is simply standard equipment. Most everyone has one; to have a family is to be "somebody" or to be part of "everyone." Even the wanderer who is a stranger to the people around him is an object of concern (Deut. 10:18) and is often to be taken into a family. This same taken-for-granted character is true of the kingdom or nation. The family or nation that gives meaning to the individual's labors is simply assumed just as is the contrast between "up" and "down" in space. For this reason, there can be no problem of meaning or of meaninglessness.

During the last two centuries, however, a basic change occurred in Western civilization. It changed from a village-farming society to a city-industrial human grouping. Relations among people in society changed from personal and sacred to business-like and secular. These changes were in great degree outcomes of the process of industrialization. Communities became organized around the needs or requirements of industry, not those of people and their relationships. So instead of the large family or clan, we have the *industrial city*. We have an entity that is organized around the processes of industry, not around sacred traditions, such as those of family or nation.

With social change going on in calm indifference to sacred traditions, the entities that are the referents of meaning are brought into question. The family, the nation, and similar realities take on a "maybe" character. They seem to be "out there" in the world. But are they *real?* Maybe. And then again, maybe they are not real.

When the fans at a football game cheer for the Home Team, is the "U" (university) that the team represents *real* as a participant in such a contest, or is it not? We may wonder what would happen if the devoted fan faced questions about it: What sort of thing is the "U"? Why do you see it as an entity that can enter into an athletic contest and win or lose? Why do you see the players on the team as somehow *being* "U" so that if they win, it wins, and if they lose, it loses? Is the "U" a mystical entity that rose above the campus and came down into the bodies of those players so that they now *are it?* Is it an incarnation? If a "U" fan faces these questions long enough or hard enough, he may begin to *doubt.* And once he starts to doubt, the question of *meaning* has arisen and the horrifying possibility of *meaninglessness* has appeared on the horizon.

Once *doubt* has arisen, an entity to which people were devoted may dissolve and its place may be taken by a collection of less exalted realities. The soldier may not be fighting for his "country" but only for a particular governing arrangement. And that arrangement may be *good* only to the extent that it is actually good for the people under its rule. To be ruled from Washington, D.C. may be better than to be ruled from, let us say, London or Berlin *only* if those who rule in Washington do so *better* than alternative rulers in those other cities. In effect, there is no longer *America;* there are only *Americans.* Do we find this a pretty dreary prospect, or do we welcome this development with open arms? Do we really know how we feel about this, and who is telling us how we *should* feel? Where are we going to get the blast of the nationalistic trumpet and the roll of the drums in the present time?

The same can be said of family. Even the genetic link, we note, thins out rapidly as we move through the family tree, and other links may be scarcely real at all. Other features that define "kinds" of people may be no more than phantoms. We quickly see that the larger family exists only because we *say* that it does, and as soon as we stop saying it exists, it disappears.

And what about the "U" whom we may "back" (support, be in favor of) and for whose football team we may cheer? It clearly will evaporate into the air, with the residue on the ground being nothing other than an educational institution, with classrooms, laboratories, teachers, students, and "courses." And these exist only to provide education for individual persons with a "research" undertaking added. So where is the cheering now?

There goes nation, family, and team! Where this takes us is right up to ourselves, what *we* do. Clearly, the same evaporation can happen to meaning as to individual achievement. A woman achieves success working for a company that produces cardboard boxes. It is hard to find glamour in a cardboard box, or in anything that is manufactured and sold. But the woman has done well "for herself." She has climbed the executive hierarchy. Impressive, right? Well, yes, but only if *people* are impressed. If people are told about the woman's "success" and they then say "that's nice" and then quickly change the subject, her "success" loses its substance. The same is true of the scholar's wonderful publication record, consisting, as it does, of a host of articles and books that no one reads and that will soon be forgotten (if they were ever noted in the first place). As we go down the list of people who do "well for themselves," we find a similar volatility of the substance of what they have achieved.

THE SPECTER OF MEANINGLESSNESS

A grim prospect emerges from all of this. The prospect is that life may be, at its core, without meaning. It may be *meaningless.* Every achievement we chalk up and every pleasure we enjoy may be just that, simply a goal arrived at in the "now," or just a moment of enjoyment. We managed to do something, or we had a good time. Neither may refer to anything beyond itself. When this possibility comes into view, we try to hunker down. We seek to view everything we do and everything we experience as just itself, with no reference beyond what it is. Life is here and now, and that is all.

The question of *meaning,* however, will not be banished so easily. Like the cat who keeps coming back from wherever you take him, the question of *meaning* will reappear again and again. It is just that way with us. We demand meaning. A possible absence of meaning is, for us, a nauseating prospect. It is an emptiness for which we see no remedy or comfort.

Imagine that someone has set out to take a trip in her car. She takes notice of her arrival at each of many immediate destinations. She arrives at a certain highway going east. She then turns onto another highway going north. She passes a certain city. She then passes another city. She arrives at a state line and goes beyond it. She sees a large hill, reaches it, and goes beyond it. She treats each of those proximate destinations as stages of her advance toward a final destination. She feels that as she passes each one, she may now focus on the next one, and, who knows, it may be the last one before her grand arrival at the Final Destination. But at some point it is revealed to her that there is no final destination. There are only the intermediate points, one after the other. She is condemned, we might say, to wander indefinitely to one proximate point and then to another. Would this not be a description of hell? More specifically, is it not a model of emptiness?

This may be a parable of our great efforts to do whatever we do. We undertake one project, and we then proceed to another. There may be a great chain of effort leading to an objective, then another objective, and another, and so on. But implicit in all of this movement from one proximate goal to another is an end-point that does not need a reference to something further. There should be a point at which we aspire to arrive that does not lead to another point, for it is the Final Destination. It is a place to which we arrive that has its value in itself and not in its service as a step leading to another value. Perhaps the term *home* could serve as a symbol for this. This home is not something that we *should* regard as a final destination. It is, rather, something that we *do* so regard. It is the End that has unconditional importance. It is important beyond all possible limit.

The anxiety of modern people, then, is that there may not be any such destination. Our mighty efforts and our great achievements do not lead to a home base to which we arrive amid the cheers of crowds and onlookers. Rather, it leads to the Great Yawn, the ultimate sigh of lethargy and indifference. And if this is where we end up, each of our proximate victories of achievements is emptied of significance. Notably, our incredible technological advances may become phantoms, marvelous in themselves but *meaning* nothing.

We sense intuitively that we could live with, or tolerate, such emptiness. There is a transcendent source of meaning that does not depend on the schemes that we construct. This ultimate focus of our efforts could be a nation or race, or both together. Fascism and Nazism illustrate this. It could be a religious group of any kind, from the august eminence of the Vatican City to the "home town" intimacy of a community dominated by

Baptists or Mormons. In all of these, one or another kind of social organism is set up and proclaimed to be the Ultimate Reality to which our many individual efforts contribute. People rally to these centers of "belonging" readily in our era, for they serve as defenses against the horrifying possibility that all of our mighty efforts may not mean anything at all.

The defenses are not, however, adequate. The specter of meaninglessness is not easily banished, and the weaknesses of our defense systems show up in a number of ways. Prominent among these are the efforts people put forth to succeed and then succeed further. No level of achievement seems to be enough. No matter how high a person rises in the company that employs him, and no matter how great his income may be, these indices of "success" are never enough. A man thinks that he will be happy with the next plateau if he can just reach it. But when he attains that proximate goal, he is not satisfied and so decrees that he needs to go still further. No level of "success" is adequate for more than a brief moment. He has perceived that his achievements are meaningless, but instead of seeing them as being by their nature without meaning, he thinks that they are just not *enough*. Or at least, so he reasons. He thinks that if he could just go a step further, all would be well. But when he gets to that next step, he will think the same thing about that plateau and will need to go further still.

This scenario helps to explain why people in business and the professions are willing to cheat to get ever more exalted positions or to acquire more money than they have already. It also explains why they are so intolerant of efforts to reform the economic order to make it more just and fair for the less prosperous. Just being reasonable, a very wealthy woman could allow some of that wealth to "trickle down" to her employees, to her customers, and to the community. But the pervasive threat of meaninglessness does not allow reason to play its proper role. She therefore becomes intent on getting and keeping wealth for herself, for the correct quantity or amount of it is always *more* than what she has at the moment.

Others seek to accomplish much the same thing by immersing themselves in pleasures and in what we might call the *expressive life*. They may choose to immerse themselves in music that is loud and rhythmic, much of it which carries within it a desperation: MAKE THIS MEAN SOMETHING, MAKE THIS MEAN SOMETHING, MAKE IT! If a viewer watches performances on "MTV" for a few minutes, she is likely to see this desperation, this hunger for meaning, to hear the expression of a young generation that sees no real future and no real hope. Immersion in the pleasures of drink and sex provides a similar escape from the yawning abyss of meaninglessness. The escape may be only temporary, but it is at least escape for a moment.

Rather different from this—or maybe it is not so different after all—is the escape into religion and "morality." The point here is to be good or on the side of the Good. A person will stake out a few issues and take his stand on them. In doing so, he feels that he is on the side of the Good, the Decent, and the Godly. If he is of rightwing "conservative" persuasion, these may include such matters as opposing abortion and being negative and even punitive about homosexuality. If his proclivities lie on the other side of the right–left spectrum, he may see racism, sexism, and homophobia under every bush and behind every tree. Whatever the issues and whatever his stand on them may be, he seeks to be, in effect, God's pet. He is one of God's "good boys." He is on the right side. This feeling of being "good" provides a defense against meaninglessness!

ADDRESSING MEANINGLESSNESS

In dealing with the modern problem of meaninglessness and emptiness, as in dealing with the more traditional fate and death issues with their guilt and condemnation, there is a "death and resurrection" structure. In the seeming meaninglessness, there is an unflinching confrontation with a powerful (seeming) negative—with the abyss of nonbeing, of condemnation to emptiness. But there is hope—some *thing* rather than no*thing*—a resurrection of being. Such a resurrection ensures *being* itself, as opposed to not being, to nothingness.

In philosophies other than those reflected in the Hebraic Bible, the concept of nothingness or the void has a neutral or even positive meaning. The ancient Greek Epicurean philosophers said that death was nothing to be feared. It is a total absence of being, and, as such, is an absence of pain and agony. And if a person can take up philosophy—the endeavor to *understand*—he will see that there is nothing to fear. He can, therefore, face death with total calm and equanimity

For Buddhists, the *void* is empty, but it is so only in the sense that it is without the particular structures that make up the visible world. It is "above" those structures and, as such, is the fullness of being. As long as people are in the world of objects and events, they will be under the reign of suffering. The realm of nature and the sphere of human civilization make up—before all else and after all else—an arena of frustration and pain. Just because they are *particular,* they cannot be anything else. The very wish to exist as an individual guarantees suffering. What is good for human beings, therefore, is to *renounce* existence in the world. They do this by "letting go" of the world of "things." They go through a step-by-step process, gradually leaving behind all attachment to the world and to the desires and ambitions that arise within it. When, after a long tutelage, this is achieved, a person's soul rises above all that is finite and suggestive of the existence of an individual. She will then drop into the Great Ocean of Being, called Nirvana. There, like a cup of water falling into a river, she will become one with the fullness of being. And this will be bliss inexpressible.

By contrast, in the concepts of emptiness and meaningless, we have a loss or a deprivation that is totally negative. In the biblical worldview, the created order is not bad, as it is for both Greek philosophies and the religions of India. It is, rather, God's creation, and, as such, is good. And the loss of it, for that reason, is pure loss. It is an emptying of all that is good. The descent into nothingness is a case of being excluded from the Good, and all that is good. It is therefore altogether bad and painful. Unlike the Epicurean view, this view sees death as a loss of the Good that is in the world. Unlike the Buddhists, the Bible sees the great void as loss of being rather than the fullness of being.

THE "EMPTY" OR THE "VOID" INSIDE
OF HEBRAIC CULTURE

We will see that the biblical faith, in contrast to Greek and Buddhist-Hindu philosophies, is "worldly." It is so in the sense that the Good for human beings does not lie in the rejection of the created order, but precisely within that order. Because the world is good, the objects and events within it refer beyond themselves to what they are "in the light" of something—of the Ultimate Good, that is, to God. But because the world is a realm of sin—the efforts of human beings to be like God—The Good always lies on the far side of a "death and resurrection" event.

The hope that is then held out is a hope for something that is on the *far side* of the Great Abyss. A person must go through the negative to get to the positive. He hits the bottom of the pit before he rises. In this, all sentimentality is avoided. Indeed, it is crushed. We do not seek to interject good feelings to push out the bad, as when perfume overwhelms a bad smell. We seek a rigid honesty that denies nothing of the negative.

This is the case with death. We deny neither the reality of death nor the anxiety that pertains to it. We love life; we see life as a gift from a good God. We therefore see death as the loss of that which is good. We fear death, but we live in the hope of resurrection from the dead. Yet that resurrection is down the road; it is on the other side of death and does not take death's place. We go through death and all that it involves. Then and only then do we see the prospect of the life that knows no death.

It is the same with guilt and condemnation. Measured by the code of our society or by any moral law, we do all right. At least most of us do all right most of the time. But we recognize that there is another demand on us to which we do *not* do justice with our nice middle-class and "respectable" lives. The commandments in the Sermon on the Mount stand over us. They issue a decisive "no" to our claims to be good and godly. The commandment to "love your enemy" is our constant reminder of this. Even if we obey every moral law we know, we stand just as guilty as the worst criminals we can find. As we face the facts of our sinfulness, we reach bottom where we find no excuse for ourselves. It is there, then, at the lowest point in the pit that we find that we are sinners, to be sure, but *forgiven* sinners. God in Jesus Christ has made every complaint against us his business and has lifted it from us. Indeed, when we had already reached the bottom, we had already been forgiven, for it was only as those already forgiven that we could even know how sinful we were. Without God's pardon, we would have been stuck in measuring ourselves by the moral code of our society. Our bourgeois morality would have been good enough for us! But with God's forgiveness, we see ourselves by God's standards, not those of society. Forgiveness and pardon begin with the *conviction* of sin that comes upon us. Then we reach the other shore where we know we are forgiven. We come to accept the fact that we are accepted in spite of being unacceptable.

This acceptance may seem easy to achieve–receive, but it is, in fact, not so at all. We need only to imagine that we have betrayed a friend in some serious way. We try to find excuses for what we did, but none seem sufficient. The fact is that, at the time, we intended wrong; there is no way of denying it or even minimizing it. Nevertheless, our friend forgives us, as we—in the present moment—wish he would, for this is our last hope. He does so in an act that is entirely *his*. We can see here that it will be difficult to accept forgiveness. We will hang on most desperately to the hope of excusing what we did on the grounds of ignorance, or some bad thing that our friend did, or perhaps a momentary insanity. Only when all of these excuses fail do we ask to be forgiven. Still, when that forgiveness is given, accepting it is one of the hardest things we will ever do. This is the way that accepting God's forgiveness feels—difficult, very difficult.

The same "down and up" structure occurs in the case of meaninglessness. Just as we cannot know death unless we first perceive life, and we cannot feel guilty unless we are aware of righteousness, so we cannot feel meaninglessness unless we first know *meaning*. We must begin with a sense of what is involved in saying that something *has* meaning. We say it has meaning in the sense that immediate outcomes of an action are not all there is. Rather, these outcomes refer beyond themselves to a sphere of value that can stand on its own as good and worthy. We say that something *has* meaning or is *meaningful*. If we set out to perform a task, we see the successful accomplishment of that task as meaningful. It refers beyond itself to a larger Good to which it contributes. If we engage in a celebration or experience a pleasure, these occurrences similarly contribute to, or form part of, a larger good that is complete in itself and "eats up" our devotion. There has to be the Larger Good or the Final Good as the end-of-the line value if we are to "see" the empty hole left by its absence, the hole of meaninglessness.

Once we have this sense of meaning or meaningfulness, we can also understand its absence, the state of meaninglessness. In that state, we deal with the great "so what?" So we achieved something in our jobs or careers. That is "nice" is it not? But perhaps it is only "nice." We are waiting for, as they say, the "other shoe to drop." We are waiting to see the *meaning* of our achievement. But lo, there is none. We sold more mousetraps that any one else. So what? We sold more mousetraps; that is all there is. There is no "what" to follow the "so." All that remains is silence or the shrug of a shoulder. The same is true when we win a victory in chess or tennis. That victory stands alone in the January cold. It does not go anywhere or *mean* anything. Or again, we experience a great pleasure, as in eating a gourmet meal or in engaging in tumultuous love-making. Again that pleasure is the end of the line. There is nothing beyond it that it can "mean." The lovers cannot "tell the world of our new love divine" (as the song said) because the world is not interested.

The very fact that we can experience the absence of meaning and can know meaninglessness supposes that we first understood meaning, just as sin supposes that we first knew righteousness. And this being the case, we can reach bottom, the realm of total emptiness. It is this excruciatingly empty hole in which there is no "wet finger placed on the parched tongue" (Luke 16:24). Such an emptiness is unbearable. It could be faced only with the utmost courage. Some writers think that Nietzsche showed such courage in the time of his life that preceded his losing his mind completely. Few wish to have such courage, and, at the cost of their integrity, most people seek one or another way out.

Even at the bottom of this pit, however, there is the fact that the experience of meaninglessness makes us aware of the meaningfulness that could have been. And then there, at the bottom with nothing more than that awareness to moderate it, we find the meaning that comes from "elsewhere." It is not the proximate and dubious meanings to which we have clung, such as family, nation, success pleasure, or even "religion." It is, rather, the meaning that comes from the ground and source of meaning, from being itself, from God. But just as Jesus was raised from the dead only after dying, so we ground our sense of meaning in God only after we come to terms with the full height and depth of meaninglessness and emptiness.

In the Great Emptiness, we have lost, or perhaps we have abandoned, the proximate centers of meaning that have been so important to us all our lives. We have "given up" on family, nation, career, wealth, and social eminence. These are all "emptied" of sacredness. But for some, the space that they vacated is filled by God and by his revelation of himself in Jesus Christ. The space that they have vacated is filled by a Christ who insists that he comes before family. We may remember that he said that we are to love him more than father, mother, son, or daughter (Matt. 10:37). And, more than that, he has to come before nation, career, wealth, and social eminence. These are all cast aside or "emptied." We now know them for what they are and only for what they *are*. They are, to us, the finite—the "so much and no more" that describes them. But the meaning that we have lost we believe we get back, so to say, from God. Just as forgiveness comes from God, so does meaning. If marriage and family, community and nation, job and career are to have meaning, it is because they first lose all meaning that originates in themselves and then receive their significance and importance from God. No matter how sacred we may have thought some of these to be, we understand them in a Christian way when we say that they have lost *all* meaning and then received it back from God.

All that was sacred before is sacred now, but it is so *again*. It has lost its sacredness and then been given it back. But its sacredness is now *from* God and *in* God and *for* God. Its sacredness is, we might say, *borrowed*. It is a sacredness that comes from God and that belongs to him. It has a conditional character about it, for it comes under the unconditional sovereignty of him who is the source of being and meaning. A husband and wife may love each other, but that love is not a whirlpool that has the two of them as its center. It is, rather, centered in God. Their love is not self-sufficient. It is first a good in and for the larger community, and then it is a good for the Good itself and for God.

The career may certainly be treasured. But it is treasured as a means and as a measure for serving people and, through the service to people, for serving God. Success in the career is therefore of value only if that success is blessed by a God who wants all job performances to be useful to the community and to be carried out justly and honestly. The American dream of "rags to riches" ceases to be a dream at all and becomes nothing more than the "increase in riches" that Psalm 62 says we should not "set our heart on" (Verse 10).

The nation similarly has lost its sacredness and then received it back from God. It now has no sacredness in itself. America is not in and of itself sacred. Its sacredness, rather, comes from God and is for God. The nation is, therefore, to be always guided by God and guided for his purposes, not its own. And it is to be judged by God. The nation is commanded to promote justice within itself and to act in the interest of peace and compassion with the rest of the world. If the nation, that is, the nation's government and its economic and military powers, acts unjustly toward its own people or toward the rest of the world, it is to be opposed. Any notion that whatever the nation does is right because it is the–or our–nation is to be rejected with all vigor and in every way possible. When it does wrong as "wrong" is defined by universal and abstract principles, it is to be opposed. When the nation does right, it is to be supported, not because it is the nation but because it is doing right. The Right—the Will of God—is always the prime consideration. Indeed, it is the *only* consideration.

THE CONCEPT OF GOD
AND MORAL JUDGMENT

Just where, however, do we locate the Good? On what basis do we distinguish, as we say, right from wrong? It is easy enough to say—within a

Christian framework—that the contrast of right and wrong has its basis in the will of God. But the term *God* poses a problem for human beings, especially for those who are "modern." Just what is its referent? There is a difficulty if we refer to God as a *being*. To do so is to refer to something that is finite, *a* being is a part of the larger totality of everything, of all that make up the realm of the "real." Even if this god is "great," he remains a part of the universe. No quantitative measure of a god's stature can change this. No superlatives will suffice.

So let us look at it another way. In lectures at the University of Chicago in the 1960s, theologian Paul Tillich spoke about German scientists who lived and worked under the Nazi regime of the 1930s. He said that these men held a mechanistic view of reality, a view that did not require a "god" as a creator. And on the matter of right and wrong, they were "relativistic." That is, they thought that people judge actions to be right and wrong because of the cultural context in which they live. Such judgments are, then, no more than what "people" think or say. Beyond the fact that people make judgments, there is no contrast of right and wrong. A judgment that what someone does is "wrong" cannot be called a "true" or a "false" judgment. It is simply one that people make.

But during the 1930s, officials of the Nazi government communicated to some of these scientists that they needed to change some of their scientific statements. They were ordered to adjust the statements to make them consistent with Nazi ideology. This had to do with ideas about the relation of heredity and human character and the like. Some of these scientists, being above all *scientists,* discovered that they were not so "relativistic" after all. The order to change the assertions that they make *as scientists* evoked a *no* that was altogether serious. The demand that they base their statements on ideology rather than on evidence and logic was unthinkable. It was important to them to always speak the truth in their capacity as scientists. It was not just important. It was not just very important. It was, rather, *unconditionally* important. It was important in a way that allowed no qualification or compromise. It took the Nazi demand made of them for the scientists to discover this about themselves.

What was it that they discovered about themselves? It would not be correct to say that they made psychological observations concerning their own nature, for they did not observe simply that they had thoughts and emotions. They discovered, rather, that they had a link to reality-as-such. Whatever it was that made it intolerable to falsify scientific statements linked them to the ground of all that they were. To compromise with the Nazi administrators would be to lose themselves, that is, to lose their being or their reality as human beings.

We may take, then, this unconditional "must" pertaining to telling the scientific truth to be a beginning point. To speak of God is *not* to talk about a being. It is, rather, to speak of the referent and basis of the unconditional "must." It is to be aware of an ultimate "up" and "down" in which no compromises, no "being reasonable," for right and wrong stand in a sharp and total contrast to one another. The biblical image of the "day of the Lord" as a "day of clouds and thick darkness" is suggestive of this total contrast. The "must" goes to the depths of a person's being. It goes to the depths of being as-such.

So what about the atheist? The term *atheist* properly means someone who holds a certain opinion. She holds the opinion that there is no god. But from a Christian standpoint, neither that nor any opinion is the crux of the matter. What is at center is being altogether or unconditionally *serious* about a matter of right and wrong—or, better stated, of Truth and Justice. If a person is thus concerned about a matter that pertains to affirming human community in all its aspects, she is a believer, regardless what her "opinions" about metaphysical matters may be.

And if these depths require a person to call his nation to account, and to do so precisely as one who cares about and "loves" his nation, the same is true of his love of people. Human beings have always treasured one another. They treasure one another as kinsmen, friends, comrades, and lovers. They treasure one another in ways that are appropriate to the relation that exists between them. In most relations, this relation in nonsexual, but in the husband–wife relation it is sexual. In all of this many-sided affection and "bonding" of one person with another, the other person is considered valuable *in view of* something. Within the family, one person is another's father, mother, brother, sister, son, or daughter. One person is another's husband or wife. Beyond the family, one person is another's friend, colleague, client, patient, or student. In every relation, there are both limit and extent. Where the relation receives its blessing from God, both are honored. Any two people have *only* the relation that they have, but they also have every bit *of* the relation that they have. It is the combination of limit and extent that makes a relation the personal relation that it is.

Out in the larger world, people are considered good and desirable because of certain attributes. A person is attractive in appearance, is "cool" in the manner in which she conducts herself, or exemplifies certain qualities such as courage, skill, or knowledge. These attributes are, in turn, grounded in one or another collective. A larger social group is armed with traditions or fashions and, in effect, blesses these attributes. If a woman is beautiful, for example, that beauty is not simply an attribute that belongs to her or emanates from her. Rather, it is grounded in a community that treasures "beauty" and then assigns it as a valued attribute to this particular woman. To either admire or love a person is always to treasure that person as an embodiment of a certain value. There is always the "in view of." And it is the world's "view."

This view changes drastically when all meaning is abandoned and then received back from God. Now a person is not treasured for what he is "in view of something." Nor is he treasured because he embodies a value that comes from or refers to a social group. Rather, he is treasured for the actual and specific person that he is. Every man and every woman is a particular person and, as that certain person, has depths that are independent of any and all social groups. He or she is this person, and that is what matters most. For this reason, we do not need to ask, for example, whether a certain woman is beautiful, for if she is a woman, she is necessarily a certain woman and *as* the woman who she is, she is beautiful. She has the beauty that belongs to her concretely and individually. A man, similarly, is definitely handsome because he is this particular man. If we have difficulty seeing men and women this way, it is because we are caught up in the "in view of" of the world. When we give it up and then receive it back from God, we will see each individual as beautiful because he or she is that person.

This is evident in those religious groups that have great Christian vitality. Many who enter the group feel themselves to be *lifted up* to an importance that they did not have before. These are people who did not have an attribute or an "in view of" that would give them importance in the world. They are "nobodies." But when the "in view of" is abandoned and the point of view of God is taken, they become important indeed. They are important and are viewed as important because they are particular persons. If a man's name is "Duane," he is important because he is Duane. If a woman is "Sophia," she is of great significance because she is Sophia. Of course, there may be people in the group who have a very good status based on the "in view of." They are important people in the world for any of a variety of reasons: they are rich, famous, knowledgeable, beautiful, talented, or the like. But even if they seem to be brought down when they lose the "in view of," they perceive as better the treasured status they have as being particular persons. It is better because it is grounded in God and not in a finite community. It is more secure because it is grounded in God and not in things that are fickle or that pass away. Most important, it is more substantial because it is grounded in God who is the *ground of reality* as such.

The expression *ground of reality* is important. Let us say that I am here. I appear. I have walked out onto the stage of life. I appear in the sense that I affirm myself as being. I say "yes" to my own reality as a human being. And once I have uttered this "yes," my being becomes of unconditional importance to me. Just in being aware of myself as being "here," I am also aware of the possibility that I could not be—or be not. And to "not be" is unconditional terror and deprivation. Yet "not being" is not the same as being unconscious or dead. It is, rather, a not being that arises from my failure to affirm myself as being myself, or simply to affirm myself as being. The person who affirms herself is authentic as a real person. And as such, she has a state of being that is not lost when she dies, for as one who is dead, she is one who did affirm herself when she had power of decision (was alive). In that sense, she has a reality as a human being that remains even when she is dead.

We may think here of someone who suffers at the hands of others because he has done what he thought was right. Or we may think of a person who passes his days in melancholy because he "feels for" people who are hungry, sick, or imprisoned. Then give this person a pill that, you say, will make him forget about what is right or about the sufferings of others. What we see here is that a person would commonly *prefer* the state of misery to that of a happiness that is grounded in indifference to right and wrong or in ignorance of the sufferings of other people. We may think that it is contradictory to say that a person could "want" to suffer. Yet we can see why it is. The person who suffers for doing right or out of compassion for others who suffer feels himself to be *real*. He is a real person. And, truth to tell, we human beings want to be real more than we want to enjoy ourselves. Psalm 1 talks about this. It says that the wicked are like "chaff which the wind drives away." The righteous, by contrast, are like "trees planted by streams of water that puts out its leaves in its season." We see here a contrast of unreality and reality. The wish is to be like a fruitful tree rather than like something that is light and that moves with the wind. Our basic wish is *not* to have pleasure and to avoid pain. It is, instead, to be real or substantial as persons who exist. If we are honest with ourselves, we would rather be miserable because we know that others are in misery than to be able to ignore those others and just "have a good time." Reality, not pleasure, is our prime desire. And to be real is to *decide* to be in community with our fellow human beings.

When we speak of the *ground of reality,* then, we talk about the basis for, or the source of, this condition of being real. I may note that I do not find the basis for my reality as a human being simply within myself. It is other than I. It is the ground from which my reality as a person derives. I affirm myself, but I affirm myself on the basis of a ground of my being that is other than I and infinitely more than I. We get a vision of this in Psalm 18. That psalm speaks of God as having heard the Psalmist's plea, and so came in clouds and "thick darkness" and then "the channels of the sea were seen, and the foundations of the world were laid bare at your rebuke, O Lord."

Or, we could say that a person would rather "know the Lord" and be in anguish about the evil and suffering in the world than to be jolly without the Lord. But the person who is in anguish because she shares the woes of all of those who suffer does, in truth, "know the Lord" regardless whether she is "of the opinion" that there is a God.

Further, when we find all meaning in what we do taken away and then given back to us by God, our actions take on a different rank-order from the one they had before. What was impressive and of great importance reappears as trivial or less. Whatever was "no big deal," goes, like Superman, into a telephone booth and reappears as very important. Big business deals, splashy commercials, famous people on stage occasion little more than a yawn. The man who thinks he has "made it big" comes face to face with a world that is bored with his exploits. On the other hand, simple acts of kindness, whether in the form of material aid or in emotional support, emerge from their obscurity and become matters or examples of prime importance. Instances of telling the truth just because it is the Truth produce flashing lights in the councils of heaven. The employer who is fair to his employees and customers because being fair is "beautiful" has a place of greater prominence in business than Bill Gates and the heirs of Sam Walton. When Jesus said, "inasmuch as you have done it to the least of these my brethren you have done it to me," he indicated this new order of priorities. When he said, "inasmuch as", he was assigning *meaning* to actions that were thought to be trivial, even by those who performed them.

And actions that appear to be part of hum-drum daily existence in fact reappear as great.

Before these meanings that are *from God* and *for God* can be discerned, all other sources or bases of meaning must be abandoned. The threat of meaningless must be confronted in all of its hurricane force and its sickening depths. *Then* there is the discovery of new meaning in God. In this discovery, things are commonly turned upside down. What was "big" in the world becomes trivial. And simple acts of kindness, justice, and truthfulness become "big deals."

JOY IN A MINOR KEY

There is in Christian faith a tension between two states of mind (and heart) to which the faithful are called. On the one hand there is the command to "rejoice in the Lord." And on the other, there is the imperative to be and to remain in solidarity with all of those who suffer. Concerning joy, the Bible is full of declarations of joy and rejoicing. Psalm 97 concludes with the words "Rejoice in the LORD O you righteous and give thanks to his holy name!" Psalms 98:4 and 100:l both urge us to "make a joyful noise unto the LORD all the earth;". There are many places in the Scriptures that speak of "joy," "rejoicing," "being glad," or "gladness." Similarly, the more liturgical churches, such as the Catholic, Episcopal, and Lutheran, include many assertions of joy and joyfulness in their songs of praise. Churches of the Pentecostal type both produce and treasure spontaneous outbursts of joy in their actions of "praising the Lord." Traditional hymns also include a great deal of singing about joy. The "Ode to Joy" in Beethoven's Ninth Symphony is present in most hymn books as "Joyful, Joyful We Adore Thee." In one hymnal, the index of first lines lists six hymns that begin with the word *rejoice*. In Scripture, in hymns, in preaching, and in the traditions of worship and prayer there are innumerable declarations of joy, rejoicing, and gladness.

In tension with these joyful notes is another major feature of Christian faith. It is that the Christian is called on to be aware of all the suffering that afflicts the peoples of the earth. And being aware of their pain, she is called to live in fundamental solidarity with them. Among the groans of the human community as a whole, none is louder and more excruciating than those of the massive numbers of people who are victims of genocidal killings. We read (if we have the right sources of news) of armies and "death squads" that have killed people by the tens of thousands and hundreds of thousands in Africa, Latin American, and elsewhere. Most Americans are shielded from the horror of these occurrences by the silence of our newspapers and by the reporters' preoccupation with local trivia. There is also some protection in the fact that Africa and South America are far away, their societies are very different from ours, and there is "nothing we can do about it anyway."

Yet the heart-wrenching terror and despair are like a stranger who is knocking at the door and who may come to our attention whether we want him to or not. One person who observed the massive array of bodies on the ground following a genocidal attack in Africa came upon the body of a little girl. He said it appeared to him that the girl knew that she was going to be killed, and she wanted to fix herself up so that the people who found her body would think that she looked nice. Such a statement is, of course, speculative. We do not know what the girl knew or thought. But even so, does this not help to bring home to us something of the horror that was involved?

Where mass murder does not occur, grinding poverty is often the order of the day. Americans may think that living in a hut with a dirt floor and subsisting on a minimal and monotonous diet is just the way some other folks live. But in my observations in Central America, I had the distinct impression that the poor of Guatemala and Nicaragua know very well that they are poor. Their one luxury is often a television set through which they see the comfort and affluence of others' lives.

Quite apart from violence and poverty, there is also terrible suffering because of distorted personal relations together with inner tensions, anxieties, and agonies. We need only to see the many in our own nation (the United States) who suffer from desperate loneliness, either because they are alone or because scolding and recrimination mark their personal relationships so vividly that they know no real communion with fellow human beings.

How then does the Christian so "rejoice in the Lord," that he remains in fundamental solidarity with all who suffer and with the indescribable suffering found in many quarters? Should he give up his joy? Or, should he wall himself off in a "godly" ghetto so that he can rejoice without having to be aware of the terrible suffering of his fellow human beings? We certainly do not want either of these options.

But what else can we do? I offer here only a tentative, feeling-my-way answer. To be honest, this is all I and others can suggest. When we think of the little girl who appeared to want her dead body to look nice, we are gripped by a heart-wrenching horror. There is, for this heartache only one possible antidote. We must be careful here; we do not want any cheap, easy, or premature "comforts." This one antidote is this statement: *God is great.* That is, God as the ground and source of all that is, is great in the specific sense of being greater *than* the horror and the rivers of tears of which we *are* aware, and indeed of which we *should* or *could* be aware. For by now we would rather have broken hearts than healthy hearts that can be kept healthy only by ignoring the horror. Truth to tell, this is the way we are. Let us admit it. It belongs to being human. It is part of being *real* human beings that we know the heartache. And we want, above all, to be *real.*

In saying "God is great," however, we are not speaking only of God. We are also talking about that little girl. We are saying that God is so great that he can hold that little girl in the palm of his hand. He can and *does* hold her in his hand. And what she is given while she is in his hand is all that she could have dreamed of. It is not just a "spiritual" compensation or booby prize to take the place of the life of which she was deprived. It is, rather, that she has all that she could have had if she had lived. Had she survived, she might have grown up, married, had children, and enjoyed a good life with family, friends, and community. All of this, we say, is what she has in the hand of God, for God is great.

It is easy to say this, but it is not so easy to "see" it. We cannot just say "God is great and has the girl in the palm of his hand," and let the matter go at that. For the reality and force of God's greatness and of his holding the girl does not "get through to us" so easily. At any given moment, we may not "see" it at all. The statement "God is great" may sound more like a pious, and even pompous, dictum. It may not sound like a report of the realities pertaining to God and human beings. As such, it could even be a cruel digression from the harsh realities of the world. So we cannot just say "God is great." What we say, instead, is that we believe that we *will see* that God is great and holds the little girl. We see God's greatness, not in the sense that we *do* see it, but in the sense that we *will* see it. We "see" it *in the mode of* "will see." We have faith in the sense that we think we will see what we do not now see. Right now, "in silence we wait patiently" for God (Ps. 62:1,5).

This does not in any way mean that it was all right that the little girl was killed. It is still our calling to oppose violence and cruelty in every way we can. It is our calling to see that the millions of little girls who are now alive do not fall victim to that little girl's fate. The God who is great and can hold that girl in his hand is the same God who issues orders to us. His orders are that we do all we can to prevent such suffering and to relieve it. These orders reach to the height and depth of all that we are. They are unconditional orders. The mountains shake and all of creation trembles as we decide to obey or not to obey these orders.

Nor can we simply acknowledge that "God is great" and that he has the little girl in his hands. It is not a lesson that we learn by reading a church magazine or being attentive in Sunday school. Nor can we, of our own power, "see" that it is true and so regard the matter as settled. Of necessity, the "we" that understands that God is great and holds the little girl is the same "we" that felt our hearts breaking when we heard about her and thought about her. Only as those who know the sickening horror of her fate can we "know" the greatness of God and the adequacy of his love. It is an existential knowing, a divinely guided taking in of the whole of this experience, the whole of this reality.

Further, it is a knowing *of* God that is of necessity a knowing *by* God. That is, God himself reveals to us that he is great and holds the little girl in his hand. We, as ourselves, are incapable of learning or knowing it, or "seeing" that it is so. *This is indeed something that God reveals to us in his own time and in his own way.* In this sense, it is something for which we *wait.* I may say "God is great," but I know that it is true in the specific sense that I *will know* that it is true—that God is great and holds the girl—when he himself reveals it to me.

Much is intended by the single statement, "God is great." Of necessity, it is a statement sung in a minor key, for it is a joy that holds sadness and sorrow within itself. It is also a joy based on a sense of the mystery of God's gracious intentions toward us. It is the joy of those who *wish* to be in solidarity with all who suffer and who can therefore rejoice only because they believe that God is greater than even the most heart-wrenching sorrow.

THE VISITOR AT THE CHURCH

A visitor comes to First Church. This visitor is "serious." He is so in a special meaning of that term. That is, he is alert to the problem of *meaning*, or may become alert to it. At the moment, he may be "caught up" in certain proximate meanings. He may be focused on developments in science or progress with "high-tech." Or he may be involved with music and the arts or with journalism and politics. These matters "eat up" his attention to such a degree that they seem to him to be the sum-total of what concerns us. Or, better stated, he sees these developments as having an implicit promise. He expects that when they reach the appropriate stage, all will be well. The progress of science needs only to reach a certain plateau—not too far off—and the world will become a wonderful place. This promise is, of course, one that science and "high tech" will not and cannot fulfill. Science cannot make good on the promise because it addresses the linking of means to ends and cannot cope with the organizing of the collective minds and hearts of human communities. To see this inability, we need only to note that the previous century was notable for the unprecedented progress of science and of technology, but it was also notable for the most brutal conflicts and wars ever to be seen in human history.

The visitor of whom we speak is capable of understanding this. She has an *ability* to "see it." She can perceive that she is expecting more of, for example, cell phones than just that they enable her to speak with a friend who is anywhere in the country, and she could do so from anywhere in the country. She can see that, implicitly, she is expecting a grand and glorious "more." And, once she realizes that she is, in fact, expecting this, she is also capable of seeing that the promise of the "more" will not be kept. Science will not keep its promise. The cell phones will do what cell phones do, and that will be all. Before long, she will see that the promised "more" is not forthcoming. Instead of the grand and glorious world that science seemed to promise, there is a globe full of war and threats of war, of widespread poverty, of political intrigue, together with the endless discussions of it to be heard on "talk shows" that lead to nowhere and, in due course, to a pervasive emptiness of the human spirit.

The authentic Christian church will help him to see this. It will do this by holding up before him the biblical and Christian motifs that the mega-church, by its nature, cannot hold up. These will be the motifs of the *holiness of God* and of *righteousness*. In Psalms 42:7–8, we read, "My soul is cast down within me, therefore I remember you from the land of Jordan. . . . Deep calls to deep at the thunder of your cataracts; all your waves and your billows have gone over me. By day the Lord commands his steadfast love; and at night his song is with me". The expressions "deep" and "thunder of cataracts" are important here. They refer to God as *holy*. And "holy," in turn, refers to the ultimate referent of meaning. The final "what it is all about" is, by its nature, overpowering. It "fills" the whole of reality, and it "fills" our consciousness. It is therefore thunder and lightning; it is a "day of clouds and thick darkness"; it is "deep calling to deep." This is what is meant by the word, *holy*. If the writer of the psalm says his soul is "cast down," it is because he has not yet seen the holiness and the "steadfast love" of God. The hope is that the visitor to First Church will experience the casting down of his soul. But that casting down will be a prelude to hearing the "thunder of the cataracts" and to perceiving the "steadfast love" of God.

And this will put the proximate goals in science, business, and politics in perspective. They may appear as good or even marvelous, but we will expect of them that which, and *only* that which, is to be expected of them. We will not look to them for fulfillment of life at either the individual or the societal level. We will, instead, look elsewhere for that fulfillment. The visitor to First Church who is "serious" will sense, whether clearly or vaguely, that the proclamation of the Gospel in the Church will open that door for him.

This "serious" visitor will also perceive that true *righteousness* is an underlying theme of the Church's proclamation. This righteousness is, by its nature, one that a person hears; she does not just assert it. We are bid to "be still and know that I am God" (Ps. 46:10). It is a choosing of the Right and a rejection of the Wrong that is what it is and *not* what we think it is, or want it to be, or think that it should be. We therefore must "hear" it. And to do this, we must "be still." We know that it always expands our community with our fellow human beings—all of them—rather than contracting those relations. But within that framework, we must be attentive; we must listen.

By its nature, what is "right" is not what the "authorities" say it is. Nor is it what is popular—what "people" say it is. It is, rather, what the God who guides us "by night" (Ps. 16:7) says it is. Or, it is what we say it is, when "we" are alone and totally responsible. It is, then, to this serious visitor that we make appeal. Certainly, we make appeal to all. But we appeal to them *as* serious. We do not address just anyone who may hear. People who sell products may appeal to "anyone." They may do so because they do not care why people buy their products. In the nature of what they do, they care only that customers do buy their products. But the Church must care. It must appeal to people for the right reasons.

Should Christian churches advertise? Attending a motion picture recently, I noticed that the Ocean Tide Church advertised before the feature began. Its "spot" was sandwiched between advertisements for car dealerships, casinos, and other businesses. Its content was simple: We are a wonderful church. Come and attend!

Should authentic churches advertise? Perhaps so, but certainly not as individual churches. Their message should have to do with the Gospel, not with this or that particular church. And it should emphasize those features of authentic Christianity that distinguish it from the mega-church. These are the holiness of God and righteousness.

The mega-church bases its entire program on a diminutive view of people. It assumes that they will respond positively only to what "appeals" to them. In this view, there must be something that takes hold of them in an immediate and dramatic way. Just as a rock concert grabs people with its rhythms and loud sounds, so the Christian Evangelist presents vivid images that "connect" with people's wish for sensations that are colorful and that "take hold of them" without demanding much of them. Neither thinking nor moral alertness must be required or "you will lose your audience." Or, you will fail to "be relevant."

It is interesting to note that the first Christians had a similar problem as they preached to people on street corners in the Greco-Roman world of their time. It is for this reason that the passages in the first three Gospels (the Synoptic Gospels), Matthew, Mark, and Luke, are very brief. The evangelists were speaking to people on street corners, and they had to be brief to hold those passers-by who were listening. But in their efforts to be brief, they did not water-down the "Good News," as they called it. It was stern and demanding. It involved a call to "repentance." It spoke of a God who was demanding yet merciful, who required righteousness, yet who offered an eternal life that was incredible in its heights and depths.

Perhaps we need to hold a higher idea of what people are. If we assume that the "hunger and thirst for righteousness" is there, we might do better.

BIBLIOGRAPHY

Barth, Karl. *The Epistle to the Romans.* London: Oxford University Press, 1965.

Bonhoeffer, Dietrich. *The Cost of Discipleship.* New York: Macmillan, 1959.

Herberg, Will. *Protestant, Catholic, Jew.* Garden City, NY: Anchor Books, 1960.

Niehbur, H. Richard. *The Social Sources of Denominationalism.* Cambridge, MA: Harvard Divinity School, 1929.

Niehbur, Reinhold. *The Nature and Destiny of Man.* Vols. 1 and 2. New York: Charles Scribner's Sons, 1943.

Schaller, Lyle. *From Cooperation to Competition.* Nashville, TN: Abingdon Press, 2006.

Tillich, Paul. *The Courage to Be.* New Haven, CT: Yale University Press, 1952.

Tillich, Paul. *Systematic Theology.* Vols. 2 and 3. Chicago: The University of Chicago Press, 1963.

INDEX

Advertise, 197, 247–48

Anonymity of attenders, 16

Atheism, 17; and the Bible, 150

Attenders and members, 15

Auditorium (for worship), 17, 49, 58–62

Authentic Christianity, 8–9, 12, 96, 173, 188; righteousness, 125–28; way back to, 202

Authenticate a performance or a group 155–57

Authenticity: of Christianity, 149, 162; of a person, 240

Authority: in a mega-church, 8–9; purpose in society, 208; top-down vs. bottom-up authority, 2–4; and value, 5–6

Barth, Karl, 66, 91, 221

Bishop and Pope, 3, 64, 200

Bonhoeffer, Dietrich, 87

Boundaries: basis of, 166–67; facing in and out, 164–66; mega-church and, 195–97, 221–22

Bridge, burned or not burned, 202, 222

Buddhism: achievement, 164, 179; and the problem of meaning, 231–32

Capitalism and "free enterprise," 175–76

Celibacy, 222

Celebrity culture, 6–7, 18–20

Charisma, charismatic authority, 12

Children, programs for, 98–99

Christmas music, 22

Communists and totalitarian state, 132

Confronting the mega-church, 8–9

Cross, salvation by the, 24, 31, 46–47, 71, 87, 117, 151, 161, 164, 166, 169, 171, 185; "emptied of its power," 165, 170; as symbol, 186, 198

Deism. See Rationalism, deism, and modernism

Denomination, deemphasis on, 27–28

Doctrine: place of in Christianity, 43, 151, 184, 210, 219–21; taken lightly in the mega-church, 41–45, 50, 116, 152, 155, 165, 197–98

Ecumenicism, 163

Egotism and pride, 48, 73, 112, 119, 137, 212

Empiricism. See Rationalism, deism, and modernism

Emptiness and problem of meaning, 194, 224, 225, 228–35

Encounter: as distinct from experience, 43–44, 115, 123, 161, 169, 181, 191; with a person, 18, 37–38

Enlightenment culture, 141, 190–91

Entrepreneurial minister, 29, 52, 182

Epistemology and faith, 169–70

Evangelical tradition and movement, 7, 29–31, 45–47, 79, 91–93, 115–18, 151, 159, 190

Evangelist, 1–5, 24, 52, 151, 201, 248; televangelist, 29

Event, central role of, 73–74, 108, 161, 169, 172–73, 190, 210, 213

"Float," and items of culture that, 51–55

Frontier, Western: faith of, 4–8, 18, 23, 107, 187, 194

Fundamentalism, 141–42; vs. cosmopolitan hauteur, 145–47; darker face of, 149–50; fundamentals of, 148–49; moment of uncertainty and, 151–52; vs. rationalism, 142–45

Gate-keeper, membership management, 16, 17, 223

Gnosticism, 171–72, 178, 179

Greek culture and philosophy, 5, 164, 190–91, 210–15, 231–32

Ground of reality, 172, 238, 240, 241

Growth, project of, 7, 40–46, 90, 104, 110, 120, 200, 202, 204, 224

Herberg, Will, 47

Hybels, Bill, and Willow Creek, 12, 17, 31, 33, 91, 198

Ideal type, 9–12

Images, projected on screen, 60

Incarnation, doctrine of, 210–12

Isaiah, scholarship and the book of, 109–10

Joy in a minor key, 242–45

Knowledge and the gospel, 41, 203–4

Large church, intention to build. *See* Growth, project of

Liberation theology, 192–95

Life adjustment tradition, 28–33, 49, 76–77; and eschatology, 84–89

"Lone Ranger" as reverberation of faith, 189–90

MacArthur, John, 108–12, 114, 116

Marxism, 173–75, 178, 192

Mass society, 156–57

Meaning, problem of, 224–28

Meaninglessness, specter of, 228–31; addressing the problem of, 231–36

Mega-church as distinct type, 12–32, 45, 49, 115

Men's class in Ocean Tide Church, 108–10

Modernism. *See* Rationalism, deism, and modernism

Moment of uncertainty: critical judgment and, 103–6, 121–22; importance for civilization, 117–18; logic and evidence and, 129–34; and love of the good, 127–28; as opposed to self-praise, 123–25; the word from God and, 134–39

"Moments" of the gospel, 188

Moral dilemmas, considered or not, 103–6

Morality as escape from meaninglessness, 231

Music: new, novel, 7, 21–26

Nationalism and idolatry, 176–77, 178, 212

Nazi government and scientists, 237–38

Nazism, 193, 229

Neo-Orthodoxy or neo-Reformation theology, 191–92

Niebuhr, H. Richard, 154

Niebuhr, Reinhold, 110, 114, 115, 168

Ocean Tide Church, 22, 27, 31, 57, 75, 97, 180, 247; ideal type and, 49–50

Otto, Rudolph, 43

Parks, Rosa, 33
Peal, Norman Vincent, 30
Pietism: individual vs. group morality, 107–8
Praise: produced, evoked, 63–67, 94–95; self-praise and immediate judgment, 123–25; songs of, 62
Pre-School Center in Ocean Tide Church, 58
Pride. *See* Emptiness and problem of meaning
Project of growing ever larger. *See* Growth, project of
Protestant Reformation, 4, 9, 191–92

Quakers, Society of Friends, 188

Rationalism, deism, and modernism, 142–43
"Real Presence" and tradition, 73–74
Regal pastor, 12–15
Reverberation of faith through culture, 188–94
Righteousness, 78, 82, 85–89, 92–93, 145; hunger for, 166, 181; makes a beacon to nations, 175; unbound to conventions, 208
Rock concert as model, 17–18, 22, 155–56, 196, 198, 248

Schaller, Lyle, 7, 40–41, 43, 204
Schuller, Robert, and Crystal Cathedral, 30–32, 77
Scientists and Nazi government. *See* Nazi government and scientists
Self-fulfilling prophecy (Robert K. Merton), 77

Self-praise. *See* Praise, produced, evoked
Senior pastor, 15
"Serve the church" as a theme, 89–91
Sin and power, 6, 54, 72, 92, 112–13, 120, 131–32, 175, 190, 206, 218
Sinner-redemption model, 29, 79–81, 217–18
Size of church. *See* Authentic Christianity
Small groups in mega-church, 16, 58–60, 100–103, 132, 224
Social gospel, 191
Spirit, as free, 200, 206–8
Status deprivation and the non-cosmopolitan, 146–47
Success (capital "S"), 25, 26, 30–32, 76, 81–91
Success and happiness as goals, 173, 226, 240

Televangelist. *See* Evangelist
Tillich, Paul, 36, 87, 143, 167, 171, 173, 221, 224, 237
Traditions: esoteric, 71–72; role of, 22, 67–68, 120–22, 220, 227
Trinity and the Spirit, 212–16
Truth, objective nature of, 122, 124, 126, 129, 130–31, 155, 161–62, 217

Virgin birth, doctrine of, 42, 148, 151–53, 165
Visitor in the church, 245–48

Warren, Rick, 12, 33, 39, 49
Weber, Max, 9, 177
Wells, David, 204
Will, as the seat of the human problem, 80, 122, 169, 172

About the Author

WILMER E. MACNAIR is retired Associate Professor of Sociology at the University of Louisiana at Lafayette. He is an ordained minister in the United Church of Christ and has served as a part-time and interim pastor on many occasions. He has published several works, including the books *Basic Thinking: On Beginning at the Beginning in Thinking about Social and Economic Problems* and *The Ten Commandments and the Crisis of Community in America.*